COMMERCIAL ARBITRATION AND MEDIATION IN NIGERIA

By

Celestine U. Ugonabo, Esq.,

B.Sc. (Est Man), MBA, LL.B, B.L., M.Sc., Ph.D.

Chidera Josemaria Ugonabo, Esq.,

ACIArb (UK), LL.B, B.L., LL.M (Wales, Cum Laude)

COMMERCIAL ARBITRATION AND MEDIATION IN NIGERIA

ISBN: 978 – 978 – 68 – 5692 - 6

Printed by:
MEMOIYKE PUBLISHING NIG. LTD
#41 Udoji Street, OGUI N/Layout, Enugu
Phone: 08037456414.

FOREWORD

It is with great pleasure that I write this foreword to a work that captures both the essence and the future of arbitration and mediation in Nigeria. Arbitration has evolved from being a niche area of law into a universal tool for resolving disputes efficiently, fairly, and without the delays often associated with litigation. In today's global and digital environment, where commercial relationships are increasingly conducted through non-physical and online platforms, arbitration has become indispensable not only within domestic transactions but also across international borders.

At the College of Arbitrators Nigeria, we strive to enthrone arbitration and other forms of ADR as practicable, acceptable and result oriented paths towards effective management and resolution of commercial disputes. As a result, we believe that the resolution and management of such disputes should not be reserved to any one particular profession.

We believe that engineers, estate surveyors, valuers, architects, bankers, accountants, and other experts have important roles to play in dispute resolution and management. Their technical knowledge and professional objectivity enrich the quality of arbitration proceedings and outcomes. This book strongly reflects that inclusive vision.

In this text, the authors present arbitration in a manner that is at once comprehensive, simplified, practical, and engaging. Their analysis of the novel provisions of the Arbitration and Mediation Act 2023 is both scholarly and accessible, bridging the gap between academic rigour and practical understanding. Importantly, the book does not confine itself to domestic arbitration alone. It extends its scope to international arbitration, enforcement of foreign awards, investor–State disputes, sovereign immunity, public policy, and the operation of global arbitral conventions such as the New York Convention and the ICSID Convention. In doing so, it situates Nigerian arbitration practice within the wider international legal order.

A particularly commendable aspect of the work is the authors' effort to painstakingly simplify complex statutory provisions, reading them in harmony with complementary Arbitration Rules to bring out their true intent and purpose. Through clear explanations, relatable examples, and practical illustrations, the authors succeed in demystifying arbitration concepts, making them easily understandable to entry-level arbitration pupils and those newly introduced to the field, while still offering depth to experienced practitioners.

The book thoughtfully situates arbitration within the context of domestic contracts in Nigeria, particularly those involving parties operating from different states or distant regions of the federation. At the same time, it recognises that modern commerce is rarely confined within national borders. Many agreements today are concluded and performed through electronic communication, digital platforms, and social media interactions, sometimes between parties located in different countries and governed by multiple legal systems. This evolving commercial reality underscores the growing relevance of arbitration as a flexible, neutral, and enforceable mechanism for resolving disputes that transcend both geographical and jurisdictional boundaries. In realization of this emerging trend, the authors devoted commendable time in resolving the complexities of arbitration as a veritable tool for efficient settlement of commercial/contractual disputes.

By bridging legal analysis with real-world application, this book makes a valuable contribution to both the study and practice of arbitration in Nigeria and beyond. It speaks to students, lawyers, and non-lawyers alike, to academics and practitioners and to all who believe that justice can be achieved through reasoned dialogue and professional expertise, away from the rigid evidential and procedural formalities of the regular courts.

Indeed, the book is a must have for anyone who is engaged in and or concerned with resolving disputes through the instrumentality of arbitration and other forms of ADR.

I warmly commend the authors for this timely and insightful contribution. It is a book for the shelf of everyone, regardless of discipline or profession.

It is with great pleasure that I commend the book and express my heartfelt congratulations to the authors.

P. I. N. Ikwueto, SAN., FCIArb (UK)
Founder and President, College of Arbitrators Nigeria
Abuja, Nigeria

March 2026

PREFACE

In an era where commercial relationships are increasingly conducted across digital platforms and social media channels, the nature of contractual obligations has evolved beyond the traditional written document or handshake. Many transactions today exist in non-physical forms executed through emails, online messages, virtual agreements, and digital exchanges that nonetheless create binding legal rights and obligations. With this shift, disputes have also taken new shapes, frequently involving parties situated in different domestic and international jurisdictions, and governed by overlapping layers of municipal law, international conventions, arbitral rules, and transnational commercial norms.

It is within this changing environment that arbitration has proven to be both relevant and indispensable. Arbitration provides a flexible, confidential, and efficient mechanism for resolving disputes arising out of modern commercial relationships, including cross-border, digital, and technology-driven contracts. The enactment of the Arbitration and Mediation Act 2023 (AMA) marks a major step forward in strengthening Nigeria's position as a modern arbitration-friendly jurisdiction, capable of addressing the demands of global commerce while reflecting our domestic legal traditions. At the same time, Nigeria's integration into the global arbitral framework through instruments such as the New York Convention and the ICSID Convention underscores the importance of understanding arbitration not merely as a local process, but as an international legal system with enforceable consequences across borders.

This book was written to clarify the principles of arbitration and mediation in Nigeria and to demonstrate how these processes can adapt to the realities of non-physical and technology-driven transactions. It also extends beyond domestic arbitration to examine international commercial arbitration, investment arbitration, enforcement of foreign awards, sovereign immunity, public policy, and emerging global trends. The work therefore bridges both domestic and international arbitral regimes, combining statutory interpretation, judicial authority, comparative jurisprudence, and professional insight.

A particular emphasis is placed on the role of estate surveyors and valuers. As professionals who routinely engage in valuation disputes, rent reviews, boundary issues, and other matters involving expert judgment, they are uniquely positioned to participate in and even preside over arbitral proceedings. Their technical expertise and professional independence make them valuable contributors to the growth of arbitration in Nigeria. This book therefore encourages estate surveyors alongside lawyers, engineers, accountants, and other professionals to see arbitration not merely as a legal process, but as a multidisciplinary platform for achieving justice, preserving relationships, and advancing professional standards.

The work also examines customary arbitration, highlighting how its communal principles of fairness, consensus, and restorative justice continue to influence the practice of modern arbitration. Together, the statutory, customary, and international systems reveal the adaptability and resilience of dispute resolution mechanisms in Nigeria and beyond.

The Tables of Cases and Statutes, List of Abbreviations, and Index have been carefully prepared to guide readers through the key authorities and provisions discussed throughout the text. It is my hope that this book will assist students, practitioners, arbitrators, judges, and professionals including estate surveyors in understanding and applying arbitration principles effectively within both traditional and contemporary contexts, whether the dispute is local, regional, or truly international in character.

I remain grateful to the Nigerian judiciary, whose decisions have illuminated the evolving principles of arbitration law, and to the many teachers, colleagues, and students who continue to inspire inquiry and reflection in this field.

May this book serve as a useful contribution to the advancement of arbitration and professional practice in Nigeria and within the wider international legal community.

Celestine U. Ugonabo, PhD

Awka, Nigeria
March 2026

DEDICATION

We dedicate this book first and foremost to Almighty God, whose wisdom and grace sustained the course of this work to fruition. To our beloved family, whose love, patience, and understanding provided the quiet strength behind our long hours of writing and research we owe you more than words can express.

To the students and alumni of the department of Estate Management, Nnamdi Azikiwe University, Awka whose curiosity and commitment over the last decades continue to inspire our passion for knowledge-sharing and professional excellence this work is for you.

We also dedicate this book to every young practitioner and non-lawyer seeking to understand the beauty and balance of arbitration, and to use it as a tool for fairness and progress in modern commercial life.

Finally, to the memory of those who instilled in us the love for justice, discipline, and scholarship, may your legacy find expression in the pages of this work and in the minds it shapes.

ACKNOWLEDGMENTS

The writing of this book has been a journey of learning, reflection, and collaboration across generations. As father and son, we have been privileged to share not only the practice of law but also the passion for knowledge and the pursuit of clarity in the understanding of arbitration and its modern relevance.

We remain profoundly grateful to Professors C.C. Egolum, J.U. Ogbuefi, F.I. Emoh, K.C. Okolie, E.I. Oladejo, C.P. Igwe, E.O.C. Obidimma of the Faculty of Law and Professor (Rev. Fr.) E.O. Ezike, as well as the rest of the academics and support staff of the Department of Estate Management, Nnamdi Azikiwe University, for their invaluable guidance, encouragement, intellectual influence, and sustained institutional support throughout the development of this work.

We also extend our sincere appreciation to P.I.N. Ikwueto, SAN, the Lead Partner of Ikwueto®, as well as the lawyers and support staff of the Abuja Office of the Firm, whose support, patience, and professional understanding particularly in granting time off regular duties greatly contributed to the successful completion of this work.

Our special appreciation goes to Ebunoluwa Chidera Igili, Esq., a distinguished lawyer, arbitration practitioner, and Fellow of the Chartered Institute of Arbitrators (CIArb), whose active engagement in practice brought practical realism, procedural depth, and a contemporary perspective to the discussions contained in these pages.

To our family, whose patience and understanding have been our constant support throughout the many late nights and long days of research and writing thank you for your love, encouragement, and sacrifice.

Above all, we give glory to Almighty God, whose wisdom, grace, and strength made this rare but pleasantly historic collaboration possible and fruitful.

This book represents not just a contribution to legal literature but a shared testament to the enduring link between generations the passing of knowledge, values, and faith in the transformative power of learning.

Celestine U. Ugonabo, PhD
Chidera Josemaria Ugonabo, Esq.
Awka, Nigeria
March 2026

TABLE OF CASES

A

A.P.C. v Karfi (2018) 14 NWLR (Pt 1640) 479 (SC)
Arenson v Casson Beckman Rutley & Co [1977] AC 405 (HL)
Armada Ship Management (S) Pte Ltd v Schiste Oil & Gas Nigeria Ltd (Unreported, High Court of Nigeria)

B

Baker Marine (Nig) Ltd v Chevron (Nig) Ltd (2000) 12 NWLR (Pt 681) 393 (SC)
Blanchard v Sun Fire Office (1894) 1 QB 344 (CA)

C

Cable & Wireless Plc v IBM United Kingdom Ltd [2002] EWHC 2059 (Comm)
CF Sonnar (Nig) Ltd v Partenreedri M.S. Nordwind (1987) 4 NWLR (Pt 66) 520 (SC)
Churchill v Merthyr Tydfil County Borough Council [2023] EWCA Civ 1416
Cukurova Finance International Ltd v Alfa Telecom Turkey Ltd [2013] UKSC 2; [2013] 1 All ER 1

D

Dallah Real Estate and Tourism Holding Co v Ministry of Religious Affairs, Government of Pakistan [2010] UKSC 46; [2011] 1 AC 763
Dunnett v Railtrack Plc (Costs) [2002] EWCA Civ 303

E

Ebokan v Ekwenibe & Sons Trading Co Ltd (1999) 10 NWLR (Pt 622) 242 (CA)

F

Federal Airports Authority of Nigeria v Nwoye (2019) 7 NWLR (Pt 1671) 200 (CA)

H

Haigh v Haigh (1861) 1 De G F & J 675; 45 ER 1081
Halsey v Milton Keynes General NHS Trust [2004] EWCA Civ 576

I

Interocean Oil Development Co v Federal Republic of Nigeria ICSID Case No ARB/13/20

J

Johnston v Cheape (1817) 5 Dow 247; 3 ER 809 (HL)

K

Kano State Urban Development Board v Fanz Construction Co Ltd (1990) 4 NWLR (Pt 142) 1 (SC)

L

Limak Construction Industry and Trade Inc v Sahelian Energy & Integrated Services Ltd (2021) 3 NWLR (Pt 1764) 85 (CA)

M

Malmesbury Railway Co v Budd (1881) 17 Ch D 443 (CA)
Mekwunye v Imoukhuede (2019) 13 NWLR (Pt 1689) 435 (SC)
Metal-Tech Ltd v Republic of Uzbekistan ICSID Case No ARB/10/3 (Award, 4 October 2013)
M.V. Lupex v Nigerian Overseas Chartering & Shipping Ltd (2003) 15 NWLR (Pt 844) 469 (SC)
M.V. Panormos Bay v Olam (Nig) Plc (2004) 5 NWLR (Pt 865) 1 (CA)

N

Neale v Ledger (1863) 2 H & C 42; 159 ER 17
Niger Gate Ltd v Niger State Government (2008) 12 NWLR (Pt 1101) 422 (CA)
Nigeria Water Resources Development Ltd v Jaiyesimi (1983) 1 SCNLR 454 (SC)
Nigerian Agip Oil Co Ltd v Kemmer (2001) 3 NWLR (Pt 701) 449 (CA)
Nigerian National Petroleum Corporation v Clifco Nigeria Ltd (2011) 10 NWLR (Pt 1255) 209 (SC)
Nigerian National Petroleum Corporation v Fung Tai Engineering Co Ltd (2023) 15 NWLR (Pt 1906) 117 (SC)
Nigerian National Petroleum Corporation v Lutin Investment Ltd (2006) 2 NWLR (Pt 965) 506 (CA)
Nigerian Ports Authority v Construction General Filli & Anor (1974) 1 All NLR (Pt 2) 463 (SC)
NML Capital Ltd v Republic of Argentina 573 US 134 (2014)

O

Onward Enterprises Ltd v M.V. Matrix (2010) 2 NWLR (Pt 1179) 530 (CA)

P

Process & Industrial Developments Ltd v Federal Republic of Nigeria [2023] EWHC 2638 (Comm)
PT Central Investindo v Franciscus Wongso & Ors [2014] SGHC 190

R

Race Auto Supply Co Ltd v Akib (1977) 11 NSCC 343 (SC)
Rossek v A.C.B. Ltd (1993) 8 NWLR (Pt 312) 382 (SC)

S

Shell (Nig) Exploration & Production Co Ltd v Federal Inland Revenue Service (2021) 17 NWLR (Pt 1806) 545 (SC)
Shell Nigeria Ultra Deep Ltd v Federal Republic of Nigeria (Unreported investment arbitration)
Solel Boneh International Ltd v Government of Cross River State (2003) 1 NWLR (Pt 802) 740 (CA)
Soufraki v United Arab Emirates ICSID Case No ARB/02/7 (Award, 7 July 2004)
Stabilini Visinoni Ltd v Mallinson & Partners Ltd (2014) 12 NWLR (Pt 1420) 134 (CA)
Statoil (Nig) Ltd v Nigerian National Petroleum Corporation (2013) 14 NWLR (Pt 1373) 1 (CA)

T

Taylor Woodrow (Nig) Ltd v Etina Werro & Sons Ltd (1993) 4 NWLR (Pt 286) 127 (SC)

U

UAC v Macfoy [1962] AC 152 (PC)
UBA Plc v Triedent Consulting Ltd (2023) LPELR-60643 (SC)

W

Well v Cooke (1857) 3 CB (NS) 672; 140 ER 698
Woluchem v Wokoma (1974) 3 SC 153
Wood v Leake (1806) 12 Ves Jun 412; 33 ER 94
World Duty Free Co Ltd v Republic of Kenya ICSID Case No ARB/00/7 (Award, 4 October 2006)

TABLE OF STATUTES AND LEGISLATION

A

C

E

F

Foreign Sovereign Immunities Act 1976 (United States)

I

ICSID (Enforcement of Awards) Act (Nigeria)

N

Nigeria Tax Act 2025

S

State Immunity Act 1978 (United Kingdom)

TABLE OF INTERNATIONAL INSTRUMENTS AND TREATIES

LIST OF ABBREVIATIONS

ACA - Arbitration and Conciliation Act (Cap A18 LFN 2004) (Repealed)
ADR - Alternative Dispute Resolution
AMA - Arbitration and Mediation Act 2023
ART - Award Review Tribunal
BCRA - Banco Central de la República Argentina
BIT - Bilateral Investment Treaty
CA - Court of Appeal
Ch - Chancery Division (England & Wales)
COAN - College of Arbitrators Nigeria
Comm - Commercial Court (England & Wales)
ECSLR - Eastern Central State Law Reports
EWHC - England and Wales High Court
EWCA Civ - England and Wales Court of Appeal (Civil Division)
FHC - Federal High Court
FIRS - Federal Inland Revenue Service
FRN - Federal Republic of Nigeria
FSIA - Foreign Sovereign Immunities Act (United States)
HL - House of Lords
HKIAC - Hong Kong International Arbitration Centre
ICC - International Chamber of Commerce
ICJ - International Court of Justice
ICSID - International Centre for Settlement of Investment Disputes
ICSID Convention - Convention on the Settlement of Investment Disputes between States and Nationals of Other States (1965)
KB - King's Bench
LCA - Lagos Court of Arbitration
LCIA - London Court of International Arbitration
LACIAC - Lagos Chamber of Commerce International Arbitration Centre
LFN - Laws of the Federation of Nigeria
LJ Ch - Law Journal Reports, Chancery Division
LR - Law Reports (England & Wales)
Model Law - UNCITRAL Model Law on International Commercial Arbitration

NWLR - Nigerian Weekly Law Reports
NNPC - Nigerian National Petroleum Corporation
PC - Privy Council
PSC - Production Sharing Contract
QB – Queen's Bench
RCICA - Regional Centre for International Commercial Arbitration (Lagos)
SAN - Senior Advocate of Nigeria
SC - Supreme Court
SCNLR - Supreme Court of Nigeria Law Reports
SIAC - Singapore International Arbitration Centre
UKSC - United Kingdom Supreme Court
UNCITRAL - United Nations Commission on International Trade Law
UNCITRAL Rules - UNCITRAL Arbitration Rules
UN - United Nations
US - United States Reports
US$ - United States Dollar

TABLE OF CONTENTS

CHAPTER 3
CONSTITUTION OF THE ARBITRAL TRIBUNAL

CHAPTER 4
JURISDICTION OF THE ARBITRAL TRIBUNAL

CHAPTER 5

CONDUCT OF ARBITRAL PROCEEDING

CHAPTER 6

THE ARBITRAL AWARD

CHAPTER 7

CHALLENGES AND POST-AWARD PROCEEDINGS

CHAPTER 8

RECOGNITION AND ENFORCEMENT OF AWARDS

CHAPTER 9
COSTS AND ANCILLARY MATTERS IN ARBITRATION

CHAPTER TEN
INTERNATIONAL ARBITRATION

CHAPTER ELEVEN
MEDIATION UNDER THE NEW ADR REGIME

CHAPTER 1

INTRODUCTION

1.1 MEANING AND NATURE OF ARBITRATION

Disputes are a second nature to human existence. Once a person has joined with another whether for business, life partnership, marriage or such other joint ventures, it is wise to anticipate the certainty of a potential dispute.

The question then is, in the event of a dispute, do all parties abandon the objective of their venture and flee or are there ways to resolve these disputes? Furthermore, if and when these disputes are resolved, are they resolved in such a cordial manner that the relationship of the parties at the point of the joint venture remains intact post dispute resolution? Does the cost of resolving these disputes substantially outweigh the economic dividends of the joint venture and can the dispute be resolved quickly such that the object of the venture is not frustrated by passing of time spent on dispute resolution?

The foregoing are the typical or realistic concerns of a party to any venture whether commercial or otherwise. Multiple forms of dispute resolution mechanism have therefore evolved and indeed continue to evolve with a view to resolving disputes particularly in commerce in a way that is most favorable to parties and the objects of their venture. Top among the mechanisms of resolving disputes in a commercial savvy way is arbitration which we buttress herein with giant scholarship.

In any organized society, there are Courts which settle differences between people in that society. If there is no such Court system, there will be chaos. Even in primitive societies there were organized systems of settling disputes, similar to what is obtainable in a Court. The Courts can coerce anyone to appear before it, failure of which will result in some sort of sanctions.

Arbitration is a way of settling disputes. Usually, parties agree to submit future or current disputes to arbitration. This means that the parties can decide before or after a dispute arises that if a dispute arises between them, it will be settled by way of arbitration. It is a mechanism in which the disputing parties appoint a person or a number of persons to settle a dispute or difference that may arise between them. Even where parties had not initially envisaged a dispute, they can, within the course of the contract at which they have the misunderstanding, submit the dispute to arbitration. It is a method of settling disputes under which the parties agree to be bound by the decision of an independent third person whose decision is, in general, final and legally binding on both parties. This process derives its force from the agreement of the parties, with the aid of the Courts which enforces these decisions.

In **DANGOTE INDUSTRIES (ZAMBIA) LTD v. IMA (ZAMBIA) LTD**[1], the Court of Appeal in defining arbitration relied on the age long Supreme Court decision in **K.S.UD.B. v. FANZ CONST. LTD.**[2], where Agbaje, J.S.C. referring to Halsbury's Laws of England 4th Edition defined arbitration as:-

> **An arbitration is the reference of a dispute or difference between not less than two parties for determination, after hearing both sides in a judicial manner, by a person or persons other than a Court of competent jurisdiction.**

---

[1] (2024) LPELR-62899(CA)

[2] (1990) 4 NWLR (PT. 142)

A person or persons to whom a reference for arbitration is made is called an arbitrator or arbitrators as the case may be. A purported arbitration panel which is created to resolve disputes between persons in a manner other than judicial is not an arbitration tribunal.

The decision rendered by an arbitral tribunal is known as an **arbitral award**. Historically, in arbitral proceedings conducted by a panel of three, it was common for parties to appoint two arbitrators one each and to designate a third person, known as an *umpire*, who would intervene only where the two arbitrators were unable to reach agreement. In such circumstances, the umpire would assume full authority to determine the dispute and issue a binding decision.

Contemporary arbitration practice, however, has moved away from this model. Modern arbitration laws, including the Nigerian Arbitration and Mediation Act 2023, no longer recognise the office of an umpire. Instead, provision is made for the appointment of a **third or presiding arbitrator**, who participates fully in the proceedings from the outset alongside the party-appointed arbitrators. Decisions of the tribunal are ordinarily reached by majority, with the presiding arbitrator exercising an equal vote rather than a substitutive or overriding one.[3]

This evolution reflects a broader shift toward collective deliberation and procedural coherence within arbitral tribunals. By ensuring that all members of the tribunal are equally engaged throughout the proceedings, modern arbitration promotes consistency, transparency, and fairness in decision-making, while preserving the finality and authority of the arbitral award.

---

[3] Gary B Born, *International Commercial Arbitration* (3rd edn, Kluwer Law International 2021) 2134–2138.

1.2 DISPUTES THAT MAY BE SUBMITTED TO ARBITRATION

It is not every dispute or difference that can be referred to arbitration. Those that can be referred must be justiciable issues which can be tried as civil matters. They must be disputes that can be compromised by accord and satisfaction. These include all matters in dispute about any real or personal property, disputes as to whether a contract has been breached by either party, or whether one or both parties have been discharged from further performance of a contract. Other examples abound, for instance terms of a deed of separation between the husband and wife can be settled by arbitration. Issues before a Court can, if the parties agree, with leave of the Court, be referred to arbitration. A specific question of law such as the construction of a document may be referred to arbitration and if this is done the award cannot be set aside merely because the decision is erroneous.

The Court of Appeal in **B. J. EXPORT & CHEMICAL CO. LTD v. KADUNA REFINING & PETRO-CHEMICAL CO. LTD**[4] in expounding on the principle of arbitrability held that:

> ***It is trite that the disputes which are the subject of an arbitration agreement must be arbitrable. In other words the agreement must not cover matters which by the law of the State are not allowed to be settled privately or by arbitration usually because this will be contrary to the public policy.***

The Court went on to cite the aged case of the **KANO STATE URBAN DEVELOPMENT BOARD v. FANZ CONSTRUCTION LTD**[5]. where it was restated that a criminal

---

[4] (2002) LPELR-12175(CA)

[5] (1990) 4 NWLR (PT.142)1 at 32-33

matter, like the allegation of fraud raised by the respondent in that case, does not admit of settlement by arbitration.

On the other hand, disputes arising out of illegal transactions cannot be referred to arbitration. Consequently, a difference relating to contract which is illegal for being inconsistent with a government order cannot be referred.

Disputes arising out of void transactions such as wagering and gaming contracts cannot be referred to arbitration. An indictment for an offence cannot be referred to arbitration.

In **ESSO EXP. & PROD. (NIG.) LTD. v. F.I.R.S.**[6] the Court of Appeal held that

> ***Only arbitrable matters are governed by the Arbitration and Conciliation Act. A matter is arbitrable if it is one that the parties to the dispute in which it arose can settle by arbitration. Generally, a matter regulated by statute or a matter of public interest cannot be settled by arbitration. Petroleum profits tax is a matter regulated by statute and a matter of public interest. So, a dispute concerning it cannot be settled by arbitration.***

Similarly, the Supreme Court in **U.B.A. PLC v. TRIEDENT CONSULTING LTD.**[7] held that

> ***Disputes which are subject of an arbitration agreement must be arbitrable. Criminal matters or disputes where fraud is alleged and raised are, as a matter of public policy, not to be settled privately by arbitration.***

---

[6] (2021) 8 NWLR (Pt. 1777) 43
[7] (2023) 14 NWLR (Pt. 1903) 95

In **MEKWUNYE v. LOTUS CAPITAL LTD & ORS**[8] per Adumein JCA. The Court of Appeal reached a historically unusual decision when it held that

> ***It is not every allegation of fraud that will oust the jurisdiction of an arbitral tribunal. What will render a dispute non-arbitrable is fraud that goes to the root of the arbitration clause or the contract itself. Where the allegation of fraud merely arises in the performance of the contract, the arbitral tribunal has jurisdiction to determine it.***

This decision seems to confer limited criminal jurisdiction on arbitral tribunals to decide on allegation of crimes or fraud committed in the performance of a contract. It is submitted with respect that this decision goes utterly against the Arbitration and Mediation Act 2023, the 1999 Constitution of the Federal Republic of Nigeria (as amended), and indeed the plethora of Supreme Court authorities on the subject. An arbitral tribunal cannot decide on a criminal allegation without reference to the standard legislations on crime. The tribunal can also not cherry pick on what criminal allegation to entertain because if for instance the tribunal decides to entertain only criminal allegations which occur in the performance of a contract, then if a party commits murder or somewhat smashes the skull of a partner during an argument at a building site where the contract is being performed, then the tribunal may as well have jurisdiction to try the offence of murder.

1.3 CAPACITY TO ARBITRATE

Section 2(2) of the Arbitration and Mediation Act 2023 provides that an arbitration agreement shall be in writing and shall be binding upon the parties capable of entering into a contract. Indeed, section 58(2)(a)(i) goes further to provide that incapacity of a party to an

---

[8] (2018) LPELR-45546 (CA),

arbitration agreement as contemplated under section 2(1) of the Act is a ground for setting aside an Award. This all means that where a person is found to be incapacitated or incapable of entering a contract which includes a contract to arbitrate, then any such arbitration which follows therefrom will be deemed unenforceable or in any event liable to be set aside. Any person who has the capacity to enter into a contract can equally enter into an agreement to arbitrate since the agreement to arbitrate is in fact a contract in itself.

In **K.S. (NIGERIA) LTD v. KOFAN DOKA (NIG.) LTD**[9] K.S. (Nigeria) Ltd and Kofan Doka (Nigeria) Ltd entered into a contract which contained an arbitration clause providing that disputes arising from the contract would be referred to arbitration. A dispute later arose between the parties concerning performance under the contract and one of the parties (K.S. Nig. Ltd) attempted to avoid the arbitration process, arguing that the arbitration agreement was not binding because there was no valid contract and that the party lacked capacity to be bound by arbitration. The other party insisted that the arbitration clause was valid and binding, since both were corporate entities capable of contracting. The Court held that

> ***Arbitration agreements are contractual in nature and that only parties who have capacity to contract can enter into a valid and binding arbitration agreement.***

The Court held further that

> ***Companies registered under Nigerian law have capacity to enter arbitration agreements as part of their contractual powers, provided the subject matter is within their corporate objects. It was then held that the arbitration agreement was valid and binding on parties.***

---

[9] (1998) 12 NWLR (Pt. 579) 538

In law, only legal persons, natural or artificial, have the capability to enter into a contract. An offer and its acceptance cannot be made to a non-existent part. **See E.T.E.C. (NIG.) LTD, v. NEVICO LTD.**[10] The law is settled that at common law infants or minors are barred from entering into contracts. The only exceptions are in respect of contracts which are for the infant's necessaries. See **OMIDIJI v. FMB & ORS**[11]

It follows from these cases that a person who has no capacity to contract in the first place cannot enter into an arbitration agreement, and where the capacity to contract is qualified, the power to enter into an arbitration agreement is qualified to some extent, e.g. an arbitration agreement made by an infant binds him only if it relates to the supply of necessaries, or to a reasonable contract of service or otherwise is for his benefit as held in **OMIDIJI v. FMB & ORS**[12.]

In other cases, the agreement is voidable at his instance during his infancy or within a reasonable time after attaining majority, unless it relates to such a contract by him as is declared to be absolutely void.

A married woman can now enter into an agreement to arbitrate just like any other person. Before **Married Women's Property Act 1882** married women were unable to independently enter a contract, but by Section 1: a married woman may contract and be contracted with as a **feme sole** (independent person). The Supreme Court decision in **OKONKWO v. OKAGBUE**[13] confirms the equality of women and married persons generally to contract independently.

An agent duly authorized in that behalf can enter into an arbitration agreement on behalf of his principal, but even where there is no express authority from the principal, agency can be implied by the

---

[10] (2004) 3 NWLR (Pt. 860) 327
[11] (2001) LPELR-10666(CA)
[12] Supra
[13] (1994) 9 NWLR (Pt. 368) 301 (SC)

existing pattern of conduct between the agent and the principal. In **GRAYSHOT ENT. LTD. v. MIN. OF AGRIC**[14], the Court held that "The capacity to contract or do any other act by means of an agent is co-extensive with the capacity of the principal himself to make the contract or do the act which the agent is authorized to make or do."

Section 5 of Partnership Act of 1890 (a statute of general application in Nigeria) provides that:

> ***Every partner is an agent of the firm for the purpose of the business of the partnership... but an act of a partner which is not done for carrying on in the usual way the business of the firm is carried on, does not bind the firm unless authorized or ratified.***

Russel holds the firm view that a partner has no implied authority to bind the firm by submitting disputes to arbitration. Authority to do so must be expressly conferred or subsequently ratified by the other partners [15] It is the onus of the person seeking to rely on the arbitration agreement to prove that he has the authority (express or implied) of the partners to execute the agreement or that the other partners have ratified it.

In **SHARPE v. FOY**[16] the Court held that

> ***one partner's submission of a partnership dispute to arbitration did not bind the other partners, as arbitration was not within the ordinary course of business.***

By the decision in **SHARPE v. FOY**[17] a solicitor has no implied authority to bind his client by submission to arbitration, but once a

[14] (2002) 9 NWLR (PT. 771) 1
[15] Russell on Arbitration (24th ed., Sweet & Maxwell, London, 2015) para. 2-080.
[16] (1868) LR 4 QB 611

dispute has been referred, counsel has an implied authority to bind his client in matters relating to the conduct of the proceedings.

A Corporation Aggregate may be a party to an arbitration agreement just like a natural person, but for the agreement to be valid it must be in conformity with the rules which normally regulate transactions by the corporation. E.g. if the corporation can only validly contract under its common seal, the submission must be under seal in order for it to be bound.

The Court in **NKPORNWI v. EJIRE**[18] elaborated on the definition and capacity of a Corporation Aggregate. It held that

> ***A corporation aggregate has been defined as a collection of individuals united into one body under a special denomination, having perpetual succession under an artificial form, and vested by the policy of the law with the capacity of acting in several respects as an individual, particularly of taking and granting property, of contracting obligations and of suing and being sued, of enjoying privileges and immunities in common and of exercising a variety of political rights, more or less extensive, according to the design of its constitution, or the powers conferred upon it either at the time of its creation or at any subsequent period of its existence.***

A corporation sole, e.g. a Bishop has full contractual capacity and so can contract to arbitrate. The contractual capacity of a corporation sole was listed in **NKPORNWI v. EJIRE**[19]. A "corporation sole" is a body politic having perpetual succession, constituted in a single person who in right of some office or

---

[17] Supra

[18] (2009) 9 NWLR (Pt. 1145) 131

[19] Supra

function has a capacity to take, purchase, hold, and demise and in some particular instances, under qualifications and restrictions introduced by statute, power to alienate lands, tenements, and hereditaments, and also to take and hold personal property, to him and his successors in such office forever, the succession being perpetual but not always uninterruptedly continuous; that is there may be, and often are, periods in the duration of a corporation sole, occurring irregularly, in which there is a vacancy, or no one in existence in whom the corporation resides and is visibly represented.

1.4 ADVANTAGES AND DISADVANTAGES OF ARBITRATION

The Court of Appeal in **S.A. AND IND. CO. LTD. v. MINISTRY OF FINANCE INCORP**[20]. per THERESA NGOLIKA ORJI-ABADUA, J.C.A held thus:

> ***The notable reasons for arbitration are:***
>
> ***a. It may reduce the risk of punitive damages awards;***
>
> ***b. It may decrease exposure to class actions or other forms of aggregate litigation;***
>
> ***c. It may result in more accurate outcomes because of the arbitrator's expertise and incentives;***
>
> ***d. It may better protect confidential information from disclosure;***
>
> ***e. It enhances the ability of the parties to have their disputes resolved using trade rules;***
>
> ***f. It may enable parties to better preserve their relationship; and***
>
> ***g. It may provide a neutral forum.***

---

[20] (2014) 10 NWLR (Pt. 1416) 515

In **NICON INSURANCE LTD v. BRIGHTHOUSE ESTATE LTD**[21] the Supreme Court in establishing the advantages of arbitration restated thus:

> ***By referring any dispute/s arising from their legal relationship to arbitration, the parties clearly intended to avoid other usual or ordinary ways or methods of settling disputes, such as litigation in ordinary Courts which involves cumbersome procedures, unimaginable delays, expenses and general inconvenience.***

There are so many other reasons why there is a growing preference for arbitration than litigation. Some of these are:

1. *Arbitration can be quicker than litigation.*
   A Court action involves conformity with laid down procedure which cannot be circumvented by the parties. An arbitration on the other hand does not have to follow any particular laid down procedure.

2. *Arbitration is generally considered to be more cost-effective than litigation.*
   Parties to Court proceedings usually retain counsel who normally charge fat fees and unnecessarily prolong cases. Again, because litigation normally lasts longer, it involves more costs to the parties. If a dispute is of a technical nature, and a technically qualified arbiter is appointed, he can conduct the arbitration effectively and quickly without the involvement of lawyers.

3. *Arbitration saves time and cost.*
   Arbitration process permits some disputes to be resolved solely on documents without a hearing, especially the

[21] (2014) 10 NWLR (Pt. 1416) 515

less contentious disputes. This not only saves time, but can significantly save costs as well.

4. *Parties can represent themselves in arbitral proceedings.* They can alternatively be represented by other persons of their choice who may or may not be lawyers. In contrast, non- lawyers have no right of audience in Courts of law, and representation therein is only by lawyers.

5. *Arbitration allows for more a single person to preside over a dispute*
   A party to a contract may not wish to be exposed to a decision of a single individual who incidentally must have his weaknesses, should a dispute arise out of the contract. This desire can be realized by stipulating for an arbitral tribunal of three persons one of whom is to be appointed by himself. This possibility is particularly important where the parties to the contract belong to different countries and cultures, each party will then have the satisfaction that the tribunal includes at least one person who is familiar with his country and culture.

6. *Arbitration is less formal than litigation*
   Litigation takes place in the open Court before the whole world. Many ordinary persons are therefore frightened by Court trials and they detest the formality, solemnity and publicity associated with them.
   Arbitration on the other hand can be made to be very informal and confidential. Parties are therefore much relaxed in arbitral proceedings.

7. *Convenience for both the parties and witnesses.* Arbitration takes care of the convenience of the parties and their witnesses in fixing the date, time and place of hearing. This of course is not the case with normal Court

proceedings which have the convenience of the Court as the paramount factor.

8. *Engagement of experts to sit on the matters.*
   Arbitration allows for the selection of experts to look into disputes on matters in which they are proficient. Because of their expertise, they are better able than others to appreciate the issues involved and return verdicts which are likely to be satisfactory to the disputing parties. A judge on the other hand deals with any dispute that is brought before him. It does not matter that he has no special knowledge of the issues involved. He must listen to the parties and their witnesses and do his best to hand down what he considers to be an equitable decision.

9. *Arbitration is conciliatory in nature and contrasts with litigation.*
   Litigation has or wears the connotation of battle/war between the litigants. At the end of the day the relationship between the litigants may not be the same again, whereas in arbitration, the parties are likely to remain cordial.

10. *Neutralization of disputes.*
    Parties to international commercial transactions may neutralize any dispute that may arise from their transactions. There are many reasons why neutralization of a dispute may be desired by the parties. A party from country A may have no faith in the Courts of country B which national he does business with. The distrust often derives from suspicion of bias, lack of experience or lack of integrity on the part of the judges. In order to avoid such Courts and neutralize any dispute that may arise in

the transaction, arbitration with an arbitrator from a neutral country C may be arranged.

11. *For reasons of national prestige.*
    States and state institutions do not readily submit to the jurisdiction of foreign Courts. But many of them accept arbitration as a machinery for dispute settlement between them and foreign business organizations.

All the foregoing refers to the general run of things in arbitration. Therefore, it is not being claimed that every arbitration is necessarily cheaper, quicker, etc. than litigation.

So it will be expedient at this juncture to consider some disadvantages of arbitration.

1. *Where intricate questions of law arise, arbitration may not be suitable.*
   In such cases it would be cheaper and more expeditious for the parties to take their differences at the outset to the Court. Where, however, such disputes go to arbitration, provision has been made in the English Arbitration Act and in our old Arbitration Act, for the questions of law involved to be stated by the arbitrator for the opinion of the Court. This, however, is no longer possible under our law as the present Arbitration Act contains no such provision.

2. *Specialized Courts where they exist, like commercial Courts, that are manned by experts, dispose of cases faster and more efficiently than arbitration.*
   One example in Nigeria is the Tax Appeal Tribunal (TAT) to settle tax disputes, the National Industrial Court of Nigeria (NICN) which was established for the purpose of settling labour disputes, the Election Petition Tribunal which provides a structured avenue for

resolving disputes and challenges that arise after an election.

Arbitration may be more costly than litigation. This is usually the case in international arbitration, where the place of the arbitration is in a foreign country and may involve employing translators to translate documents. Costs will also increase on account of transport fares to a distant foreign country, coupled with hotel bills and other incidental expenses during the period of arbitral proceedings.

3. *Limited powers of the arbitral tribunal*
   Another major weakness of the arbitral process is the limited powers which the arbitral tribunal has. The arbitral tribunal's powers fall short of those conferred upon a Court of law. For example, the arbitral tribunal does not possess the power to compel the attendance of witnesses under penalty of fine or imprisonment, or to enforce awards by attachment of a bank account or the sequestration of assets. In practice, if it becomes necessary for an arbitral tribunal to take coercive action in order to deal with the case before it, such action must usually be taken indirectly, through the machinery of the Courts, rather than directly, as a judge himself can do.

1.5. ARBITRATION V. OTHER FORMS OF ADR

What is ADR?

The term 'Alternative Dispute Resolution (abbreviated as ADR) is generally used to describe the methods and procedures used to resolve disputes either as alternatives to the traditional dispute resolution mechanism of the Court or in some cases as supplementary to such mechanism.

Curiously, arbitration is not included in ADR. This is because:

> ***Arbitration presents an alternative to the judicial process in offering privacy to the parties as well as procedural flexibility. However, it is nonetheless fundamentally the same in that the role of the arbitrator is judgmental. The function of the judge and the arbitrator is not to decide how the problem resulting in the dispute can most readily be resolved so much as to apportion responsibility for that problem.***[22]

ADR began to gain prominence because of the high cost of arbitration and also because of the judicial interventions in the arbitral process. Although arbitration is informal and has advantages over litigation, still people looked at it as not satisfying the quest for complete freedom of the parties in settling their disputes. People were becoming dissatisfied with the nature of arbitration process, and the negative effect of Court litigation both of which sees disputes in terms of right and wrong, and the disputants as either winners or losers.

The attitude of the Courts in Nigeria also support the dividends of ADR and its ability to decongest the Court's cause list. Hence even when parties have commenced proceedings in Court, parties may still elect to consider ADR and the are obligated to encourage parties to vacate their cases and settle out of Court.

In **POPOOLA v. UGHAOGARANYA & ORS**[23] the Court restated its firm support for ADR thus:

> ***The law is trite beyond per adventure that where a matter has been filed in Court parties are not***

[22] Brown, Henry J. & Marriott, Arthur L.,
ADR: Principles and Practice (2nd ed., London: Sweet & Maxwell, 1999), p. 19.

[23] (2020) LPELR-50033(CA)

> ***precluded from exploring avenues for amicable settlement of their grievance. As a matter of fact, Courts are enjoined to encourage parties to peacefully settle their disagreement. No Court can insist and should insist or compel parties to complete their case before it where there is room for amicable settlement and parties have indicated to take that option.***

In **ABEY v. ALEX**[24], the Supreme Court held thus:

> ***It is in consonance with the right of parties to settle civil actions out of Court and the established practice is that this should be encouraged by the Courts whenever there is such a move by parties at any stage or pending civil proceedings save in specified circumstances in which public interest or policy element is involved.***

Other State High Courts like Abuja, Lagos inter alia have very clearly shown support for ADR in their Courts rules. **High Court of Lagos State (Civil Procedure) Rules 2019**, Order 25 urges parties to consider ADR.

Let us now consider some forms of ADR.

a. **Mediation**

One of the most novel innovations of the to Arbitration and Mediation Act (AMA) 2023 is that by section 82 of the Act, a settlement agreement resulting from mediation is binding and enforceable in Court as a contract, consent Judgment or award.

By the said Act, Mediation means a process, whether referred to by the expression, "mediation", "conciliation" or an

---

[24] (1999) 14 NWLR (PT. 637) Pg. 138 at 150

expression of similar import, where parties request a third person (the mediator) to assist them in their attempt to reach an amicable settlement of their dispute arising out of or relating to a contractual or other legal relationship but the mediator does not have the authority to impose a solution upon the parties.

Mediation is at the heart of ADR. It is a process through which parties who have failed to resolve a dispute themselves can settle it through an independent third party called a mediator. A mediator is therefore a person who is trusted and accepted by both parties to a dispute. His role is to assist the parties to reach an agreed settlement of the dispute. The procedure he adopts to achieve this is to meet each party privately so as to understand that party's own side of the story. In this regard he shuttles between the parties, and discusses with them in separate meetings known as "caucuses". He attempts to persuade each party to focus on his real interests, rather than on what he thinks to be his contractual or legal right. Thereafter, he tries to bring the parties together so that they may themselves work out a compromise solution to the dispute. He does not himself suggest a solution to the parties and cannot compel them to reach a settlement.

One illustration of the process of mediation that is sometimes given is that of a dispute over a consignment of oranges, to which both parties claim title. It was discovered after careful enquiry by the mediator that one party needs the oranges for their juice and the other needs them for their peel - and so an amicable solution to the dispute was happily found.

This process however does not stop or limit the rights of parties to explore the litigation or other dispute resolution part ways in the event that the outcome of the mediation is not amicably accepted or transformed in to a settlement agreement which is *strictu sensu* an enforceable contract. In **CBN v. ADANI MEGA SYSTEM LTD**[25] The Court held that:

> ***the Mediators' role in the mediation was merely advisory and not enforceable in law. The Mediators' advice did not fully and finally determine or dispose of the parties' rights and obligations to the extent that the parties did not adopt same as their settlement agreement.***

b. **Conciliation**

Conciliation and Mediation are sometimes used interchangeably, but this is not right. The two are not quite the same. We have already looked at mediation. In conciliation, a conciliator goes a step further than the mediator in that he would draw up and propose the terms of agreement that he or she considers to represent a fair settlement of the dispute.

Conciliation is therefore a process according to which a neutral third party trusted by the disputing parties intercedes between them in order to persuade them to settle the dispute themselves. This is easily distinguished from arbitration. While an arbitrator is concerned with imposition of a solution on the disputing parties, a conciliator does not himself hand down a decision in respect of a dispute. Rather he assists the parties in reaching a decision on the dispute often by suggesting a solution for their consideration.

Indeed, if the disputing parties are able to settle their differences by themselves, they would have conserved much energy and expense. It is of course much better for the parties

[25] (2025) LPELR-81108(CA)

that differences do not arise in the first place. That is why Professor Schmitoff observed that:

> ***It is a truism to state that arbitration is better than litigation; conciliation better than arbitration; and prevention of legal disputes better than conciliation.***[26]

c. **Mini-trial**

This is a form of evaluative mediation which enables the parties to reach a better understanding of the issues involved in their dispute, thus disposing them to enter into a negotiated settlement in an informal way. It works by trying to put, e.g. two high-level executives, one from each party, into an environment in which the strengths and weaknesses of their respective cases are drawn to their attention. When confronted in this way, they will focus on the risks involved in taking to litigation, and then reality of the time and costs likely to be wasted in litigation, will induce them to reach a compromise solution.

Mini-trial has no fixed procedure. However, it usually takes the form of a hearing of one or two days when lawyers from both sides make a brief presentation, outlining possible evidence they would call in the event of a trial. The hearing is presided over by a neutral adviser (generally a retired judge or a senior lawyer, who gives a preliminary opinion as to how a Court would be likely to react). After this information exchange, the executives retire and try to negotiate a settlement either with or without the assistance of the neutral adviser. This will enable them view their dispute in a more dispassionate manner and help them to settle. If a settlement is not reached, the parties may ask the neutral

---

[26] F.A. Mann, *Commercial Law in a Changing Economic Climate* (2nd edn, London: Sweet & Maxwell, 1981)

adviser to give a non-binding opinion as to the likely result of litigation. This in itself may well help them to arrive at a compromise settlement.

d. **Med-Arb (Mediation/Arbitration)**

In Med-Arb process, there is first an attempt to resolve the matter by mediation, but with the agreement of the parties that if mediation does not produce a settlement, the mediator will change and act as their arbitrator to decide on the dispute.

The advantage of this is that if mediation fails, the initial mediator can now be appointed the arbitrator entrusted with the duty of making a binding decision, especially where the parties have, during the course of mediation, developed a relationship of trust and confidence with the mediator.

On the other hand, it raises some questions to a lawyer. For example, how open are the parties likely to be in their discussions with the mediator, if they know that he might be called upon to act as arbitrator in the same dispute? And how can the arbitrator satisfy or appear to satisfy the requirements of impartiality and a fair hearing, if he has previously held private discussions with the parties separately and indicated his views on the issues to them?

However, it appears that the advantages outweigh the disadvantages. In Med- Arbitrator the decision to go to arbitration if mediation fails is one which the parties commit themselves in advance, before the process begins. That is why Evans-Lombe J. held thus:

> ***It is said that this offers the advantages, real or perceived, that first, the process will produce a resolution, one way or another; secondly, that parties may perhaps try harder to be reasonable***

> ***and to resolve the matter during the mediation phase; and thirdly, that if adjudication is required, there will be no loss of time or cost in having to re-acquaint a new neutral with the facts of the case and the issues between the parties.***[27]

1.6 ACTIVITIES DISTINGUISHED FROM ARBITRATION

There are other forms of ADR that are in existence and are being used mostly in the United States. Some examples are the "Neutral Listener Agreement", "Baseball" or "Last Offer" arbitration; "Medaloa" (which stands for "mediation and last offer arbitration) and Summary Jury Trial (SJT). [28]

a VALUATION

Many times, experts in various fields are invited to carry out a valuation for the benefit of the parties to the transaction. A common example is where a rent review clause in a lease provides that a new rent shall be fixed by a qualified valuer or surveyor, or where the articles of association of a private company provides that the company's auditor shall determine the price at which shares are to be sold when an existing shareholder decides to sell his shares to the directors. An arbitrator decides the issues before him and makes an award normally on the basis of evidence led before him by the parties and their witnesses and on the basis of arguments canvassed by the parties.

An expert, i.e. a surveyor or auditor on the other hand is asked to exercise his professional judgment on a matter

---

[27] Kalmneft v. Glencore International AG [2002] 1 Lloyd's Rep 128, 137 (Comm) (Evans-Lombe J)

[28] Henry Brown and Hugh Marriott, *ADR: Principles and Practice* (4th Edn, Sweet & Maxwell / Thomson Reuters, London, 2018).

within his expertise in the light of whatever enquiries and methods he chooses to employ.

Sometimes the distinction is understood by the saying that "an arbitrator determines an existing dispute whereas a valuer seeks to prevent a dispute from arising". This is, of course, not to say that a valuer or an auditor or other experts cannot be appointed an arbitrator. Of course he can. Whether an expert is an arbitrator or a valuer depends on the intention of the parties as evident in their arbitration agreement or the surrounding circumstances. But it is not always easy to22222 determine whether an expert is just a valuer or an arbitrator, particularly where the expert is a mutual valuer. This is because both are required to give decisions which will bind parties with conflicting interests. Both have a duty to act impartially between the parties. Both can reach their decisions by using their own skill and judgment without hearing evidence.

However, the main difference between them is that an arbitrator, like a judge has to decide a dispute that has already arisen and he usually has rival contentions before him, while the mutual valuer is called in before a dispute has arisen in order to avoid it.

b. CERTIFICATION

Building contracts usually provide that some works should be done to the satisfaction of a third party who is required to issue a certificate as evidence of such satisfaction. E.g. A contract may provide that a third party such as an architect has to indicate his satisfaction with a party's performance of a contract before that party's right to payment arises. Such a certificate may or may not be classified as arbitration. Whichever, it depends on the circumstances of a particular case. However, the answers to certain questions will indicate whether what has taken place or will take place is arbitration or mere certification. The questions include whether the certifier is employed by both parties or by one of them, or whether a dispute has arisen or is contemplated.

If he is appointed and controlled by one of the parties, the transaction is a certification and not arbitration, because it means that the certifier is not independent, and independence is the essence of an arbitral function. If he is appointed by both parties, then he is independent and there is an arbitration.

Again, if a dispute has arisen or is contemplated, the transaction is arbitration, otherwise it is certification.

1.6.1 DIFFERENCE BETWEEN ARBITRATOR, VALUER AND CERTIFIER

The arbitrator does his job for the parties judiciously and must act on the basis of evidence of the parties. A certifier or a valuer does not talk to the parties and his job is dependent on his expert knowledge. Apart from this, the greatest distinction is that an arbitrator is immune to actions for negligence but a valuer or certifier is not. Under Nigerian law:

- The **Arbitration and Mediation Act 2023** governs **arbitrators**.
- **Valuers** are regulated by the **Estate Surveyors and Valuers (Registration, etc.) Act Cap E13, LFN 2004**.
- **Certifiers** (architects, engineers) operate under **standard forms of contract** (e.g., Federal Ministry of Works Conditions of Contract) and professional codes like the **Architects (Registration, etc.) Act Cap A19 LFN 2004**.

The respective outcomes of these professionals are distinguished thus:

- Arbitration Award for an Arbitrator
- Valuation Report for a Valuer
- Certificate (e.g., payment, completion)

It has long been established that arbitrators like judges, enjoy immunity because policy requires that they should not be harassed by disappointed parties against whom they handed down decisions.

But for the immunity "no man but a beggar or a fool or other worthless person" would accept to be judges or arbitrators[29].

The liability of valuer or certifier may be illustrated with references to English cases. In the first case of **SUTCLIFF v. THACKRAH**[30], the plaintiff purchased a building site and engaged the services of the defendants, a firm of architects, to design the building, supervise its construction and advise on the appointment of a builder. A builder was appointed and the defendants were named architects and quantity surveyors in the building contract.

Progress on the building works was slow and the plaintiff complained that work so far done was of inferior quality. As a result, he dismissed the builder and other contractors were appointed to complete the building.

The plaintiff then commenced this action against the defendants, claiming damages for negligence and breach of duty in supervising the construction of the building and in certifying work not done at all, or improperly done by the builder in consequence of which he was obliged to pay the builder more than he was entitled to.

---

[29] Anderson v. Gorrie (1895) 1 Q.B. 668, at 670 (CA).

[30] [1974] AC 727 (HL)

The official referee to whom the dispute was referred held that the plaintiff was justified in dismissing the builder from site, that negligence in supervision was not proved but that the defendants were negligent in issuing two interim certificates. He awarded £2,000 damages to the plaintiff.

This decision was reversed by the Court of Appeal on the ground that the defendants were acting in an arbitral capacity and were therefore absolved from liability for negligence. The plaintiff appealed to the House of Lords which allowed the appeal, holding that in issuing the interim certificates the defendants were not acting as arbitrators but as valuers and certifiers. Unless a contract expressly stipulates otherwise a valuer or an architect is not an arbitrator. Since as valuers and certifiers they were not entitled to judicial immunity, they were consequently liable in negligence, i.e., for over-certifying. The decision of the official referee was therefore restored.

In the second case of **ARENSON v. CASSON BECKMAN RUTLEY & CO**[31], the first defendant, Archy Arenson, was the controlling shareholder and chairman of a private company, A. Arenson Ltd. He took his nephew, Ivor Arenson, the plaintiff in this case, into the business and gave him a parcel of shares in the company. The plaintiff, Ivor, agreed with his uncle, Archy, that in the event of Ivor's employment with the company terminating he would sell his shares to the uncle at a fair value. "Fair value" was defined in the agreement as meaning the value of the shares as determined by the auditors of the company "whose valuation acting as experts and not as arbitrators shall be final and binding on all parties".

In 1970 the plaintiff's employment with the company ceased. The second defendants, the auditors of the company, valued the

[31] [1975] 3 All ER 901

plaintiff's shares at £4,916:13:4 and the plaintiff transferred them to his uncle, Archy Arenson, at that price. A few months later the company went public and the transaction involved a report by the second defendants as to the value of the assets of the company.

The plaintiff then claimed that the later valuation showed that the shares which he sold to his uncle, the first defendant, were worth £29,500, that is, six times their value as assessed by the second defendants a few months earlier. He therefore commenced this action against the defendants, claiming damages against the second defendants for negligence.

Both the trial Court and the Court of Appeal dismissed the suit, holding that the second defendants in valuing the shares, had been performing a function of an arbitral or quasi-judicial character and were immune from liability for negligence in respect of the valuation. The House of Lords held, applying **SUTCLIFF v. THACKRAH**[32], that the immunity of judges and arbitrators were exceptional to the general rule of liability for negligence, that there would be no sufficient reason to treat a "mutual" valuer who was not exercising any judicial function as an exception to that rule. Consequently, the plaintiff had a cause of action against the second defendants.

1.7 CUSTOMARY ARBITRATION

The Court in **AGU v. IKEWIBE**[33] has defined customary arbitration as "an arbitration in dispute founded on the voluntary submission of the parties to the decision of the arbitrators who are either the chiefs or elders of their communities, and the agreement to be bound by such decision"

---

[32] Supra

[33] (1991) 3 NWLR (Pt.180) 385 (SC)

The Court of Appeal in **IKEZUAGU v. OKONTA**[34]" held that Customary arbitration is essentially a native arrangement by selected elders of the community who are vast in the customary law of the people and takes decisions which are mainly designed or aimed at bringing some amicable settlement, stability and social equilibrium to the people and their immediate society or environment.

The existence of customary arbitration in Nigeria has received judicial and extra-judicial recognition. In Nigerian traditional communities, extra-judicial settlement of disputes by chiefs, elders, age grades, masquerade institutions, family members etc, is accepted and forms part of our customary law.

Where disputes or matters in difference between two or more parties are by consent of the disputants submitted to a domestic forum, inclusive of arbitration or a body of persons who may be invested with judicial authority to hear and determine such disputes and matters for investigation in accordance with customary law and general usages, and a decision is duly given, it is as conclusive and unimpeachable, unless and until set aside on any of the recognized grounds, as the decision of any constituted Court of the land. Such a decision is consequently binding on the parties and the court inappropriate cases will enforce it. **See ACHOR v. ADEJOH** [35]

Note the unpopular view of Uwaifo J.C.A.(as he then was) in the case of **OKPURUWU v. OKPOKAM**[36] that:

> ***No community in Nigeria regard the settlement by arbitration between disputing parties as part of native law and custom,*** *and that* ***there is no concept known***

[34] (2017) LPELR-42788(CA)

[35] (2010) 6 NWLR (Pt. 1191) 537

[36] 4 NWLR (Pt. 90) 544

> ***as customary or native arbitration in our jurisprudence.***

Of course there is such a concept. Ample evidence abounds. Oguntade, J.C.A. (as he then was) who sat on the same case with Uwaifo J.C.A. did not hide his dismay at Justice Uwaifo's pronouncement. In his dissenting judgment, Oguntade, J.C.A., said:

> ***I find myself unable to accept the proposition that there is no concept known as customary or native arbitration in our jurisprudence.... If parties to a dispute voluntarily submit their dispute to a third party as arbitrator, and agree to be bound by the decision of such an arbitrator, then the Court must clothe such decision with the garb of estoppel per rem judicatam.***

It is respectfully submitted that Justice Uwaifo's statement on this matter is very unsatisfactory and does not represent the law. His brother, Justice Oguntade's opinion is preferred. The correct position of the law is that in our jurisprudence, the practice of chiefs and elders of the community in settling disputes between contending members of their community is recognized by the Nigerian Legal System as forming part of our customary law.

The Courts are directed to observe and enforce the observance of native law and customs provided always that such a custom is not repugnant to natural justice, equity and good conscience, nor incompatible either directly or by implication with any law for the time being in force. Pursuant to this directive they recognize customary arbitrations and enforce awards resulting therefrom. Accordingly,

> ***Where matters in dispute between parties are, by mutual consent, investigated by arbitrators at a meeting held in accordance with native law and***

> ***custom and a decision given, it is binding on the parties and the Court will enforce such decision.***[37]

It should be noted, however, that an award of a customary arbitration is not a judgment of a Court of law. It has no force of law and therefore cannot be enforced as such a judgment until it has been carefully examined and approved by a competent Court. But the Court will not pronounce upon the award unless it is specifically pleaded and proved in proceedings before it involving the parties to the arbitration or their privies.

When the award is proved and accepted by the Court, it creates an estoppel by way of *res judicata*, provided that the person or body that conducted the arbitration is a judicial tribunal which hands down judicial decisions.

If there is a disagreement as to whether there was in fact a properly constituted arbitration between the parties, the Court makes a specific finding of fact on the question. The award will not be ratified and enforced unless the Court is satisfied that the arbitrators gave the parties a fair hearing and that the award itself is certain, final, reasonable, legal, capable of execution and disposes of all the differences submitted to arbitration.

If the award is conditional or contingent upon something which may or may not happen, then it is not final and will not be enforced by the Courts. Thus, in **OFOMATA v. ANOKA,**[38] there was a dispute over a piece of land between the plaintiffs and the defendants. Parties agreed that the elders of the village would settle the dispute by arbitration. The elders took evidence from the parties and found that the land belonged to the plaintiffs, but decided that if the defendants disputed the decision, they should produce an oath to be sworn by the plaintiffs. The oath swearing did not take place

---

[37] Agu v. Ikewibe (1991) 3 NWLR (Pt. 180) 385

[38] (1974) 4 E.C.S.L.R. 251 at 253

because parties did not meet for the purpose. The plaintiffs by this action sought the Court to enforce the award. It was held that the award was not final because it was conditional on the swearing of an oath, which might or might not take place. It was also held that the arbitrators should have supervised the oath-swearing ceremony.

The above case may be contrasted with **NJOKU v. EKEOCHA.**[39] Here the plaintiff sued the defendants claiming title to two pieces of land, damages for trespass and injunction against further trespass. Evidence led before the Court revealed that the plaintiff's father had, some years earlier, claimed to be the owner of the lands, which he alleged were pledged to the defendants' father who was then dead. The parties then mutually agreed to submit the dispute to arbitration by the elders, the *amalas*, and to be bound by their decision. The elders examined the case and came to the conclusion that the lands belonged to the defendants, but directed that if the plaintiff's father was not satisfied, he would produce an oath to be sworn by the defendants. If they did not die within one year after the swearing, the lands would belong to the defendants, but if they both died within the year, the lands would be lost to them in favour of the plaintiff's father. This decision was accepted by the parties.

The oath was produced and sworn as agreed and the defendants did not die within the year. The plaintiff's father accepted the decision and no longer disputed the defendant's ownership of the lands. On his death, the plaintiff commenced this action, claiming the lands all over again. It was held that the plaintiff, just like his father was bound by the decision of the arbitrators and was therefore estopped from reopening the case. This is particularly so as the defendants were led by the plaintiff's father to take a step prejudicial to their interests by being put in peril of losing their lives by swearing the oath.

---

[39] (1972) 2 ECSLR (Pt. II) 199

Another condition to be met is that the Court must be satisfied that the parties voluntarily submitted to arbitration, that they expressly or impliedly agreed beforehand to accept the decision of the arbitrator and that the arbitrator was selected in accordance with customary law. If these are proved to the satisfaction of the Court the decision will bind the parties, and can be enforced, through the Court by the successful party.

It follows that if the parties have not voluntarily submitted their dispute to a person or persons for settlement, then an arbitration has not taken place, and an award made pursuant to that cannot be enforced by the Court. In the case of **EKWUEME v. ZAKARI**,[40] the defendant started a hotel business at Abakaliki and employed the plaintiff as one of his workers. There was an understanding between them that the business could be converted into a partnership of the two if after about three months they were both satisfied that they could work together. Unfortunately, they could not work together and had dispute regarding their business. Five mutual friends of the parties on their own initiative undertook to look into the dispute with a view to settling it. The panel took evidence from the parties, and awarded the sum of £631:6:3 to the plaintiff as his share of the profits of the partnership. The plaintiff commenced this action to enforce the decision. It was held that there was no arbitration because the parties did not voluntarily submit the dispute to the panel, nor did they agree to be bound by its decision. That being the case the so-called award cannot be enforced.

Parties to a valid customary law arbitration must be given a fair hearing. As a result, proceedings leading to a customary award must be conducted in accordance with the rules of natural justice. For example, the parties and their witnesses must have adequate opportunity to present their case to the arbitrator.

---

[40] (1966) NMLR 123

If the parties voluntarily agree to submit their dispute to arbitration and to abide by the decision of the arbitrator, none of the parties will be allowed to repudiate the decision merely because it does not favour him. The question will be asked whether a party can in the circumstances above, withdraw from the proceedings midstream. The answer is that he cannot do that. This was so held in the case of **KWASI v. LARBI**[41] where the Court noted that once a party has voluntarily submitted to arbitration and agreed to abide by the decision of the arbitrator, he has no right to resile from the arbitration before the award since he has no such right after the award.

1.7.1 INGREDIENTS OF CUSTOMARY ARBITRATION

The conditions which a customary arbitration must fulfill before it becomes binding on parties was set out in **GABRIEL AKPUKPU & ORS v. MEETING ELAGHA & ORS**[42] as follows:

a. There must have been a voluntary submission of the dispute by the parties to a non- judicial body.

b. The parties must have agreed to be bound by the decision of the non-judicial body as final.

c. The decision must be in accordance with the custom of the people or their trade or business.

d. The arbitration must have reached a decision and published their award.

See also the Supreme Court's decision in **OKOYE v. OBIASO.**[43]

There has been a chequered history of the customary law arbitration ingredients in Nigeria. The Supreme Court has on different

---

[41] (1952) 13 WACA 76
[42] (2014) LPELR 22588
[43] (2010) 8 NWLR (Pt.1195) 145 at 171.

occasions decided different ingredients as prerequisites for the validity of customary law arbitration.

The first unsettling of the law started in the case of **AGU v. IKEWIBE**[44] where the apex Court wrongly added two extra ingredients as vital in the making of a valid customary law arbitration. The Court held that in addition to the above ingredients there must also be non-withdrawal of a party from the arbitral process until an award is made, and secondly there must be acceptance of the award by both parties when it is made.

This decision is wrong and does not represent the correct position of the law. It has been criticized severely by learned authors and commentators. Happily, the Supreme Court has tidied up the law and restated it as it should be. It did this in a number of cases and finally came up with the four ingredients enumerated above.

1.7.2 DISTINCTION BETWEEN CUSTOMARY ARBITRATION AND NEGOTIATION FOR SETTLEMENT

The Courts have rightly drawn a distinction between a customary arbitration and a mere negotiation for settlement. In the former, the award binds the parties and their privies and is enforceable by the Courts once it is a valid award. In the latter the decision does not bind the parties unless it is accepted by both of them.

An example of negotiation for settlement can be seen in the case of **Ekwueme v. Zakari.**[45] There, five friends of the contending parties on their own initiative invited the parties and took evidence from them with the intention of settling the dispute between them. In the end their decision was not accepted by one of the parties. The other commenced this action to enforce the decision. The Court declined

---

[44] Supra
[45] Supra

to do so partly because there was no evidence that the parties voluntarily agreed to submit their dispute to the group.

These two practices, viz customary law arbitration *stricto sensu* and a mere negotiation for settlement exist alongside and are recognized as separate and independent practices with different consequences in our jurisprudence. But Allott[46] sees this separation as mere illusory. He says that arbitration as it is known in English Law is alien to our customary law, and that all cases of "so called arbitration" under that law are mere negotiations for settlement and the parties thereto are always free to resile from the arrangement at any time before the award. The parties are also entitled to reject the award when it is made.

With due respect, Allot's view is untenable. The foregoing discussions on customary law arbitration bear overwhelming testimony to the existence and recognition of customary law arbitration in Africa in general and Nigeria in particular. It is an indisputable fact that customary law arbitration which is a voluntary submission of a dispute by the disputing parties to an independent third party who makes an award which is final and binding on the parties, exists and is part of our customary law.

Indeed, it is urged that it should be further judicially developed in order to enable it play an increased role in the country's dispute settlement machinery. Professor Ezejiofor wrote that:

> ***At the moment a large number of simple disputes (about 25-30 per cent) in the hinterland are settled in this way...This dispute settlement mechanism is popular because of its informality and cheapness compared with litigations in the ordinary Courts***

---

[46] Allott, A.N. (1970). *New Essays in African Law.* London: Butterworths.

which are usually located many miles away from the rural areas.[47]

[47] Ezejiofor, G. (1964) — *The Development of Customary Law in Nigeria* (London: Sweet & Maxwell), pp. 105

CHAPTER 2

THE ARBITRATION AGREEMENT

2.1 FORMS OF ARBITRATION AGREEMENTS

An arbitration agreement is the bedrock of jurisdiction for an arbitral tribunal to deal with the matters before it. Sometimes, that conferment of jurisdiction may come in the form of a submission agreement which is usually entered upon the occurrence of a dispute. This submission agreement binds parties to submit their dispute to arbitration. Section 91(1) of AMA 2023 in recognition of submission agreements provide that "A written agreement by the parties to submit to arbitration all or certain disputes which have arisen or may arise between them in respect of a defined legal relationship… shall be valid and enforceable. In **NIGER PROGRESS LTD v. NORTH EAST LINE CORPORATION**[48] The Supreme Court recognized that parties may submit existing disputes to arbitration even if there was no clause in their original contract.

In **U.B.A. Plc v. TRIEDENT CONSULTING LTD. (2023) 14 NWLR (Pt. 1903) 95, the Supreme Court held thus:**

> ***Arbitration is a procedure for the settlement of disputes under which the parties agree to be bound by the decision of an arbitrator whose decision is in general, final and legally binding on both parties. The process derives its force principally from the agreement of the parties and, in addition, from the State as a supervisor and enforcer of the legal process. So where two or more persons agree that a dispute or potential dispute between them shall be decided in a legally binding way by one or more***

---

[48] (1989) 3 NWLR (Pt. 107) 68

> ***impartial persons of their choice, in a judicial manner, the agreement is called an arbitration agreement.***

Section 2(1) of AMA provides that arbitration agreement may be in the form of an arbitration clause in a contract or in the form of a separate complete agreement While Section 2(2) provides that an Arbitration agreement shall be in writing.

In **MAINSTREET BANK CAPITAL LTD & ANOR v. NIGERIA REINSURANCE CORPORATION PLC,** the Supreme Court held that an arbitration agreement is an agreement by which two or more parties agree that present or future disputes shall be resolved by arbitration. An arbitration clause is often included as part of the terms of a broader contract.[49]

According to Section 2(3) of AMA, an arbitration agreement shall be in writing where its contents is recorded in any form, whether or not the arbitration agreement or contract has been concluded orally, by conduct or by any other means. As provided in Section 2(4) of AMA, the requirement for arbitration agreement to be in writing is met where it is-

a. By an electronic communication as defined in Section 91, and the information contained in it is accessible so, as to be useable for subsequent reference. Section 91, defines electronic communication as any communication that the parties make by means of data messages, that is any information generated, sent, received or stored by electronic, magnetic, optical or similar means, including electronic data interchange (EDI), electronic mail, telegram, telex or telecopy.

---

[49] (2018) LPELR-44905(SC)

b. It is contained in an exchange of points of claim and defence in which the existence of an agreement is alleged by one party and not denied by the other.

Reference in a contract or separate arbitration agreement to a document containing an arbitration clause constitutes an arbitration agreement in writing, provided that the reference is in a manner that makes it part of the contract or the arbitration agreement (Section 2(5) of AMA).

Section 3 of AMA provides that arbitration agreement is irrevocable except by agreement of the parties or leave of Court as provided in Section 5(1) of this Act.[50]

2.1.1 DEATH OR CHANGE OF STATUS OF PARTY TO AN ARBITRATION AGREEMENT

1. An arbitration agreement shall not be invalid by reason of the death of any of the parties to the agreement.

2. The authority of an arbitrator shall not be revoked by the death, bankruptcy, insolvency or other change in circumstances of any party by whom the arbitrator was appointed.

"Death" according to Section 91 of AMA includes in case of a non-natural person, dissolution or other extinction by process of law. The AMA provides that an arbitration agreement shall not be invalid by reason of the death of any of the parties neither shall the authority of the arbitrator to act in arbitral proceedings be revoked by the death or bankruptcy of the party by whom he was appointed. This provision therefore encourages continuity of proceedings since

---

[50] BCC TROPICAL (NIG) LTD v. GOVERNMENT OF YOBE STATE OF NIGERIA & ANOR
(2011) LPELR-9230(CA)

it is only on the death of the arbitrator that his authority is revoked unlike in the case of the ACA where the death of the appointing party revoked the authority of the arbitrator.

All that is necessary is that whatever document that is in issue must clearly set out the intentions of the parties to arbitrate. It is not necessary that the intentions of the parties must be elicited from a simple document. Indeed, it can be incorporated into a contract by reference or distilled from several letters, telegrams, electronic communications or other means forming part of a correspondence between the parties, however, in most cases arbitration agreement takes the form of a clause in a contract entered into by the parties. Building Contracts and Insurance Policies for example provides that any difference or dispute arising out of them shall be referred to arbitration.

Generally, the arbitration agreement must satisfy the normal legal requirements of any valid contract such as consensus, capacity to contract[51] etc. It must be in writing if it must come under the Arbitration and Mediation Act. And if in the course of the arbitration the parties make any amendment to their agreement, it must also be in writing. The agreement need not be under seal for it to be valid, except where one of the parties is a corporation. If the subject matter relates to a document which must be perfected by deed, then a deed has to be employed in the arbitration agreement. In **NUTCHINASON v. WHITEHEAD**[52] it was held that a partnership agreement should be by deed only. Hence any agreement to arbitrate in relation to the partnership should also be by deed, where it isn't then the agreement to arbitrate thereof may be unenforceable.

---

[51] K.S. (Nigeria) Ltd v. Kofan Doka Nigeria Ltd (2006) 3 NWLR (Pt. 968) 246 (CA)

[52] (1826) 3 Bing. 70; 130 ER 469

An arbitration agreement must be intelligible and unambiguous in order to be upheld by the courts. If it is not, it will be set aside by the Court.

In **K.S. (NIG.) LTD v. KOFAN DOKA NIG. LTD**[53] the Court held that:

> ***An arbitration clause must be clear and unequivocal as to the parties' intention to submit their disputes to arbitration and the scope of disputes covered. Where there is ambiguity, the court cannot supply meaning by conjecture.***

Similarly in **MACAULAY v. R.Z.B. AUSTRIA**[54] the Court of Appeal held that:

> ***For an arbitration clause to be enforceable, the language must disclose with certainty an intention to refer disputes to arbitration, and not merely to negotiation or mediation.***

The Supreme Court in **OWNERS OF THE M/V LUPEX v. N.O.C. & S. LTD**[55] held that The Court must uphold arbitration agreements that are clear and binding, but it cannot enforce one that is uncertain or lacks mutual intention. Another important requirement of an arbitration agreement is that it must be mutual. An arbitration agreement must bind both parties equally. This means that each must have the same right and obligation to refer disputes to arbitration and to be bound by the arbitral award. If the agreement gives one party the exclusive power to choose arbitration while denying it to the other, courts will often hold it void for lack of mutuality or contrary to fairness and equality of parties.

---

[53] (2006) 3 NWLR (Pt. 968) 246 (CA)
[54] (2003) 18 NWLR (Pt. 852) 282 (CA)
[55] (2003) 15 NWLR (Pt. 844) 469 (SC)

The great Professor Ezejiofor restated succinctly that an arbitration clause must be mutual; if it empowers one party alone to refer disputes to arbitration, it is void for want of mutuality.[56] The Court of Appeal in **NNPC v. LUTIN INVESTMENTS LTD**[57] held that the Court will not enforce an arbitration clause that is one-sided or allows only one party to initiate arbitration proceedings. Arbitration must operate on the basis of equality and reciprocity.

2.2 AUTONOMY AND SEPARABILITY OF THE ARBITRATION CLAUSE

Where the arbitration agreement is part of a contract, it is regarded in law as a separate contract. That being the case, the failure or total breach of the main contract does not affect the arbitration clause. This is also referred to as the principle of separability and it ensures that even if the main contract is found to be invalid, void or terminated, the arbitration clause can remain valid and enforceable on its own. This has been statutorily entrenched in the Act. Section 14(2) of AMA provides that:

> ***For the purpose of subsection (1), an arbitration clause which forms part of a contract shall be treated as an agreement independently of the other terms of the contract and a decision by the arbitral tribunal that the contract is void does not entail ipso jure the invalidity of the arbitration clause.***

In **POLARIS BANK v. MAGIC SUPPORT (NIG) LTD**[58] the Court of Appeal held that:

> ***The agreement of parties cannot in anyway be equated with an arbitration clause. The law is settled to the effect that an arbitration clause is a separate***

---

[56] G. Ezejiofor, *The Law of Arbitration in Nigeria* (1997), p. 33

[57] (2006) 2 NWLR (Pt. 965) 506 (CA)

[58] (2020) LPELR-53106(CA)

> ***agreement of its own and distinct from the general agreement containing the arbitration clause.***

In considering the effect of the autonomy of arbitration clause in a contract, the court in **Heyman v. Darwin LTD**[59] said that:

> ***...an arbitration clause in a contract is quite distinct from the other clauses. The other clauses set out the obligations which the parties undertake towards each other, but the arbitration clause does not impose on one of the parties an obligation in favour of the other. It embodies the agreement of both parties that, if any dispute arises with regard to the obligations which the one party has undertaken to the other, such dispute shall be settled by a tribunal of their own constitution.***[60]

Continuing, the Court went on to add that,

> ***...although further performance of the obligations undertaken by each party in favour of the other may cease, the contract survives for the purpose of measuring the claims arising out of the breach and the arbitration clause survives for determining the mode of their settlement. The purposes of the contract have failed, but the arbitration clause is not one of the purposes of the contract.***

The Nigerian Courts in **OWNERS OF THE M/V LUPEX v. N.O.C. & S. LTD**[61], **MACAULAY v. R.Z.B. AUSTRIA**[62] *inter alia* have affirmed the doctrine of separability in the Heyman case.

---

[59] (1942) 1 All ER 337 (HL)

[60] See also NNPC vs Clifco Ltd (2011) 10 NWLR (pt 1255) 209

[61] Supra

[62] Supra

In **ERTEL BIEBER & CO. v. RIO TINTO CO**[63] The doctrine of separability of an arbitration clause was yet again tested where a contract between Britons and Germans became illegal at the brink of the World war I between both nations.

The facts are that before the outbreak of the First World War, the parties entered into a contract for the sale of copper. The contract contained an arbitration clause, providing that any dispute arising under the contract should be referred to arbitration. When war broke out between Britain and Germany in 1914, trade with enemy nationals became illegal under wartime regulations. As a result, the British government terminated all contracts with German entities, including this one. Later, a dispute arose as to whether money already paid under the contract should be refunded. *Rio Tinto* argued that the arbitration clause survived and that the dispute should go to arbitration. *Ertel Bieber* contended that since the contract had been terminated by war, the arbitration clause (being part of the contract) was also extinguished.

It was held that the arbitration agreement is a collateral and separable contract from the substantive agreement. Therefore, even though the contract became illegal due to war, the clause providing for arbitration remained operative for resolving disputes arising before the frustration or concerning rights accrued up to that time.

This independence of arbitration clause was illustrated in the case of **SOJUZNEFTEEXPORT (SNE) USSR v. JOC OIL LTD** [64] decided in the Bermuda Court of Appeal in a case for the enforcement of an award. This case was reported by Redfern and Hunter." Bermudian company (Joc Oil) entered into a contract with a Soviet foreign trade organization (SNE) for the purchase of billions of tonnes of oil. SNE brought arbitration proceedings in the Soviet Union, in accordance with the terms of the contract, for

[63] 1918] A.C. 260 (House of Lords)

[64] *(Bermuda)*, (1989) XV Y.B. Comm. Arb. 384.

payment under the contract. Joc Oil was ordered to pay SNE almost two hundred million dollars. The defence of Joc Oil, both at the time of the arbitration and during enforcement proceedings in Bermuda, was inter alia that there was no valid agreement to arbitrate, because there was no valid contract. The basis of the argument was that under Soviet law, a contract for the foreign sale of oil required the signature of two authorized officials and this contract was signed by only one official.

The arbitral tribunal accepted that there was no valid contract, as did the court of Appeal of Bermuda. But this was not a "non-existent contract as claimed by Joc Oil. The Court held that, even if the main agreement was void *ab initio*, the arbitration agreement did come into existence; and it was open to the arbitrators to award the sum otherwise payable under the contract on the basis of restitution or unjust enrichment.

The learned authors gave the rationale for the decision as follows:

> ***The distinction made is between the nullity of a contract and its non- existence. If the contract does not exist (for example because the signature of one of the parties was a forgery, or because the signature of the person who signed was procured under duress) it is difficult to see how such a document can give rise to a valid arbitration clause and hence to a valid arbitration. However, where there is a main contract, even if it was always a legal nullity, the arbitration clause that it contains constitutes a genuine juridical "platform" upon which the arbitral tribunal may stand, to judge the validity of the main body of the contract.***

If therefore a contract has ceased to exist by the time of the arbitration, an arbitral tribunal still has the platform on which it may stand. But if the contract never existed at all, then there was never an agreement. So, the arbitral tribunal can have no valid existence, authority or jurisdiction.

The arbitration agreement and the underlying contract need not rise and fall together. It is trite that an arbitration agreement is not terminated by a breach of the underlying contract. It is only where a contract is void ab initio because one of the parties is a minor, or of unsound mind or on a matter not arbitrable etc. that this ground would also affect the arbitration clause.[65]

2.3 ESSENTIAL TERMS AND DRAFTING CONSIDERATIONS

The terms of the agreement will very much depend on whether the arbitration is for *ad hoc* arbitration or an institutional arbitration as both are recognized and supported by Section 91(1) of the AMA 2023.

Arbitrations are of two broad types – **Institutional and Ad hoc.**

a. Institutional Arbitrations

In this case, institutions formulate rules, provide facilities, and support for the conduct and supervision of arbitrations which take place in countries other than those in which they have their seats. Parties often elect that their arbitration will be administered by them in accordance with the procedural rules of the institution they have elected. Their most important function is to assist in the constitution of arbitral tribunals and to ensure a smooth arbitral proceeding.

In Nigeria, we have institutions like the Lagos Court of Arbitration established by the Lagos Court of Arbitration Law

[65]See the decision in BCC TROPICAL (NIG) LTD v. GOVERNMENT OF YOBE STATE OF NIGERIA & ANOR
(2011) LPELR-9230(CA)

2009. There is also the Regional Centre for International Commercial Arbitration, Lagos (RCICAL) - established in 1989 under the auspices of the Asian–African Legal Consultative Organization (AALCO), recognized by UNCITRAL. Very recently there's has been created the College of Arbitrators Nigeria (COAN) an indigenous Arbitral Institution in Nigeria which offers trainings and accreditation to arbitrators and is actively developing its rules and arbitration Courts to support arbitration references made to the institution.

Other international institutions include International Chamber of Commerce (ICC), International Centre for Settlement of Investment Disputes (ICSID) etc.

b. Ad hoc Arbitrations:

This type of arbitration involves no permanent institutions which administers and supervises the arbitral proceedings. Ad hoc arbitration sometimes arises under submission agreements which often establish the arbitral tribunal and set out the procedural rules which the parties have adopted. More often, they are carried out under arbitration clauses in contracts which do not designate any arbitral institution and which do not refer to any particular institutional rules.

As earlier stated, the terms of the agreement will depend on whether the arbitration is for an ad hoc arbitration or an institutional arbitration. If it is ad hoc, the parties are free to incorporate into their agreement such lawful terms as they wish. The powers of the arbitral tribunal must be clearly spelt out. If any matters are to be excluded from the reference, such matters should be clearly set out, so that the tribunal will not be in any doubt as to what to do or what not to do.

The parties do not have to name an arbitrator or arbitrators in the agreement. But if they wish that a particular individual or a particular class of professionals should be appointed, they should so state. And if they also wish that the arbitrator should be appointed by a specific appointing authority for instance a particular individual or a particular office holder they should so stipulate in their agreement. It is equally important that the parties stipulate the number of arbitrators they desire, because if they do not, the law provides that the number shall be deemed to be one as provided in Section 6(2) of AMA.

It should be emphasized that the essence of an arbitration agreement is to refer disputes between the parties to arbitration. To this end, the reference must be clear, precise and unambiguous, and capable of conferring power and jurisdiction on the arbitrator. An example of an arbitration clause is quoted below.

> **Any dispute, controversy, or claim arising out of or relating to this contract, including its interpretation, performance, breach, termination, or validity, shall be finally settled by arbitration by a sole arbitrator appointed in accordance with the Arbitration and Mediation Act 2023/ applicable institutional rules.**
>
> **The seat of arbitration shall be Enugu, Nigeria. The language of the arbitration shall be English.**

This sample provision is comprehensive enough to confer the widest possible jurisdiction. This is because "disputes" or "differences" alone may not be sufficient enough to cover the resolution of matters between the parties. For example, there may be a claim which is not disputed and about which there is no difference. If the reference does not cover claims, then it may not be possible to go to arbitration for such claims. The expression "arising out of" has also been given a very wide meaning. In **NIGERIAN NATIONAL PETROLEUM CORP. v. STATOIL (NIG.) Ltd**[66], the Court of Appeal held that:

> ***Arbitration clauses must be construed broadly and generously to cover all matters in connection with the contract, except those expressly excluded.***

If the arbitration agreement is for Institutional arbitration, it is sufficient for the parties to adopt the procedure and rules of a specified arbitration institution. The parties are however, free to modify or supplement the rules of such institution if they so wish. Some arbitration institutions recommend arbitration clauses for inclusion in contracts where the arbitration is to be held under their control. Under the I.C.C. the model arbitration clause run thus:

> **All disputes arising out of or in connection with the present contract shall be finally settled under the Rules of Arbitration of the I.C.C. by one or more arbitrators appointed in accordance with the said Rules.**

Under the UNCITRAL Arbitration Rules, the recommended model arbitration clause is as follows:

> **Any dispute, controversy or claim arising out of or relating to this contract, or the breach, termination or invalidity thereof, shall be settled by arbitration in accordance with the UNCITRAL Arbitration Rules as at present in force.**

[66] (2013) 14 NWLR (Pt. 1373) 1 (CA)

The parties are free to modify the sample arbitration clause by adding provisions in respect of arbitrators, the place of arbitration, the language of arbitration and the applicable law.

2.4 ENFORCEMENT OF ARBITRATION AGREEMENTS

In **S.A. AND IND. CO. LTD. v. MINISTRY OF FINANCE INCORP.**[67], the Kaduna Division of the Court of Appeal held thus:

> ***Parties generally should not be encouraged to circumvent arbitration agreement since both parties manifested their respective intention in the contract agreement signed by them to refer the matter to arbitration when dispute arises. Arbitration agreements are enforceable even if vague, so long as the parties' intention to arbitrate as a final and binding mechanism for the resolution of their dispute is evinced therein. In the instant appeal, the arbitration agreement could not be said to be improperly or inconclusively drafted.*** *(P. 534, paras. B-C)*

One must be careful, however, not to misinterpret the purport of an agreement to arbitrate as capable of limiting the constitutionally guaranteed right to seek redress in a Court of competent jurisdiction. It has been held that an agreement to arbitrate merely postpones the parties' rights to seek redress in the public Courts.

In **KANO STATE GOVT & ANOR v. A.S.J. GLOBAL LINKS (NIG) LTD**[68] the Court of Appeal held that:

> ***An arbitration clause in a contract is only procedural, setting out that parties agree to submit their dispute to arbitration, but where by the State***

[67] (2014) 10 NWLR (Pt. 1416) 515
[68] (2017) LPELR-46215(CA)

> ***Law governing the contract, the dispute becomes unarbitrable, the arbitration clause should not exclude the right of the parties to resort to litigation but may only postpone such a right.***

In **H.R.H IGWE K. ONYE KWULUJE & ANOR v. BENUE STATE GOVT. & ORS[69] PER KEKERE-EKUN, JSC at PAGE 65 PARAS[A-G]** of the Report held *inter alia:*

> ***In Magbagbeola v. Sanni (2002) 4 NWLR (pt. 765) 193 it was held that an arbitration clause is only procedural in that a provision whereby parties agree that any dispute should be submitted to arbitration does not exclude or limit rights or remedies but simply stipulates a procedure under which parties may settle their differences. In other words, the existence of an arbitration clause in a contract merely postpones the right of the contracting parties to resort to litigation.***

In **GLOBAL FORMWORK NIGERIA LIMITED v. MRS. AISHA AHMED MUSA & ORS**,[70] it was held that:

> ***The law is that where an agreement contains arbitration clause, that parties should first refer any issue arising between them to arbitration, no party will be allowed or permitted to breach such.***

It may happen that a party may be reluctant to go to arbitration when a dispute which is covered by the arbitration agreement arises. It may also happen that one of the parties ignores the arbitration and takes out an action in Court over the very matter covered by the arbitration clause. In this sort of situation, the party who is ready

---

[69] (2015) LPELR 24780 (SC)
[70] (2022) LPELR-57776(CA)

and willing to go to arbitration will have to enforce the arbitration agreement against the reluctant party or against the party who has gone to Court in disregard of the arbitration clause provided in their contract. The question is, what then will the innocent party do in order to compel the reluctant party to arbitrate, or to stop the party who has gone to Court?

This question will be answered in two parts.

a. **Actions which may be taken to compel a reluctant party to arbitrate**

First, the aggrieved party may bring an action for a breach of the agreement to arbitrate. This is an available remedy for every breach of contract. The issuance of a writ of summons against the reluctant party may induce him to arbitrate. But if it does not and he proceeds to trial, the aggrieved party may be awarded damages for the breach of the contract to arbitrate, but the dispute remains unresolved. This action is therefore unsatisfactory and is hardly resorted to.

Secondly, if an arbitrator has already been appointed, the arbitral tribunal may commence arbitration at the instance of the aggrieved party. In that case it may peremptorily fix a day for hearing and after due notice to the reluctant party and he fails to appear without a satisfactory reason for his absence, the tribunal may proceed ex parte. Section 41(1)(c) of the Act gives an arbitrator this power where it provides that

> **If without showing sufficient cause a party fails to appear at a hearing or to produce documentary evidence, the arbitral tribunal may continue the proceedings and make the award on the evidence before it.**

The decision in **NNPC v. STATOIL (NIG.) LTD**[71] affirms the position of the law that once a valid arbitration agreement exists, refusal to participate does not stop the proceedings [72]. It is important to note however that in the light of natural justice "*audi alterem partem*" the arbitrator must give the reluctant party a peremptory notice of the hearing for the ex parte proceedings to be valid. The decision in **KANO STATE URBAN DEV. BOARD v. FANZ CONSTRUCTION CO. LTD**[73] emphasized that even though arbitration may proceed in default, the reluctant **party must first be given notice and opportunity to be heard.**

Adebanjo & the renowned jurist, Prof Fabian Ajogwu, SAN[74] state clearly that

> **Proceeding ex parte without adequate notice to the defaulting party offends the principles of due process and fair hearing and may amount to misconduct on the part of the arbitral tribunal.**

They contend further that this misconduct may qualify as a ground for setting aside an award under Section 55(3)(a)(iii) and that a mere notice for a meeting with the word "peremptory" marked on it is enough to satisfy this requirement.

Thirdly, if an arbitrator has not been appointed in the agreement and one of the parties refuses to participate in making an appointment, the aggrieved party, may request the appointing authority designated by the parties or failing such

---

[71] Supra
[72] (1897) 2 QB 124
[73] (1990) 4 NWLR (Pt. 142) 1
[74] O. Adebanjo and F. Ajogwu, *Commercial Arbitration in Nigeria: Law and Practice*
(Centre for Commercial Law Development, Lagos, 2019) at p.

designation, by an arbitral institution in Nigeria or by the Court to appoint an arbitrator or arbitrators pursuant to Section 7 of AMA.

After the appointment the arbitral tribunal may peremptorily fix a date to commence the proceedings and may proceed in the absence of defaulting party as in the previous case.[75]

b. Action by the defendant to induce arbitration when a party has commenced legal proceedings: STAY OF PROCEEDINGS

Indeed, a party to a contract may refer disputes to arbitration and has a perfect right to bring an action in Court in respect of those disputes, and the court has jurisdiction to try such disputes. Any provision to the contrary would be an ouster of the jurisdiction of the Courts. However, if the matter goes ahead at trial, it will be a breach of the agreement to arbitrate. It is in order to realize the intention of the parties that the AMA in Section 5(1) has provided that the defendant in such an action could apply to the court to stop the action in order to enable arbitration take place in accordance with the agreement of the parties.

Erudite Prof, Fabian Ajogwu, SAN in his text on Commercial Arbitration cites Mustill & Boyd and notes that:

> **if the court has refused to stay an action, or if the defendant has abstained from asking it to do so, the court has seized of the dispute, and it is by its decision, and by its decision alone, that the rights of the parties are settled**[76]

---

[75] See the decision in NNPC V STATOIL (NIG.) LTD, Supra

[76] *Mustill & Boyd, The Law and Practice of Commercial Arbitration in England* (2nd ed., 1989), p.136; cited in Fabian Ajogwu, Commercial Arbitration in Nigeria: Law and Practice (3rd ed., 2020), pp.126–127.

Where the application for stay is granted, the plaintiff will have no other remedy than to submit to arbitration in order to settle the dispute. In this way, the original agreement to submit the matter to arbitration is indirectly enforced. Before the intervention of the AMA, the court could not refuse to settle any such dispute which was brought to it because it had not only the jurisdiction, but also the duty to settle disputes if called upon to do so.

It is important to add that in practice, it will strengthen the application for stay of proceedings if the Defendant/Applicant established in his supporting affidavit that steps have been taken to arbitrate. See **UBA PLC v. TRIEDENT CONSULTING LTD.**[77]

Section 5 of AMA

The stay of proceedings is dealt with in Section 5 of the Act which provides as follows:

> 1. Notwithstanding the provisions of any other law, a court before which an action is brought in a matter, which is the subject of an arbitration agreement shall, if any of the parties request, not later than when submitting their first statement on the substance of the dispute, refer the parties to arbitration unless it finds that the agreement is void, inoperative or incapable of being performed.
>
> 2. Where an action referred to in Sub-section (1) has been brought before a court, arbitral proceedings may be commenced or continued, and an award may be made by the arbitral tribunal while the matter (Motion for Stay) is pending before the Court.
>
> Where a court makes an order for a stay of proceedings under Sub-section (1), the court may, for the purpose of

[77] (2023) LPELR-60643(SC)

preserving the rights of parties, make an interim or supplementary order as may be necessary.

Under this Section 5, a party who intends to apply for a stay of proceedings must do so before or at the time of filing his statement of claim or defence. Once a request is made, a mandatory obligation is placed on the court to refer parties to arbitration and stay proceedings unless the arbitration agreement is "void, inoperative or incapable of being performed".

Sub-section 2 implies that while the action referred to in Sub-section 1 is before the court, arbitral proceedings may be commenced or continued if they had started before the institution of judicial proceedings. The implication of this is that both judicial and arbitral proceedings over the same dispute may go on simultaneously resulting in two decisions which may be in conflict. This is probably to avoid delay in the arbitral proceedings since a mandatory obligation is placed on the court to stay proceedings and refer the parties to arbitration at the instance of any of the parties, unless the arbitration agreement is void, inoperative or incapable of being performed.

The simple way to interpret Section 5(1) is that where there is a dispute between party A and party B and their dispute is covered by or purportedly covered by an arbitration agreement, yet party A proceeds to court to litigate the dispute which should have otherwise been submitted to arbitration in party B's view, Party B may before he takes any steps in defence of the suit make an application to the Court to Stay Proceedings in the litigation pursuant to the purported arbitration agreement and the Court may upon considering the argument of parties on the application either stay proceedings and uphold the subsistence of the arbitration agreement, or refuse the application and assume jurisdiction over the matter.

The innovation in Section 5(2) is that the Act recognizes that litigation takes a lot of time, and that it is possible that an application for stay of proceedings may remain pending before a Court for more than one year. The Act therefore gives deliberate consideration to the commercial nature of arbitration matters and therefore empowers the arbitral tribunal to either continue or commence hearing once an application for stay of proceedings has been filed and is pending hearing and determination.

This way, even if the hands of litigation remain slow, it cannot clog the wheel of arbitration. It would then seem that whilst an application for stay of proceedings is pending in Court, Arbitral proceedings may go on.

The obvious danger to this innovation in Section 5(2) is that parties may have expended resources to continue arbitration up to the point of an Award, and then if the Court refuses the application for stay of proceedings, it would seem then that the entire arbitral proceedings and the Award therefrom is a nullity and an errant waste of resources.

The provision of Section 5 of AMA is a new innovation in the new Act which resolved the previously existing ambiguity within Sections 4 and 5 of the ACA regarding whether granting an order for a stay of proceedings pending arbitration was a mandatory or discretionary function of the court.

Under the ACA the Court had the discretion to allow or reject an application for a stay of proceedings depending on the ability of the applicant to show sufficient reason or willingness to proceed with the arbitration as per the arbitration agreement. This can be seen in the case of **ENYELIKE v. OGOLOMA**[78], where it was held that "An application seeking a stay of proceedings to enable parties refer to arbitration is not granted as a matter of course. Under the old law,

---

[78] (2008) 14 NWLR (Pt 1107) 247 (CA)

for such an application to be granted, the applicant must have taken no step in the Court proceedings.

With the advent of Section 5 in the AMA, a mandatory obligation has been placed on Courts to refer parties to arbitration and stay proceedings unless the arbitration agreement is void, in operative or incapable of being performed."

2.5 ARBITRATION AS A CONDITION PRECEDENT: STAY OF COURT PROCEEDINGS

Although parties cannot oust the jurisdiction of the Courts, they can agree that no right of action shall be maintained in respect of any dispute that may arise between them until such a dispute has been submitted to an arbitrator and an award has been made. The effect of this is that a party will have no right of action in respect of a claim covered by an arbitration clause, unless and until an award has been made, or unless the clause is annulled by the Court, or the party has by his conduct waived his right to rely on it.

A clause like the above is technically called a *"Scott v. Avery Clause"*, from the leading case of **SCOTT v. AVERY**[79] where the issue was considered by the House of Lords. In that case an insurance company had inserted in all its policies a condition that when a loss occurred, any member who suffered loss or damage would be paid such an amount of money as would be determined by a committee. If the member refused to accept the amount so determined, the matter would be submitted to arbitration, provided that such a member would not be entitled to maintain an action at law, or a suit in equity, on the policy until the matter has been decided by the arbitrators. The obtaining of the decision of the arbitrators was expressly declared a condition precedent to the maintenance of an action at law. In considering the scope of these

---

[79] (1856) 5 HLC 811; 10 ER 1121 (House of Lords)

provisions, the Court held that the condition was valid and not illegal as ousting the jurisdiction of the Court.

Here in Nigeria, the Supreme Court had the opportunity to consider the issue in the case of **OBEMBE v. WEMABOD ESTATES LTD.**[80] There the apex court observed as follows:

> ***...arbitration clauses, speaking generally, fall into two classes. One class is where the provision for arbitration is a mere matter of procedure for ascertaining the rights of the parties with nothing in it to exclude a right of action on the contract itself, but leaving it to the party against whom an action may be brought to apply to the discretionary power of the court to stay proceedings in the action in order that the parties may resort to that procedure to which they have agreed. The other class is where arbitration followed by an award is a condition precedent to any other proceedings being taken, any further proceedings then being, strictly speaking, not upon the original contract but-upon the award made under the arbitration clause. Such provisions in an agreement are sometimes termed 'Scott v. Avery.***

The arbitration clause under consideration in the case of **OBEMBE v. WEMABOD**[81], was an example of the first class, according to the Supreme Court. There the arbitration clause was that:

> **Any dispute or difference arising out of this agreement shall be referred to arbitration of a person to be mutually agreed upon or, failing agreement, of some person appointed by the President for the time being of the Institute of Consulting Engineers.**

---

[80] (1977) 5 Supreme Court (SC) 115.

[81] Supra

This provision making arbitration and an award a condition precedent to an action constitutes a defence to any proceedings commenced before the making of an award. It is not the same thing as the statutory right of application for a stay of proceedings embodied under section 5 of the Act. The latter is entirely mandatory obligation of the court to grant. And the application will of course not be granted, if the defendant had taken a step in the proceedings before making the application. On the other hand, if the arbitration clause contains a Scott v. Avery clause, and there has been neither arbitration nor award, the court has no jurisdiction to entertain the matter but to terminate the proceedings and order the parties to arbitration.

It should be noted that failure of the defendant to apply for a stay of proceedings does not disentitle him from relying on the clause. Again, if he makes an application for a stay and takes a step in the proceedings, this does not equally disallow him from the protection afforded by the *Scott v. Avery clause.*

Two cases may be cited to illustrate the point. In **OYEDELE v. NEW INDIA ASSURANCE CO. LTD.**[82] the plaintiff comprehensively insured his car with the defendants. The policy contained a clause which stated that all differences arising under the Policy shall be referred to arbitration and that the making of an award shall be a condition precedent to any right of action against the defendant. The insured car was destroyed in an accident, and the plaintiff claimed the sum of ₦2,552.55 (£1,276:5:6) from the defendants, and on their refusal to pay commenced this action claiming the same amount as special and general damages for breach of contract.

Pleadings were ordered and filed. In their pleadings the defendants contended that the arbitration clause was a complete answer to the

---

[82] (1990) 3 NWLR (Pt. 141) 194

plaintiff's claim, in that being a condition precedent, the plaintiff was precluded from taking any action unless he first submitted to arbitration, that the procedure for a stay of proceedings in section 5 is merely an alternative remedy available to the defendants and not a substitute for the remedy under the Scott v. Avery clause.

The plaintiff argued that the only remedy open to the defendants was to apply for a stay and that failure to do so amounted to a waiver by them of the right to arbitration. It was held that the defendants had an option to proceed by way of application for a stay of proceedings, or to rely on the defence open to them under the *Scott v. Avery clause*. In this case the defendants clearly chose to rely on the clause. The plaintiff's action was therefore dismissed and the parties ordered to resort to arbitration.

In the second case of **JEBARA v. MERCURY ASSURANCE CO. LTD**[83]. an insurance policy under which the plaintiff was insured contained the *Scott v. Avery* clause. The plaintiff initiated an action on the policy, whereupon the defendants filed their defence. Later, however, the defendants applied to the court to amend their pleadings by adding a plea that the condition precedent to the bringing of an action which is contained in the policy had not been fulfilled. The application was opposed by the plaintiff who contended that to take advantage of the arbitration clause, the defendants' only course of action was to obtain a stay of proceedings under section 5, which was no longer possible because they had taken a step in the proceedings. That being the case, they had waived their right to insist on arbitration.

It was held, granting the application for amendment, that

> ***the defendants were not debarred from using the condition as a defence without reference to the arbitration clause.***

---

[83] (1927) AC 369 (House of Lords)

Very recently, in **TOPHER ZHANG INVESTMENT LTD. & ANOR v. MASTERS ENERGY OIL & GAS LTD**[84] the Court of Appeal restated the applicability of the Scott v Avery clause to our Nigerian Jurisprudence. The Court per **OBANDE FESTUS OGBUINYA, JCA** held:

> ***The Scott v. Avery Clause traces its paternity to the English case of Scott v. Avery (1856 5 H.L Cas. 811. The Clause has been, firmly, planted and assimilated in our jurisprudence, see A.I.D.C. v. Nigeria L.N.G. Ltd. (2000) 4 NWLR (Pt. 653) 494. In the Obembe v. Wemabod Estates Ltd. (1977) 11 NSCC 264 at 271, the locus classicus on it, Fatai-Williams, JSC (later CJN), graphically, paraphrased the classes of the Scott v. Avery Clause in these illuminating words: As the learned counsel for the plaintiff/appellant has rightly pointed out, arbitration clauses, speaking generally, fall into two classes. One class is where the provision for arbitration is a mere matter of procedure for ascertaining the rights of the parties with nothing in it to exclude a right of action on the contract itself, but leaving it to the party against whom an action may be brought to apply to the discretionary power of the Court to stay proceedings in the action in order that the parties may resort to that procedure to which they have agreed. The other class is where arbitration followed by an award is a condition precedent to any other proceedings being taken, any further proceedings then being, strictly speaking, not upon the original contract but upon the award made under the arbitration clause. Such provisions in an agreement are sometimes termed***

[84] (2023) LPELR-60279(CA)

"Scott v. Avery" clauses, so named after the decision in Scott v. Avery (1856) 5 H.L. Cas. 811.

From these cases, it can be deduced that if an arbitration agreement contains a *Scott v. Avery* clause, a defendant has the option to challenge an action commenced by the other party either by applying for a stay of proceedings under section 5, or by relying on the clause. If he chooses to apply for a stay, he must be subjected to all the rigors and rules which regulate the application under the section. But if he chooses to rely on the clause, he is not bound by any rules, and it will not lie in the mouth of the plaintiff to contend that he has filed pleadings or taken some other steps in the proceedings.

It should be noted that the *Scott v. Avery* clause may take one of two forms:

1. It may take the form of an express or implied term of the contract that no action shall be brought until an arbitration has been conducted and an award made.
2. It may also be a provision that the only obligation of the defendant shall be to pay such sum as the arbitrator shall award.

An example of an express provision can be seen in this sample of *Scott v. Avery* clause: "Where by this clause any dispute or differences is to be referred to arbitration the making of an award shall be a condition precedent to any right of action by either party against the other."

An implied provision can take many forms. It has been held that making the award of a specified tribunal or an expert, a condition precedent to an action at law is a *Scott v. Avery* clause, even though not embodied in express terms. An example is found in the case of

HICKMAN v. ROBERTS [85]where a building contract provided that the decision of the building owners' architect relating to any matter, or thing, or the goodness or sufficiency of any work, shall be final, exclusive and binding on all parties and that payment will be made to the contractor as the work progresses, on the certificate of the architect. This was held to be a *Scott v. Avery* clause.

Another example is found in the case of **CIPRIANI v. BURNETT**[86]. A sweepstake ticket was sold subject to a condition that "in the event of any dispute arising with respect to any matters connected with the drawing of the sweepstake, or the awarding of the prizes, the decision of the stewards of the Trinidad Turf Club thereon shall be accepted as final."

At the end of the race, one Guevara was declared the winner of the first prize. Burnett contended that he should have been declared winner. According to him, the winning number had been incorrectly declared because the figures were wrongly read. He therefore commenced this action against Cipriani, the Chairman of the Turf Club, and others, for a declaration that his ticket won the first prize and for payment to him of the amount of the prize.

It was held by the Privy Council that the action must be dismissed. The decision of the stewards, of the Turf Club was a condition precedent to any action at law in accordance with the principle in *Scott v. Avery*. According to Lord Macmillan:

> ***It is not essential in order to exclude a right of action at law that the contract should in terms prescribe that the award of the specially constituted tribunal shall be a condition precedent to any legal proceedings.***

---

[85] (1915) 1 Ch 881 (Chancery Division)
[86] (1960) 3 All ER 168 (Privy Council)

2.6 EXCEPTIONS TO SCOTT V. AVERY

The Court can deny the defence of *Scott v. Avery* clause to the defendant where his conduct disentitles him from relying on it. This can happen in two ways:

1. Where the defendant has waived reliance on the clause, for example by defending the action without relying on the clause, or by himself instituting proceedings in breach of it.

2. Where the defendant has, by unduly influencing the arbitrator or hindering the progress of the reference, deprived the claimant of a proper opportunity to fulfill the condition precedent.

A vivid example of this is the case of **HICKMAN v. ROBERTS**[87]. In that case the arbitrator was under the influence and control of the defendants to such an extent that he lost his independence and ceased to be a free agent. At the instance of the defendants, he refused to issue the certificate which was a condition precedent to any claim of money under the contract. It was held by the House of Lords that the builders were entitled in view of this "collusion" to sue upon the contract notwithstanding the absence of a certificate for the amount claimed, and that the defendants were precluded from setting up as a defence to the action that the issuance of the certificate was a condition precedent to the bringing of an action.

In **NEALE v. RICHARDSON**[88], in a building contract, it was agreed that in the case of disputes arising, the architect was to act as arbitrator, his certificate being a condition precedent to payment. The architect withheld his certificate as to final payment and refused to arbitrate. In an action by the builder, against the building owner,

---

[87] Supra

[88] (1938) 1 All ER 753

in respect of the balance alleged to be due to him, the defendant took no steps to appoint a new arbitrator or to stay the action. It was held by the Court of Appeal that notwithstanding that an award was a condition precedent to liability, the arbitrator under the contract having refused to arbitrate, the court had jurisdiction to determine the amount due to the builder and then to make an order for its payment.

2.7 LIMITATIONS ON ENFORCEMENT OF ARBITRATION AGREEMENTS

2.7.1 The Atlantic Shipping Clause

This clause has been sanctioned by the Courts as not excluding the jurisdiction of the Courts. The clause is sometimes embodied in an arbitration agreement, and it is to the effect that arbitration must commence within a given period of time, and if it is not so commenced, then the claim by the injured party is barred. Sometimes it may take the form of a provision that if arbitration is not commenced within a given period of time, the parties will lose their rights to arbitrate.

The clause takes its name from the case of **ATLANTIC SHIPPING COY LTD v. LOUIS DREYFORCE**[89]. In that case the respondents chartered a ship to carry a cargo of linseed from Rasario to Hull. The charter-party contained an arbitration clause to the effect that all disputes under the contract should be referred to two arbitrators appointed by the parties and that the arbitrators may appoint an umpire. The charter-party also provides that

> ***Any claim must be made in writing and claimant's arbitrator appointed within three months of final discharge and where the provision is not complied with the claim shall be deemed to be waived and absolutely barred.***

---

[89] (1922) 2 AC 250 (House of Lords)

Shortly after the arrival of the ship, the charterers/respondents informed the ship owners/ appellants that they intended to put in a claim in respect of damage occasioned to the linseed in the course of the voyage. However, they neither claimed arbitration nor appointed their arbitrator within three months of the final discharge of the cargo. Later, they commenced this action in respect of the alleged damage to the cargo. The appellants opposed the action, contending that they (the charterers) failed to appoint their arbitrator within three months.

The trial Court held that the making of a claim in writing and appointment of the claimant's arbitrator within three months was a condition precedent to the bringing of any action at all. The Court of Appeal reversed the decision, holding that the clause was contrary to public policy as it was meant to oust the jurisdiction of the Court. The House of Lords held that the clause was not objectionable as the effect of it was not to oust the jurisdiction of the Courts.

If, however, in spite of the clause, the parties submit to arbitration after the expiration of the stipulated period of time and an award on the merits of the case is made, then that constitutes a defence to an action at law. Once an award is made it becomes incompetent for the injured party to litigate the same matter in an action at law, though he may take action to set aside the award. See **OYEDELE v. NEW INDIA ASSURANCE CO. LTD**[90]

---

[90] Supra

CHAPTER 3

CONSTITUTION OF THE ARBITRAL TRIBUNAL

3.1 ARBITRAL TRIBUNAL

Arbitral tribunal means a sole arbitrator or a panel of arbitrators. So irrespective of the number of arbitrators constituting an arbitral tribunal whether one or more, it is simply referred to as arbitral tribunal. This could be inferred from the provision of Section 91(1) Arbitration and Mediation Act 2023.

This chapter is devoted to examination of arbitrators in the conduct of arbitral proceeding as follows: their appointment, challenge, removal and replacement.

The arbitral process will be meaningless if there were inadequate provisions for the appointment and functions of arbitrators like other judicial officers. To this effect the Act has in Sections 6-12 made adequate provisions and arrangements for the appointment of arbitrator(s) by the parties themselves, appointing authority, arbitral institution or by the Court; also grounds for challenge, the challenge procedure, termination of the mandate of the arbitrator due to failure or impossibility to act, the appointment of substitute arbitrator and withdrawal, death and cessation of office of an arbitrator.

3.2 APPOINTMENT OF ARBITRATORS

Pursuant to section 6 of Arbitration and Mediation Act 2023, the parties to an arbitration agreement have the right and freedom to determine the number of arbitrators to be appointed. But where they do not specify, the number shall be deemed to be one as provided specifically in Section 6(2) of the Act.

The parties to an arbitration agreement possess considerable autonomy in determining the composition of the arbitral tribunal. Under Section 7 of the Arbitration and Mediation Act 2023, parties are free to agree on the number, qualifications, and method of appointment of the arbitrator or arbitrators. This expression of party autonomy is fundamental to arbitration, as it allows disputing parties to shape the procedure according to their preferences. However, it is generally inadvisable to name a specific arbitrator within the arbitration agreement itself. The reason is practical: the named individual may, at the time of the dispute, be unwilling, unable, or even deceased, thereby frustrating the arbitral process. As observed in *Russell on Arbitration*[91], the better practice is to specify only the number of arbitrators and the method of their appointment, leaving the actual nomination until after the dispute arises. This approach ensures flexibility and avoids the complications illustrated in cases such as **JEBARA v. ARABIAN GULF OIL CO. LTD**[92], where the unavailability of a named arbitrator impeded the arbitration process.

In **KANO STATE URBAN DEVELOPMENT BOARD v. FANZ CONSTRUCTION CO. LTD**[93] the Court of Appeal recognized the difficulties that may arise when an arbitrator is specifically named in the arbitration clause but becomes unavailable when the dispute arises and held that the inability of the named arbitrator to act did not render the arbitration clause inoperative; rather, the court could intervene to appoint a substitute under Section 7 of the Arbitration and Conciliation Act 1988. This approach, now reflected in Section 11 of the **Arbitration and Mediation Act 2023**, ensures that the unavailability of a named arbitrator does not frustrate the arbitral process.

---

[91] Russel, *op cit. p.37*
[92] (1942) A.C. 52
[93] Supra

Parties may also provide in their agreement that a specified office holder may be the arbitrator or may appoint the arbitrator. For example, they may provide that the president of the Nigeria Institution of Estate Surveyors and Valuers or the Chairman of the Anambra State branch of the Institution will be the arbitrator or appoint the arbitrator.

The parties may also provide in their agreement for appointment of arbitrator(s) to be done by a designated appointing authority, any arbitral institution in Nigeria or the Court. An agreement may provide that the parties shall appoint a sole arbitrator and that in the event of a disagreement, appointment shall be made by a designated appointing authority. In that case the parties must first of all attempt to make the appointment and fail, before resorting to the appointing authority to make the appointment. Sometimes the agreement may just provide that the dispute shall be referred to arbitration in accordance with the Arbitration and Mediation Act, 2023. In that case the number shall be one and the appointment made in accordance with the provisions of the Act. Note that a person shall not be precluded, by reason of the persons nationality from acting as an arbitrator, unless it is agreed by the parties. See Section 7(1) of the Act.

Section 7(3)(a) of the Act provides that where the agreement does not specify the procedure to be followed in appointing an arbitrator, then in the case of arbitration with three arbitrators each party appoints one arbitrator and the two arbitrators appointed will appoint the third arbitrator who acts as the presiding arbitrator. Note that in the old law, he was called an umpire. The difference between an umpire and a presiding arbitrator is that an umpire does not take part in the negotiation. He will be there as a disinterested third party listening to the parties and the arbitrators. At the end of the proceedings the arbitrators will hand down an award. However, if they disagree in their award, it is then that the umpire takes over the proceedings and hands down an award himself.

The presiding arbitrator is just the third arbitrator to create an odd number in order to facilitate a majority decision. He has no more powers than the other two arbitrators.

For the purpose of Article 9 paragraph 1, where three arbitrators are to be appointed and there are multiple parties as claimant or as respondent, unless the parties have agreed to another method of appointment of arbitrators, the multiple parties jointly whether as claimant or as respondent, shall appoint an arbitrator as provided in Article 10(1) of the Rules. According to the provisions of Article 10(2) of the Rules, where parties have agreed that the arbitral tribunal is to be composed of a number of arbitrators other than one or three, the arbitrators shall be appointed according to the method agreed upon by the parties.

Care must be taken by the arbitrator in appointing the third arbitrator. If, for example, the choice is restricted to a particular class of persons, a member of such a class must be appointed, and the selection must be an act of the will and judgement of the two arbitrators. In other words, it must be a matter of choice deliberately made by them. It must not be a matter of chance. In the matter of **CASSEL & CO. LTD AND BROOME,**[94]. It was agreed that each party should nominate an arbitrator and the two should select a third one. They were unable to select a third one. It was agreed that each should name two persons and that the third arbitrator should be selected from the four by lot. An appointment was made in that manner. It was held bad appointment, since the choice was not the act of the will and judgement of the arbitrators. It must be a matter of choice and not of chance.

However, if in the opinion of the arbitrators, each and every one of the persons nominated by them is a fit and proper person to act as the third arbitrator, they can select one of them by lot. Thus, in

---

[94] (1932) A.C. 161 (H.L.),

NEALE v. LEDGER[95] the parties appointed two arbitrators who were to appoint the third. Each arbitrator proposed a person who was admitted by the other to be fit and proper person to act, but they were unable to agree on which of the two should be selected. They then agreed to decide the matter by lot. It was held that the selection was good.

The above case should be distinguished from the case of **WELL v. COOKE**[96]. Here the two parties named two arbitrators who were to select an umpire. Each arbitrator named a person to whom the other objected. Whereupon they agreed to decide by lot which of them should nominate the umpire. The arbitrator who won the lot named the person to whom the other had previously objected. It was held that the selection of the umpire in this way was bad and that the award made by him must be set aside.

In **MEKWUNYE v. IMOUKHUEDE**[97] the Court held that An arbitration conducted by an **improperly appointed arbitrator** is **invalid**.

Appointment **must strictly comply** with the arbitration agreement unless the court intervenes properly under the Act.

3.2.1 APPOINTMENT BY THE APPOINTING AUTHORITY

Section 7(2) of AMA gives the parties the mandate to adopt whatever procedure to be followed in appointing an arbitrator subject to the provisions of Subsections (4) and (5). But where there is no provision for the procedure or where the parties fail to agree on the procedure for appointing an arbitrator under Subsection (2); Section 7(3) (a-e) stipulates what is to be done. According to the subsections in an arbitration:

---

95 (1863) 10 C.B. (N.S.) 391

96 (1858) 2 H. & N. 846

97 (2019) 13 NWLR (Pt. 1690) 439 (SC)

a. **With three arbitrators, each party shall appoint one arbitrator, and two arbitrators appointed shall appoint the third arbitrator. Where a party fails to appoint the arbitrator within 30 days of receipt of a request to do so from the other party, or where the two arbitrators appointed by the parties fail to agree on the third arbitrator within 30 days of their appointment, the appointment shall be made upon request of a party, by the appointing authority designated by the parties or, failing such designation, by an arbitral institution in Nigeria or by the Court.**

b. **With the sole arbitrator, where the parties are unable to agree on the arbitrator within 30days after the receipt of a written communication containing a request for the dispute to be referred to arbitration by the other party or parties, the arbitrator shall be appointed, upon request of a party, by the appointing authority designated by the parties or, failing such designation, by any arbitral institution in Nigeria or by the Court;**

c. **Where the parties to a dispute are more than two, and the arbitration agreement entitles each party to nominate an arbitrator, if within 30 days of the receipt of a written communication containing a request for the dispute to be referred to arbitration, the parties have not agreed in writing that the disputing parties represent two separate sides for the formation of the arbitral tribunal as claimant and respondent respectively, then the appointing authority designated by the parties or, failing such**

designation, any arbitral institution in Nigeria or the Court shall, upon request of a party, have the power to appoint the arbitral tribunal without regard to any party's nomination.

d. **Where the designated appointing authority or, failing such designation, any arbitral institution in Nigeria or the Court is requested to appoint an arbitrator under the provisions of this section, the party which makes the request shall send to the appointing authority, arbitral institution or Court, a copy of the request for a dispute to be referred to arbitration, a copy of contract out of or in relation to which the dispute has arisen and a copy of the arbitration agreement if it is not contained in the contract. The appointing authority, arbitral institution or Court may require from either party such other information as it deems necessary to fulfill its functions under this Act; and**

e. **Where a party propose the names of one or more persons for appointment as arbitrators, their full names, addresses and nationalities shall be indicated, together with a description of their qualifications.**

Appointment of arbitrator(s) by the appointing authority, arbitral institution or Court comes into play where one of the parties fails to appoint his own arbitrator after 30 days of being asked to do so by the other party or where the two appointed arbitrators fail to agree on the third arbitrator or where the parties fail to agree on the arbitrator when this happens, the appointing authority, arbitral institution or Court comes in to help to get the arbitration going.

When the appointing authority is required to appoint an arbitrator in pursuance of the list procedure, the party making the request shall send to the appointing authority a copy of the request for the dispute to be referred to arbitration, a copy of the contract out of or in relation to which the dispute has arisen and a copy of the arbitration agreement if it is not contained in the contract. The appointing authority may require from either party such other information as it deems necessary to fulfill its functions under the Section7 (3) of the Act.

It is important to note that where a party proposes the names of one or more persons for appointment as arbitrators, their full names, addresses and nationalities shall be indicated together with description of their qualifications as required in Section 7(3)(e) of the Act.

In appointing a sole or presiding arbitrator, the appointing authority, arbitral institution or Court pursuant to Article 8(2) of the Arbitration rules shall employ the following list procedure unless the parties agree that the procedure should not be used or unless the appointing authority determines in its discretion that the use of the list-procedure is not appropriate for the case.

a. **The appointing authority shall communicate to each of the parties an identical list containing at least three names.**

b. **Within 15 days after the receipt of this list, each party may return the list to the appointing authority after having deleted the name or names to which it objects and numbered the remaining names on the list in the order of preference.**

c. **After the expiration of the above period of time, the appointing authority shall appoint the sole arbitrator from among the names approved on the list returned**

to it and in accordance with the order of preference indicated by the parties and

d. **Where for any reason the appointment cannot be made according to this procedure, the appointing authority may exercise its discretion in appointing the sole administrator.**

The appointing authority may have difficulties in making an appointment under the list procedure. It may be that the parties returned to the appointing authority after deleting all the names therein indicating that both parties did not consider any of the names appointable. This may happen several times. The parties may also return the lists, but the undeleted names do not match in the two lists, showing that no single nominee is acceptable to both parties. If this happens several times, the appointing authority may exercise its discretion and appoint the sole or presiding arbitrator as provided in Article 8(2) (d) of the Rules.

The parties' arbitration agreement may contain a procedure to be followed in appointing the arbitrator or arbitrators in the event of a dispute. But the parties may not be able to make the appointment in accordance with the procedure when a dispute arises. For this reason, the Act in Section 7(4) provides that where under an appointment procedure agreed by the parties-

a. **A party fails to act as required under the procedure**

b. **The parties or the two arbitrators appointed by the parties are unable to appoint the third and presiding arbitrator.**

c. **The appointing authority, a third party including an arbitral institution fails to perform any function entrusted to it under such appointment procedure, any party may request the Court to take the**

> **necessary action, unless the appointment procedure agreed by the parties provides other means for securing the appointment.**

Similarly, Section 7(5) of the Act provides that the appointing authority, arbitral institution or the Court in exercising its power of appointment under this section shall:

> a. **Appoint within 30 days of the request**
>
> b. **Have due regard to the qualification required of an arbitrator in the arbitration agreement and to the considerations as are likely to secure the appointment of an independent and impartial arbitrator, and**
>
> c. **In the case of a sole or third arbitrator, take into account the advisability of appointing an arbitrator of a nationality other than those of the parties.**

Section 7(6) of the Act is to the effect that the constitution of the arbitral tribunal shall not be hindered by any controversy with respect to the arbitral institution chosen by a party.

Whatever happens, Art 10(3) of the rules provide that in the event of any failure to constitute the arbitral tribunal under the Arbitration Rules, the appointing authority shall at the request of any party constitute the arbitral tribunal and in doing so, may revoke any appointment already made and appoint or reappoint each of the arbitrators and designate one of them as the presiding arbitrator.

3.2.2 APPOINTMENT OF EMERGENCY ARBITRATOR

Emergency arbitration is permissible where a party seeks urgent relief. The AMA in Section 16 provides parties with the option of a speedy and efficient procedure to obtain urgent interim reliefs on urgent issues prior to the constitution of an arbitral tribunal. Section 16 of AMA envisages that an application for the appointment of an emergency arbitrator would be filed either alongside or after the

filing of a request for a dispute to be referred to arbitration but before the constitution of the arbitral tribunal Such an application could be made either to the arbitral institution designated by parties or the Court where no arbitral institution is designated by parties.
The applicant shall provide sufficient copies of the application for notification of the other parties and include the following information unless the parties agree otherwise (Section 16(3)(a-f) of the Act):

a. **A statement of the emergency relief sought**

b. **The name in full, description, address and other contact details of each party;**

c. **A description of the circumstances that give rise to the application and the underlying dispute referred to arbitration.**

d. **The reason why the applicant needs the emergency relief on an urgent basis that cannot await the constitution of an arbitral tribunal.**

e. **The reason why the applicant is entitled to the emergency relief and**

f. **Any relevant agreement and in particular the arbitration agreement.**

An arbitral institution or Court before whom an application for appointment of an emergency arbitrator is filed is expected to appoint an emergency arbitrator within two (2) business days of receipt of the application.

A challenge of the appointment of an emergency arbitrator must be decided within three (3) business days and an emergency arbitrator is required to render a decision within 14 days from the date of receipt of the file. Section 28 of AMA provides that the decision of the emergency arbitrator is binding on the parties, and if a party fails to comply, the other party can enforce the decision by applying to the Court.

The Emergency Relief Procedure according to Section 16(9) of the Act is to be conducted in accordance with Article 27 of the 1st schedule to the AMA i.e. of the Arbitration Rules. Section 16(10) & (11) of AMA provides that application for appointment of emergency arbitrator does not prevent a party from seeking urgent interim measures from a Court and an application to Court for an urgent interim measure does not constitute either an infringement or waiver of the arbitration agreement.

Note however, that Section 17(1)(b) of AMA provides that the grounds for the challenge of an emergency arbitrator shall be the same as that of an arbitrator as provided in Section 8 of the Act unless. Section 18 of the Act is to the effect that the seat of emergency relief proceedings shall be as agreed by the parties or as determined by the arbitral institution or the Court that appointed the emergency arbitrator in absence of an agreement. Section 18(3) of the Act provides that any meeting with the emergency arbitrator may be conducted through a meeting in person at a location which the emergency arbitrator considers appropriate or by video conference, telephone or similar means of communication.

3.3 CHALLENGE AND REPLACEMENT OF ARBITRATORS

An arbitrator may be challenged if circumstances exist that give rise to justifiable doubts as to his impartiality or independence or if he does not possess the qualification agreed by the parties. Challenging an arbitrator in order to disqualify him from acting is a serious issue. An arbitrator so challenged will surely be embarrassed. To guard against this embarrassment, the Act in Section 8 provides:

> 1. **Where a person is approached in connection with possible appointment as an arbitrator, the person shall disclose any circumstances likely to give rise to**

justifiable doubts as his impartiality or independence.

2. **An arbitrator shall from the time appointed and throughout the arbitral proceedings, disclose to the parties any relevant circumstances not within the knowledge of the parties.**

3. **An arbitrator can only be challenged where circumstances exist that give rise to justifiable doubts as to his or her impartiality or independence or if he does not possess qualifications agreed by the parties.**

4. **A party may only challenge an arbitrator it appointed or in whose appointment it has participated for reasons of which it becomes aware after the appointment has been made.**

The intention of the Act is undoubtedly to afford the would-be arbitrator an opportunity to disclose any relationship that may jeopardize his function as an arbitrator. Such relationship like social, business, blood or financial may occasion bias in favour or against any of the parties to the arbitration proceedings. A person discharges this duty imposed by the Act once he discloses the circumstance to the parties. If the parties, despite the disclosure, do not object to his acting or his continuing to act, they cannot later challenge him on the basis of suspicion that he may be partial on account of that circumstance. They have to accept him for what he is.

In **GLOBAL GAS & REFINERY LTD v. SHELL PETROLEUM DEVELOPMENT CO OF NIGERIA LTD** [98] The dispute concerned a gas-supply contract (Gas Processing

---

[98] Lagos State High Court, Suit No LD/1910GCM/2017, 25 February 2020) (unreported) reported in 'Court Sets Aside $2 Billion Arbitration Award Against Shell' This Day (Lagos, 1 March 2020).

Agreement) between Global Gas & Refining Ltd and Shell. The parties submitted to an arbitration under the International Chamber of Commerce (ICC). Global Gas challenged the appointment of the presiding arbitrator (Professor Oba Nsugbe, QC, SAN) and another arbitrator on grounds of non-disclosure of prior connections with Shell (or its parent company) and related institutional links. The ICC Court dismissed the challenge; arbitration proceeded and the tribunal (majority) dismissed Global Gas's claims. Global Gas then applied to the Lagos High Court to set aside the award, on the ground that the arbitrators' non-disclosure amounted to misconduct and had impaired fairness of the proceeding. The Lagos High Court held that

> ***the non-disclosure by the majority arbitrators did amount to misconduct, and set aside the award.***

The Court also stated that

> ***once an arbitrator is challenged for bias or independence, they should resign rather than resist the challenge, irrespective of whether the relationship or disclosure would objectively have given rise to doubts under international guidelines***

3.3.1 GROUNDS FOR CHALLENGE

As stated earlier, Section 8(3) of the Act provides that an arbitrator may be challenged if circumstances exist that give rise to justifiable doubts as to his impartiality or independence, or if the arbitrator does not possess the qualifications agreed by the parties. Over the years, it has been observed that interest or bias are factors which adversely affect a person's impartiality or independence. And it will be good to examine these notions in some details.

i. IMPARTIALITY

An arbitrator, like a judge, must be impartial and independent in the performance of his adjudicatory functions. He must not be influenced by bias, prejudice, or any extraneous considerations. It is not enough that justice is done; it must also be manifestly seen to be done. This principle, rooted in natural justice and the doctrine of *nemo judex in causa sua* (no one should be a judge in his own cause), applies with equal force to arbitral proceedings. As held in **K.S.U.D.B. v. FANZ CONSTRUCTION CO. LTD**[99], the credibility of the arbitral process rests on the arbitrator's neutrality and fairness.

Similarly, in **GLOBAL GAS & REFINERY LTD v. SHELL PETROLEUM DEVELOPMENT CO OF NIGERIA LTD**[100] the court set aside an arbitral award on the ground that the arbitrator's failure to disclose potential conflicts of interest amounted to misconduct.

The test, as reiterated in these authorities, is whether a fair-minded and informed observer would apprehend a real likelihood of bias.

An arbitrator should avoid communicating with one party, especially the party who appointed him, without the knowledge of the other, with regard to the issues in dispute. Thus it has been said that:

> **An independent and impartial arbitrator must not engage in any ex parte communications with the parties regarding the merits of the case during the course of the proceedings".**[101]

In practice however, it is generally accepted that there will be communication with a party-nominee before his appointment

---

[99] Supra
[100] Supra
[101] *K.S.U.D.B. V FANZ CONSTRUCTION CO. LTD (1990) 4 NWLR (Pt. 142) 1*

and also in respect of the choice of a third arbitrator. There is no problem about this, as it is only sensible to ensure that the presiding arbitrator who is to be appointed will be acceptable to both parties

ii. INDEPENDENCE

Independence in arbitral process is concerned with the relationship between arbitrator and one of the parties (usually the party appointing him). This relationship may be blood, business, financial or otherwise. The question is whether the proposed arbitrator is likely to be influenced by the interest of the party who appointed him. If a solicitor or an engineer acts for a client in a matter which subsequently goes to arbitration, there is the like-hood that he will be influenced by the party who is his client.

Interest and bias are two factors which will adversely affect a person's impartiality and independence. It is worthwhile to examine these concepts in greater details.

iii. INTEREST

Interest in the arbitrator in a matter which is the subject of arbitration may take several forms. In each case the arbitrator cannot be successfully challenged if the interest was known to the parties at the time of appointment. In **JOHNSTON v. CHEAPE**[102] the parties individually owned land along the banks of a river. They decided to deepen the channel of the river. In that connection they appointed an arbitrator from the neighborhood to execute the work and apportion the amount which each of the parties should pay so as to defray the cost depending on the benefits which the lands belonging to him will derive from the work. The arbitrator made an award which was objected to by the appellant who commenced this

[102] (1817) 5 Dow 247

action to have the amount payable by him reduced on the grounds among other things that the arbitrator has interest because his own land will benefit from the deepening of the channel.

Lord Eldon held that his action must fail. The parties, he said knew whom the arbitrator was and he was chosen on account of his own skill in such matters and there was nothing to show that he acted corruptly or improperly.

The most common situation that raises concerns about the interest or partiality of an arbitrator arises from the existence of an employer–employee or professional relationship between the arbitrator and one of the parties. In building and engineering contracts, it is customary for the architect, who is employed by the building owner, or an engineer, engaged by the contractor, to be named as the arbitrator in the agreement. Where such a relationship was known to both parties at the time the contract was executed, the law does not necessarily preclude the named person from acting as arbitrator when a dispute subsequently arises, even though he may be required to pass judgment on his own professional conduct or decisions.

This practice, though seemingly inconsistent with the principle that *no one should be a judge in his own cause*, has been tolerated in the construction industry on grounds of **commercial convenience and technical competence**. Building owners often insist on such clauses because they believe the resident architect or engineer is most familiar with the technical details of the project, while contractors, eager to secure the work, accept these terms despite their inherent risks. As observed in **K.S.U.D.B. v. FANZ**

CONSTRUCTION CO. LTD[103], such arrangements are not automatically invalid, provided the relationship and potential conflict were known and consented to by the parties. However, under modern standards reflected in **Section 8(1) of the Arbitration and Mediation Act 2023**, such situations require full disclosure, and continued impartiality is subject to challenge if a reasonable doubt arises.

It should be noted that for the interested arbitrator to be protected as in the Johnston Case, he must have been named in the contract or arbitration agreement before the dispute arises.

After the dispute has arisen, an employer will not be allowed to appoint his employee, or servant or dependent, who has not been previously named in the agreement as an arbitrator. Any such appointment will be set aside by the Court.

In the case of **RE FRANKENBERG & SECURITY COMPANY** [104] the Court described as a "really monstrous" action which could not be entertained for a moment, the appointment by a company of its manager as arbitrator after a dispute had arisen.

Another example of interest in the arbitrator is the relationship of creditor and debtor between any of the parties and the arbitrator. In such a case, the question is whether or not the indebtedness arises directly out of the matter included in the arbitration. If it does, the arbitrator will be disqualified. But he will not be disqualified if it does not.[105]

---

[103] Supra

[104] (1899) 1 QB 190

[105] See *Re Chalmers and The North British Railway Co* (1876) 1 App Cas 127

In **MALMESBURY RAILWAY COY v. BUDD** [106] two contractors Budd and Holt made a claim against the railway company for jobs done for the company. An arbitrator was appointed to determine the amount payable by the company. The company moved the Court for an injunction to restrain the arbitrator from acting on the reference because there was an allegation that he (the arbitrator) advanced money to Budd and Holt. It was argued that the advance funds might have given him an interest in making an award in their favour. The Court granted an interim injunction, observing that it has jurisdiction to grant an injunction if corruption is proved in such circumstances.

Another example of financial interest in the arbitrator can be seen in the case of **BLANCHARD v. SUN FIRE OFFICE**[107]. In this case, an insurance policy issued by the Sun Fire Office contained an arbitration clause that required disputes between the insurer and the insured to be referred to arbitrators appointed under the policy. When a fire occurred and a claim was made, the insured objected to the appointment of one of the proposed arbitrators on the ground that he was a shareholder in the insurance company - that is, he had a pecuniary interest in one of the parties to the dispute.

The English Court of Appeal held that the arbitrator was disqualified from acting because his financial interest as a shareholder in the defendant insurance company gave rise to a real likelihood of bias. The court reasoned that it would be contrary to the principles of natural justice for a person with a direct pecuniary stake in the outcome to act as arbitrator, even if the amount of interest was small.

---

[106] (1867) LR 2 Ex 279

[107] (1890) 25 QBD 241

iv. **BIAS**

Bias is a state of mind which inspires prejudice in favour of, or against a person or an issue, and can arise from all sorts of reasons. When it can be shown that an arbitrator has a bias for or against any of the parties, then it raises the possibility that he will not do justice between them. If therefore there is reasonable ground to suspect that a person is biased, it is not advisable to appoint him arbitrator or to allow him continue if he has already been appointed.

The grounds on which bias can exist in the arbitrator include the following:

1. Ill- feeling against any of the parties
2. Prejudice against any of the parties
3. A strained relationship between him and any of the parties. For example, if there is a litigation between them.
4. Corrupt receipt of money or other gratification from any of the parties.

Although an arbitrator may be free from any form of bias at the time of appointment, but if it arises after the appointment, he can be challenged on that ground with a view of stopping him from acting.

It has always been held by the Courts that the arbitral tribunal would be biased where they accepted a bribe from any of the parties before making the award. In **SHEPARD v. BRAND**[108] a dispute between A and B was referred to arbitrators. Before making their award, the arbitrators demanded three guineas each from both parties as payment for their fees and expenses. A complied and paid his share

[108] 171 ER 684 (K.B.)

but B refused to pay. The arbitrators nonetheless proceeded to make the award in the matter and B moved to have the award set aside.

The Court held that:

> ***Where arbitrators receive money from one of the parties singly, whether for charges or any other purpose, before making their award, it is sufficient ground for setting aside the award.***

Indeed, the reasoning of the Court was that the payment created an appearance of bias and partiality, undermining the neutrality and integrity of the arbitral process. The principle is strict — even the appearance of corruption or partiality is fatal to the validity of the award.

An arbitrator can be challenged with a view of removing him, if it was discovered after his appointment that he does not possess the qualifications on the basis of which he was appointed. As regards qualifications for arbitrators, there is no specific legal qualification required, it is therefore those qualifications that are agreed upon by the parties that are required of the arbitrators.

But if a party or the parties knew the arbitrator did not have the qualifications agreed by the parties but nevertheless appointed him to arbitrate, they will be estopped from challenging him on the basis of qualification after the appointment.

3.3.2 PROCEDURE FOR CHALLENGE

Section 9 of AMA provides that parties may determine the procedure to be followed in challenging the arbitrator. However, where no such procedure is stipulated, then a party who wishes to challenge an arbitrator shall send to the arbitral tribunal written statement of the reasons for the challenge. But he must do so within 14 days of becoming aware of the constitution of the arbitral tribunal or becoming aware of any circumstances likely to give rise to any justifiable doubts as to his impartiality or independence.

Article 13 of the Rules sets out the detailed procedure for the challenge but extends the time within which to challenge an appointment from 14 days under the Act to 15 days. He must notify the challenge to the other parties, the other arbitrators and the arbitrator who is challenged. The notification shall be in writing and the reasons for the challenge clearly stated. Unless the challenged arbitrator withdraws, or the other parties agrees to the challenge, the arbitral tribunal shall decide on the challenge. According Section 9(3) of the Act, where a challenge under any procedure agreed by the parties or under Sub-section 9(2) is not successful, the challenging party may within 30 days after having received notice of the decision rejecting the challenge, request either:

a. **The appointing authority, arbitral institution or the Court that appointed the arbitrator or**

b. **Where a party appointed the arbitrator, the Court, as may be appropriate to decide the challenge and while the request is pending, the tribunal, including the challenged arbitrator, may continue the arbitral proceeding and make an award.**

In simplifies terms, Party A challenges an arbitrator for bias within 14 days of appointment or of knowing of the facts of the arbitrator's bias and the arbitral tribunal (including that arbitrator) decides the that the challenge has merit then the challenged arbitrator is removed. If instead the tribunal decides that the challenge has no merit, then Party A being dissatisfied, may apply within **30 days** to:

i. The appointing authority (if the arbitrator was appointed by it); or

ii. The Court (if appointed by a party or by the court).

Because the Act recognises once again that applications can pend in Court for years, the Act goes on to state that while the application/appeal is pending before the Court or appointing authority, the arbitral proceedings shall **continue uninterrupted**, and the tribunal **may even render an award.**

Section 9(4) of the Act provides that the appointing authority, arbitral institution or the Court shall decide on the admissibility or merits of the challenge after giving opportunity to the arbitrator concerned, the other party or parties and any other members of the tribunal to comment in writing within a suitable period of time. The submitting party shall communicate the comments to the other party or parties and to the arbitrators. Section 9(5) of the Act put rather simply and in practical terms; if Party A challenges an arbitrator for bias (say, the arbitrator accepted a payment or had a prior relationship with Party B); the challenge is sent to the appointing authority (e.g., Lagos Court of Arbitration) then the said appointing authority requests written comments from:

a. The arbitrator concerned,
b. Party B, and
c. Any co-arbitrators.

Each has time to respond, and all comments/responses are circulated among all the stakeholders/participant before the authority then **decides** on the challenge, i.e. to uphold it or dismiss it.

3.4 TERMINATION OF ARBITRATOR'S MANDATE

Section 10 of the Act provides that:

1. **Where, by reasons of law or fact an arbitrator is unable to perform his or her functions or fails to act without undue delay, the arbitrator's mandate shall terminate upon his or her withdrawal or by the agreement of the parties on the termination.**

2. **Where dispute remains between the parties as to the grounds upon which the arbitrator's mandate is sought to be determined, any party may request the Court to decide on the termination of the mandate.**

3. **Where under this section or section 9(2), an arbitrator withdraws from office or a party agrees to the termination of the mandate of an arbitrator, this shall not imply acceptance of the validity of any ground referred to in this section or sections 8(3) and (4).**

The Act is very clear and explicit on the termination of the mandate of an arbitrator. Where the mandate of an arbitrator has been terminated, he cannot thereafter act in the proceedings. Apart from withdrawal following a challenge, an arbitrator may withdraw from proceedings for a variety of reasons. These include ill-health, conflict of interests, lack of time or other commitments. Death of an arbitrator also terminates his mandate.

The parties also reserve the right to terminate the mandate of the arbitrator. This they can do if the arbitrator is incompetent to handle the particular arbitration or that he is not performing satisfactorily in the conduct of the arbitral proceedings, either because he is not devoting enough time to the matter or he is causing unnecessary and undue delay.

The meaning of Section 10(3) seems to be that the fact that an arbitrator withdraws from office either on his own volition or following a challenge; or the termination of his mandate should not be construed to mean that his impartiality or independence is in doubt or that he is incapable of performing his function or that he is guilty of undue delay.

It is probably to assuage the feelings of an arbitrator whose mandate is terminated and protect his public image that this provision is inserted by the legislature, otherwise it will be difficult to appreciate the purpose of its presence.

3.5 APPOINTMENT OF A SUBSTITUTE ARBITRATOR

As provided in Section 11 of the Act, where the mandate of the arbitrator terminates under Sections 9 or 10 of this Act or because of withdrawal from office for any other reason or because of revocation of the mandate by agreement of the parties or for any other reason whatsoever, a substitute arbitrator shall be appointed according to the rule that were applicable to the appointment of the arbitrator being replaced.

Article 14(2) of the Rules which complements Section 11 of the Act provides that if at the request of a party, the appointing authority determines that, in view of the exceptional circumstances of the case, it is justifiable to deprive a party of the right to appoint a substitute arbitrator, the appointing authority may after hearing from the other arbitrators, appoint a substitute arbitrator or authorize the other arbitrators to proceed with the arbitration and make any decision or award.

This rule acts as a safeguard against abuse of the appointment process.

Normally, under Section 11 of the Act, the same party who appointed an arbitrator originally also has the right to appoint a replacement if that arbitrator's mandate ends (e.g., by withdrawal, resignation, death, or removal).

Article 14(2) however recognizes that in exceptional circumstances, allowing the same party to re-appoint could lead to delay, obstruction, or unfair advantage. So, the appointing authority (for example, the Lagos Court of Arbitration, the Chartered Institute of Arbitrators (UK) Nigeria Branch, or the High Court if acting as appointing authority) can at the request of a party intervene to protect the integrity and efficiency of the proceedings by stopping a party from appointing the substitute arbitrator.

The Act is silent on what constitutes the "exceptional circumstances" which may convince the appointing authority to deprive a party from the appointment of a substitute arbitrator. However, the situations listed herein below may qualify as exceptional circumstances.

The appointing authority may deprive a party of its right to reappoint or appoint a substitute arbitrator in any of the following circumstances:

1. **Repeated Misconduct or Delay:** Where party's first appointee resigns after causing serious delay or procedural obstruction this may be a ground for depriving the appointing party of his right to a substitute appointment. The ICC Court deprived a respondent of the right to reappoint after its arbitrator resigned following multiple dilatory tactics.[109]

2. **Tactical Withdrawal:** Where a party's arbitrator withdraws shortly before an award to delay proceedings and the same party seeks to exploit the right to appoint a

[109] ICC Case No 16775/GZ (Final Award, 2011) (2012) 23(1) ICC International Court of Arbitration Bulletin 105.

substitute arbitrator, an opposing party may establish the special circumstance to deprive the appointment of a substitute arbitrator on this ground. In **PT CENTRAL INVESTINDO v. FRANCISCUS WONGSO AND OTHERS**[110] one of the main issues for determination was whether the arbitral institution (SIAC) had the power, in **exceptional circumstances**, to deprive a party of its right to appoint a substitute arbitrator, and whether such deprivation was justified in this case. It was held that the resignation of the respondents' arbitrator at such an advanced stage constituted **exceptional circumstances**, since it was likely intended to **delay proceedings** or **undermine the tribunal's continuity**. Therefore, the SIAC was entitled to **deprive the respondents of their right to re-appoint** and to allow the remaining arbitrators to continue and issue the final award.

3. **Conflict of Interest Re-creation:** Where a party attempts to re-appoint another arbitrator closely linked to the first one or sharing the same conflict, the opposing party may on this fact establish a special circumstance capable of depriving the said party from appointing a substitute arbitrator.

   In **AT&T CORP v. SAUDI CABLE CO**[111] Court approved the ICC Court's refusal to confirm a replacement arbitrator who had a similar conflict to the previous appointee.
4. **Unreasonable Non-cooperation:** Where a party deliberately refuses or fails to appoint a substitute arbitrator within the prescribed time, with intent to stall

[110] [2012] SGHC 216 (Singapore High Court)
[111] [2000] 2 All ER (Comm) 625 (CA)

proceedings then the opposing party may on this fact establish a special circumstance capable of depriving the said party from appointing a substitute arbitrator.

In **OLAWOYIN v. ADEYEMI**[112] the Nigerian Supreme Court held that where one party refuses to cooperate in arbitration, the Court or agreed authority may validly appoint in substitution.

5. **Impartiality Concerns:** Where evidence suggests the re-appointment would compromise the appearance of neutrality of the tribunal then the opposing party may on this fact establish a special circumstance capable of depriving the said party from appointing a substitute arbitrator. In **FEDERAL AIRPORTS AUTHORITY OF NIGERIA v. NWOYE**[113], Nigerian Court of Appeal stressed that arbitral integrity and impartiality override procedural technicalities.

Article 15 of the Rules provides that where an arbitrator is replaced, the proceedings shall resume at the stage where the arbitrator who was replaced ceased to perform his or her functions, unless the parties decide otherwise.

Section 13 of AMA confers arbitrators, appointing authorities, arbitral institutions as well as their employees with immunity against acts or omission that might arise in the discharge of their duties, unless it can be established that they acted in bad faith. This immunity as granted under AMA does not exempt an arbitrator from any liabilities that might arise from his withdrawal. This shields arbitrators, appointing authorities, arbitral institutions from the fear of liabilities, thus promoting independence and impartial decision.

---

[112] (1967) NMLR 167 (Nigeria, SC)

[113] (2017) LPELR-43845(CA)

In **NIGERIA MACHINE TOOLS LTD v. TOKUNBO AKINLAJA**[114], the Court held that:

> ***An arbitrator, once properly appointed, is expected to act independently, impartially and without fear or favour. The Court will not intervene merely because one party is dissatisfied with the outcome unless there is clear evidence of misconduct or bad faith.***

The Court further noted that:

> ***the independence and impartiality of arbitrators are fundamental to the integrity of arbitration, and judicial interference must be sparing and consistent with the parties' agreement.***

Although decided before the 2023 Act, *the Nigeria Machine Tools Ltd's* ***case*** reflects the same policy foundation now codified in Section 13 to the effect that:

a. **Arbitrators act as neutral decision-makers and must be free from intimidation or fear of liability for acts done in good faith.**

b. **Judicial oversight should be limited to cases of bad faith, bias, or misconduct - not mere error of judgment.**

c. **The independence and impartiality of arbitrators is a "fundamental condition of fairness", aligning with the modern principle of immunity for good-faith conduct under the AMA 2023.**

---

[114] (2018) LPELR-44505 (CA)

CHAPTER 4

JURISDICTION OF THE ARBITRAL TRIBUNAL

4.1 ARBITRAL TRIBUNAL JURISDICTION

Jurisdiction is the threshold inquiry in every arbitration. It answers, in juridical terms, a deceptively simple question: by what authority may a private tribunal constituted by agreement of the parties rather than by direct act of the State render a decision that is final, binding, and enforceable with the coercive assistance of public courts? In Nigerian law, the answer is neither purely contractual nor purely public. The arbitral tribunal derives its mandate from party consent, yet its award is accorded legal consequences that are recognizably judicial: it may be recognized as binding and enforced in the same manner as a judgment, subject to the limited supervisory jurisdiction of the courts.[115]

The conceptual structure of arbitral jurisdiction in Nigeria therefore rests upon a calibrated balance: party autonomy is respected as the engine of arbitration, but autonomy is not permitted to displace mandatory norms of public law. The Arbitration and Mediation Act 2023 (AMA) which repealed the Arbitration and Conciliation Act embodies this balance by affirming the competence of arbitral tribunals to determine their own jurisdiction in the first instance, limiting judicial intervention to instances expressly provided by the Act, and prescribing defined grounds upon which the courts may set aside, or refuse enforcement of awards tainted by jurisdictional defects.[116]

---

[115] *Arbitration and Mediation Act 2023 (AMA) ss 57–58 (recognition and enforcement of awards).*
[116] *AMA s 64(1) (extent of court intervention) and s 14 (tribunal's competence to rule on jurisdiction).*

For the practitioner and the scholar alike, 'jurisdiction' in arbitration is not a monolith. It encompasses multiple dimensions jurisdiction over the parties (ratione personae), the subject matter (ratione materiae), the time period (ratione temporis), and the place or seat (ratione loci). It also includes the tribunal's jurisdictional authority to adopt measures necessary to decide the dispute, including the power to determine whether the arbitration agreement exists, is valid, or covers the dispute that has arisen. Nigerian courts have long insisted that these jurisdictional questions must be approached with commercial realism: the law should enforce genuine bargains to arbitrate, while refusing to convert arbitration into a mechanism for ousting mandatory statutory regimes or for insulating illegality from judicial scrutiny.[117]

4.2 COMPETENCE–COMPETENCE PRINCIPLE

Statutory foundation and conceptual content

The competence–competence principle is the doctrinal bedrock of modern arbitral jurisdiction. In its positive aspect, it authorizes the arbitral tribunal to rule on its own jurisdiction in the first instance, including any objections with respect to the existence or validity of the arbitration agreement. In its negative aspect, it restricts premature recourse to the courts in a manner that would interrupt or stultify the arbitral process. Nigerian law now places the principle on an explicit statutory footing: Section 14(1) of the AMA provides that 'the arbitral tribunal shall rule on its own jurisdiction, including any objections with respect to the existence or validity of the arbitration agreement'.

The AMA's formulation is materially aligned with Article 16 of the UNCITRAL Model Law, a deliberate policy choice that signals Nigeria's commitment to international best practice. The Model Law approach performs two systemic functions. First, it protects the tribunal from tactical obstruction: if every jurisdictional plea could

---

[117] *See; M V Panormos Bay v Olam (Nig) Plc (2004) 5 NWLR (Pt 865) 1 (CA).*

automatically trigger a full-blown judicial inquiry, arbitration would be reduced to a prelude to litigation. Second, it reinforces the separability of the arbitration agreement: disputes about the main contract do not necessarily destroy the tribunal's authority to decide whether the contract (and the arbitration agreement) is binding.[118]

4.2.1 Separability as an incident of competence–competence

Section 14(2) of the AMA codifies the doctrine of separability in terms that are both orthodox and significant. It provides that an arbitration clause forming part of a contract 'shall be treated as an agreement independent of the other terms of the contract' and that a decision by the tribunal that the contract is void does not entail, ipso jure, the invalidity of the arbitration clause. In practical terms, this means that allegations of rescission, frustration, misrepresentation, breach, or even illegality of the main contract may not automatically deprive the tribunal of jurisdiction; the tribunal may still decide, as a preliminary question, whether the arbitration agreement survives and covers the dispute.[118]

Separability does not, however, operate as a legal alchemy that conjures jurisdiction where none was ever agreed. If the challenge is one of contract formation namely, that no contract (and therefore no arbitration agreement) was concluded at all, then the tribunal must first examine whether there was a concluded arbitration agreement in accordance with ordinary principles of consent. Separability addresses defects of validity in an existing contract, not the non-existence of assent. In this sense, separability is a doctrine of survival, not a doctrine of creation. The ancient decision of the Supreme Court in **CF SONNAR (NIG) LTD v.**

---

[118] UNCITRAL Model Law on International Commercial Arbitration 1985 (as amended 2006) art 16; AMA s 14(1)–(2).

PARTENREEDRI M S NORDWIND is instructive on this point.[119]

4.2.2 Judicial recognition of competence–competence in Nigeria

Long before the AMA, Nigerian courts had already embraced the policy underlying competence–competence, though expressed through the framework of the repealed Arbitration and Conciliation Act and the courts' general pro-arbitration posture. The Supreme Court has repeatedly emphasised that where parties have freely chosen arbitration, courts should be slow to encourage dilatory manoeuvres designed to derail arbitral proceedings. **IN NNPC v. CLIFCO (NIG) LTD**[120], although the Supreme Court was seized of issues arising from an application to set aside/refuse enforcement of an award, its reasoning underscores a deeper point: arbitral proceedings and awards enjoy legal efficacy and are not to be treated as optional or advisory simply because one party regrets the bargain.

Similarly, appellate authority has deprecated attempts to procure premature judicial determinations of issues better left, in the first instance, to the tribunal. In **STATOIL (NIG) LTD v. NNPC**[121], the Court of Appeal reaffirmed that arbitration is intended to be efficient and final within the statutory limits, and that the courts' role is supervisory not managerial except where the statute expressly empowers intervention.

The competence–competence principle also shapes the manner in which jurisdictional objections should be raised. Nigerian courts have stressed the importance of procedural discipline: a party who participates in arbitration without timely objection, and later seeks to challenge the tribunal's authority only after an unfavourable turn,

[119] *(1987) 3 NWLR (Pt 66) 520 (SC).*
[120] *(2011) 10 NWLR (Pt 1255) 209 (SC).*
[121] *(2014) 14 NWLR (Pt 1373) 1 (CA).*

is likely to face the doctrinal barriers of waiver and estoppel embedded in the statutory scheme.[122]

4.3 SCOPE OF JURISDICTION

4.3.1 Sources of arbitral jurisdiction: agreement, law, and mandate

The primary and indispensable source of arbitral jurisdiction is the arbitration agreement, whether as a clause within a broader contract or a standalone submission agreement. Under Nigerian law, the arbitration agreement is construed as a specialised contract: it must satisfy the ordinary requirements of consent, certainty, and legal capacity, while also meeting statutory form requirements where applicable. The tribunal's jurisdiction is therefore not inherent; it is conferred. That conferral is typically express (through words of reference) but may sometimes be implied from the parties' conduct where the statute permits and the facts justify such inference.[123]

Yet the arbitration agreement does not operate in a legal vacuum. The scope of jurisdiction is also shaped by mandatory provisions of the AMA, by other statutes that reserve certain matters for judicial determination, and by constitutional norms. Section 65 of the AMA provides in general terms that the Act does not affect any other law by virtue of which certain disputes may not be submitted to arbitration, or may be submitted only in accordance with the provisions of that or another law. The significance of section 65 is that it preserves the architecture of non-arbitrability without attempting an exhaustive catalogue; the question whether a particular dispute is 'capable of settlement by arbitration' therefore requires attention to the substantive law governing the dispute.[123]

4.3.2 Dimensions of jurisdiction: personae, materiae, temporis and loci

---

[122] *See AMA s 14(3)–(4) (timing of pleas) and s 63 (waiver of right to object).*
[123] *See;* ***M V Panormos Bay v Olam (Nig) Plc*** *(2004) 5 NWLR (Pt 865) 1 (CA).*

A disciplined analysis of arbitral jurisdiction benefits from distinguishing its principal dimensions. Jurisdiction ratione personae concerns a person who is bound by the arbitration agreement and who may properly be brought before the tribunal. The general rule is that only parties to the arbitration agreement are bound; however, modern commercial practice raises recurrent questions concerning assignment, agency, novation, group-of-companies arrangements, guarantors, and non-signatories. The Supreme Court in **SONNAR (NIG) LTD v. PARTENREEDRI M S NORDWIND**[124] adopted the ultimate approach to such questions through orthodox doctrines of contract and agency, cautious not to impose arbitration obligations in the absence of demonstrable consent.

Jurisdiction ratione materiae concerns what disputes are covered by the parties' submission. The interpretive task is performed by construing the arbitration clause in context. Nigerian courts, notably in **SONNAR (NIG.) LTD v. PARTENREEDRI M.S. NORDWIND**[125], consistent with international commercial practice, have adopted a liberal and commercially sensible approach in construing arbitration clauses employing phrases such as "arising out of," "in connection with," or "relating to." Such expressions are generally interpreted expansively to encompass disputes possessing a sufficiently close nexus to the contractual relationship.

However, this liberal approach is not without limits. Where the arbitration clause is narrowly framed, its boundaries must be strictly respected. An arbitral tribunal is a creature of the parties' mandate and derives its jurisdiction solely from the agreement; it is not a court of general jurisdiction and cannot assume authority beyond the scope expressly or impliedly conferred by the arbitration agreement.

Jurisdiction ratione temporis concerns time. It asks when an arbitral tribunal's authority begins and how far in time it extends. In

---

[124] *(1987) 3 NWLR (Pt 66) 520 (SC).*
[125] *Supra*

particular, it examines whether the tribunal can hear disputes that arose before an arbitration clause was introduced, after the contract has been terminated, or are said to be out of time.

Assuming as estate surveyor is appointed in January to manage a residential property under a written property management agreement which initially contains no arbitration clause. The surveyor begins collecting service charges and managing the property from January. In March, the parties execute a variation of the agreement introducing an arbitration clause.

If a dispute later arises concerning service charges collected in January and February, the question is whether the arbitral tribunal has jurisdiction over disputes that pre-date the arbitration clause. This is a classic question of jurisdiction ratione temporis.

Similarly, if the property management agreement is terminated in December, but a dispute arises afterward concerning handover of records, outstanding service charges, or unpaid management fees, the tribunal may still have jurisdiction if the arbitration clause is drafted to survive termination. This position is reinforced by the doctrine of separability, which treats the arbitration agreement as independent of the main contract.

Questions of limitation introduce a further distinction. A claim that is brought late may not necessarily deprive the tribunal of jurisdiction; rather, depending on the governing law and the wording of the arbitration agreement, it may go to admissibility, that is, whether the claim should be heard, rather than jurisdiction, which concerns the tribunal's power in the first place.

In practise however, Nigerian jurisprudence has not always sharply distinguished between jurisdiction and admissibility. Accordingly, careful pleading is required. Objections based on limitation periods or contractual preconditions such as mandatory notice, valuation, or prior negotiation before reference to arbitration must be framed with precision to avoid conflating distinct legal concepts.

4.3.3 Jurisdiction ratione loci

This is about place specifically, the legal seat of the arbitration. The seat is not just where meetings are held or where the parties are located; it determines which country's arbitration law applies and which courts supervise the arbitration.

If an estate surveyor and valuer enters into a property management agreement with a property owner and the agreement contains an arbitration clause stating that "the seat of arbitration shall be Lagos, Nigeria". Even if the hearings later take place in Abuja or online, the legal seat remains Nigeria.

Because Nigeria is the seat:

a. the Arbitration and Mediation Act 2023 (AMA) governs the procedure (unless the parties validly agree otherwise); and
b. Nigerian courts have supervisory jurisdiction to:
   i. grant interim measures,
   ii. hear challenges to the tribunal's jurisdiction, and
   iii. entertain applications to set aside the award.

If, however, the same agreement provides that the seat of arbitration is London, Nigerian courts will generally not supervise the arbitration. Their role will be limited mainly to recognising and enforcing the international award in Nigeria, under Sections 57 – 60 of the AMA and the New York Convention as incorporated into Nigerian law.

In short, for an estate surveyor and valuer's illustration or like dispute, the chosen seat decides which courts are in charge, not where the property is located or where the work was done.

4.3.4 Arbitrability and public policy limits

A major limit on an arbitral tribunal's jurisdiction is arbitrability. Even if parties agree to arbitrate, not every dispute can legally be resolved by arbitration under Nigerian law.

Under the Arbitration and Mediation Act 2023 (AMA), section 65 preserves the principle that only arbitrable disputes may be submitted to arbitration while Sections 55 and 58 empower the court to set aside an award or refuse enforcement where:

a. the subject matter is not capable of settlement by arbitration under Nigerian law, or
b. enforcement would be contrary to public policy.

These provisions reflect the same policy found in Article V(2) of the New York Convention, which allows national courts to refuse enforcement on grounds of non-arbitrability or public policy.

For instance, an estate surveyor and a property owner agree to arbitrate disputes arising from a property management contract. A dispute over management fees or service charges is clearly commercial and therefore arbitrable.

However, if the dispute involves allegations of criminal misappropriation of tenants' funds, issues affecting title to land vested by statute, or matters where a statute confers exclusive jurisdiction on a court or regulatory body, such issues may fall outside the scope of arbitration, regardless of the parties' agreement. In those circumstances, arbitration cannot be used to sidestep the courts or statutory processes.

In **M V PANORMOS BAY v. OLAM (NIG) PLC**[126], although the dispute was commercial and therefore arbitrable, the Court of Appeal emphasised that arbitration cannot be employed to defeat mandatory legal norms or public policy considerations. Where such

---

[126] Supra

issues arise, the supervisory jurisdiction of the court is engaged, notwithstanding the existence of an arbitration clause.

Simply while most estate-management or professional disputes are arbitrable, arbitration stops where public interest begins. Parties cannot, by agreement, remove from the courts, matters that Nigerian law reserves to judicial determination.

4.4 PRELIMINARY OBJECTIONS AND JURISDICTIONAL CHALLENGES

4.4.1 Timing, form and waiver

Section 14 of the Arbitration and Mediation Act 2023 (AMA) does more than recognise that an arbitral tribunal may rule on its own jurisdiction; it also sets strict timing rules for raising jurisdictional objections.

In simple terms:

a. If a party says "this tribunal has no jurisdiction at all," that objection must be raised no later than the statement of defence.

b. If a party says "the tribunal is going beyond what the arbitration clause allows," the objection must be raised as soon as that excess arises during the proceedings.

c. The tribunal may allow a late objection only if the delay is justified.

The policy behind this is straightforward: jurisdictional objections must be raised early, within the arbitration itself, and not saved as a fallback in case the final award is unfavourable. Assume that an estate surveyor and valuer is in arbitration with a Landlord over unpaid management fees. If the Landlord believes that there is no valid arbitration agreement, or that the dispute is tainted with element of crime and therefore falls outside the scope of an arbitrable matter, the Landlord must raise that objection promptly, either in the defence or immediately the issue arises. If the Landlord participates fully in the arbitration and waits until after losing to complain about jurisdiction, the objection will likely fail.

This approach is reinforced by Section 63 of the AMA, which provides that where a party knows that a procedural requirement under the Act has not been complied with, but continues with the arbitration without objecting promptly, that party is deemed to have waived the right to object.

In the estate surveyor context above, if a landlord knows that the tribunal was improperly constituted or that a procedural step was skipped, but still attends hearings, files submissions, and cross-examines witnesses without protest, the landlord cannot later repackage that complaint as a jurisdictional defect.

Arbitration therefore rewards vigilance, and not ambush. Parties are expected to raise objections as they arise, not litigate in stages or hold objections in reserve as insurance against an adverse award.

4.4.2 The tribunal's ruling: preliminary decision or award on the merits

An arbitral tribunal may rule on a jurisdictional objection either as a preliminary issue or in the final award on the merits. Where the tribunal decides, as a preliminary question, that it has jurisdiction, Section 14(6) of the Arbitration and Mediation Act 2023 (AMA) allows an aggrieved party to apply to the court, within 30 days of receiving notice of the ruling, for a determination of the issue.

Crucially, Section 14(7) provides that the arbitral proceedings may continue and the tribunal may make an award, notwithstanding that a jurisdictional challenge is pending before the court. These provisions reflect a deliberate legislative compromise: they maintain judicial oversight of jurisdiction while preventing the arbitral process from being stalled by interlocutory court proceedings.

While this mechanism is a commendable innovation of the AMA, it is not without practical risk. Where arbitration proceeds to a full award incurring substantial costs, fees, and time while the jurisdictional question remains unresolved before the court, the process operates under a degree of uncertainty. If the court ultimately upholds the jurisdictional challenge, the arbitral proceedings conducted in the interim may be rendered nugatory, resulting in a significant waste of resources.

The scheme promotes efficiency in the arbitration system as a whole, but it shifts significant risk onto the parties and the tribunal. For example, where an estate surveyor and valuer is engaged in a high-value property valuation dispute, the tribunal may continue with the arbitration while a court is still deciding whether it even has jurisdiction. If the arbitration proceeds to a full hearing incurring professional fees, expert valuation costs, and legal expenses and the court later rules that the tribunal lacked jurisdiction, all that effort and expense would have been wasted.

Accordingly, the provision demands careful tactical judgment by parties and tribunals, especially in complex or high-value property disputes where the financial consequences of an adverse jurisdictional ruling can be substantial.

4.4.3 Relationship with court proceedings: stay, referral and anti-stultification

Jurisdictional challenges often arise where court proceedings and arbitration run side by side. A common example is a property dispute in which an estate surveyor and valuer is engaged to value a commercial property or assess compensation, but one-party files a court action despite an arbitration clause in the valuation or development agreement. The other party then applies to the court for a stay of proceedings and a referral to arbitration.

The Supreme Court has made it clear that a stay will not be granted automatically. In **KANO STATE URBAN DEVELOPMENT BOARD v. FANZ CONSTRUCTION CO LTD**[127], the Court stressed that there must be a real dispute.

Applied to an estate surveying and valuation context, if a developer admits owing a professional valuation fee to an estate surveyor and valuer but simply fails to pay, the court may find that there is no genuine dispute to refer to arbitration only a debt to be paid in which case an undefended list procedure may appropriately deal with a liquidated or fixed money demand of this nature.

In **M. V. LUPEX**[128], the Supreme Court further explained that:

> ***the decision to stay proceedings is discretionary and must be exercised judicially.***

For instance, where a landlord drags a valuation dispute to court, files pleadings, and actively participates in the case before suddenly invoking an arbitration clause, the court may refuse a stay, having regard to the party's conduct.

Recent cases also emphasise that a party seeking arbitration must show real readiness and willingness to arbitrate. In **ONWARD ENTERPRISES LTD v. MV MATRIX**[129], the Court held that

> ***it is not enough to merely state an intention to arbitrate.***

In practical terms, the client of an estate surveyor and valuer seeking a stay must show concrete steps such as proposing arbitrators, paying arbitral fees, or activating the arbitration clause rather than using arbitration as a delay tactic to avoid paying valuation or consultancy fees.

---

[127] *(1990) 4 NWLR (Pt 142) 1 (SC)*
[128] *Supra*
[129] *(2010) 2 NWLR (Pt 1179) 530 (SC)*

Finally, it is important to distinguish between the court's jurisdiction and the parties' right to insist on arbitration. The court's jurisdiction over land and property matters is constitutionally guaranteed and cannot be removed by a private contract. An arbitration clause in a valuation or development agreement merely gives the parties a personal right to insist on arbitration. That right can be waived. Thus, where a party to a property valuation dispute takes substantial steps in court proceedings without invoking arbitration, the Court of Appeal has recognised that such conduct may amount to a waiver of the right to arbitrate, even though the court retains full jurisdiction over the matter.

4.5 CONSEQUENCES OF LACK OF JURISDICTION

4.5.1 Conceptual consequences: nullity, partial nullity and curial control

A tribunal that acts without jurisdiction does not merely commit an error; it exceeds the foundational consent upon which arbitral authority rests. The juridical consequence is that the award is vulnerable, either to being set aside at the seat or to being denied recognition and enforcement at the enforcement stage. The AMA treats jurisdictional defect as a paradigm ground of curial intervention. It is important to appreciate that 'lack of jurisdiction' may present itself in varying degrees. At one end is total absence of jurisdiction (for example, no arbitration agreement). At the other is excess of authority (for example, the tribunal decides matters beyond the submission), a situation for which the Act expressly provides the possibility of partial setting aside or partial enforcement where separable.[130]

4.5.2 Setting aside for jurisdictional defect under Section 55

Section 55 of the AMA is the primary set-aside provision for arbitrations seated in Nigeria. It stipulates that recourse to the court

[130] See; AMA ss 55(3)(a)(v), 58(2)(a)(v).

against an arbitral award may be made only by an application for setting aside in accordance with the prescribed grounds. The grounds include incapacity, invalid arbitration agreement, lack of proper notice or inability to present one's case, non-arbitrable subject matter, public policy, and critically where the award deals with a dispute not contemplated by or not falling within the terms of the submission, or contains decisions on matters beyond the scope of the submission. The latter ground is the statutory expression of excess of jurisdiction.

Section 55(4) imposes a limitation period: an application to set aside must be made within three months from the date the applicant received the award (or, where a request for correction/interpretation has been made, from the date that request is disposed of). This time limit is central to finality. It ensures that jurisdictional challenges are not weaponized indefinitely. Notably, section 55(5) empowers the court, once grounds are proved and substantial injustice is shown, to remit the award to the tribunal for reconsideration in whole or in part, or to set it aside in whole or in part. This remedial flexibility is important where the jurisdictional defect is curable or confined to distinct parts of the award.

4.5.3 Refusal of recognition and enforcement under Section 58

Where the question of jurisdiction arises at the enforcement stage, Section 58 becomes central. It permits the court to refuse recognition or enforcement only on specified grounds that substantially mirror Article V of the New York Convention. Of particular relevance are the grounds that the arbitration agreement was invalid, that proper notice was not given, that the award deals with matters beyond the submission, and that the subject matter is not capable of settlement by arbitration under Nigerian law or that enforcement would be contrary to public policy. The statutory logic is evident: an award should not be enforced if it was rendered without jurisdiction, whether because the agreement was invalid or because the tribunal exceeded its mandate.

4.5.4 Nigerian judicial attitude: the binding force of awards and supervisory restraint

Nigerian courts have repeatedly reiterated that arbitral awards are not to be treated lightly, and that the grounds for curial intervention are narrow and circumscribed. In **BAKER MARINE (NIG) LTD v. CHEVRON (NIG) LTD**[131], the Supreme Court affirmed that:

> ***the court will not lend its authority to enforce an award where statutory grounds for setting aside or refusal of enforcement are established.***

The decision is frequently invoked for the proposition that parties must live with the consequences of their choice of arbitration, and that courts will resist invitations to re-litigate the merits under the guise of jurisdictional complaint while remaining firm where jurisdiction is truly absent.

This restrained supervisory posture accords with the broader jurisprudence on obedience to subsisting decisions and the preservation of legal order. The Supreme Court has consistently emphasised, in the context of court orders, that decisions of courts of competent jurisdiction remain binding on the parties until they are set aside. In **ROSSEK v. A.C.B. LTD**[132] and **A.P.C. v. KARFI**[133], the Court reaffirmed that parties are not at liberty to treat judicial decisions as optional or provisional.

Although arbitral awards are not identical to court judgments, the same systemic concern underpins arbitration law: legal processes must command respect and certainty. Accordingly, where an arbitral tribunal is properly constituted, has jurisdiction, and has made an award, the courts will not lend their authority to acts of non-compliance. Conversely, where jurisdiction is absent, the courts will

---

[131] *(2006) 15 NWLR (Pt 1002) 276 (SC).*
[132] *(1993) 8 NWLR (Pt. 312) 382 (SC)*
[133] *(2018) 6 NWLR (Pt. 1616) 479 (SC),*

equally decline to enforce the award. This balanced approach preserves both the integrity of arbitration and the supervisory role of the courts.

4.6 Practical implications and guidance

From a practical standpoint, jurisdictional discipline requires both tribunal and counsel to adopt a structured approach. First, counsel should plead jurisdictional objections promptly in accordance with Section 14, and should document the objection so as to preserve it for any permissible curial review. Second, tribunals should, where appropriate, bifurcate jurisdictional issues and deliver reasoned preliminary rulings, bearing in mind the statutory 30-day window for court review. Third, parties seeking to resist enforcement on jurisdictional grounds should align their arguments with the strict statutory language of Sections 55 and 58, avoiding merit-based complaints dressed up as jurisdictional defects. Finally, courts should maintain the statutory balance to intervene where jurisdiction is genuinely absent, but to resist being drawn into managerial supervision of arbitral process.

4.7 Conclusion

Jurisdiction in arbitration is both the gateway and the guardrail of the arbitral process. In Nigerian law, it is now governed by a modern statutory architecture that combines competence–competence and separability with carefully delimited judicial oversight. The result is a system that aspires to commercial efficacy without sacrificing public law control. For Nigeria's arbitration project to succeed in practice, parties and counsel must internalize the discipline demanded by the AMA: timely objections, faithful adherence to the tribunal's mandate, and respect for the limited grounds upon which courts may intervene. In this way, arbitral jurisdiction becomes not a battleground for procedural gamesmanship, but a principled framework that supports both party autonomy and the rule of law.

CHAPTER 5

CONDUCT OF ARBITRAL PROCEEDINGS

5.1 COMMENCEMENT OF PROCEEDINGS

Before an arbitrator begins his or her duties, the individual must first be formally notified of the appointment in writing and must accept the appointment in writing as well. The parties are then required to provide the arbitrator with the documents conferring authority to act, such as the arbitration agreement, the arbitration clause within the main contract, the contract itself, or where applicable, a Court Order referring the dispute to arbitration.

Upon receiving these documents, the arbitrator must carefully verify that the appointment is valid and that he or she meets all the qualifications or conditions agreed upon by the parties. Where the arbitrator discovers any deficiency - for instance, a lack of required expertise or a potential conflict of interest - it is essential to inform the parties immediately, who may then decide whether to waive the deficiency or appoint another arbitrator.

Once the arbitrator (or panel of arbitrators) confirms their qualifications and formally accepts the appointment, they are constituted as the arbitral tribunal. At this stage, the tribunal should ensure that the scope of its authority, as defined in the arbitration agreement, is broad enough to cover all issues in dispute. Addressing such jurisdictional and procedural matters early helps to prevent complications or challenges later in the proceedings, when amending the agreement may be far more difficult.

5.2 PROCEDURAL AUTONOMY AND CONDUCT OF HEARINGS

The Act in Section 31(1) allows parties to adopt the procedural rules that shall apply to their proceedings however where parties do not agree on any rules of procedure, then the Act requires that the arbitral tribunal conducts the arbitral proceedings in accordance with the procedure contained in the Arbitration Rules which complements the Act. Where the Rules or the agreed procedural rules of parties are silent on a procedural matter then the arbitral tribunal shall rely on section 30 of the Act in applying discretion to act fairly, treat parties equally with a view to resolving the dispute of parties without unnecessary expense.

It is considered good practice for the arbitral tribunal to hold a preliminary meeting with the parties to settle procedural issues and give necessary directions before the hearing begins. During this meeting, the parties may agree on several fundamental matters, such as the place of the arbitral proceedings, whether there will be oral hearings, whether the proceedings will be conducted solely on documents, or a combination of both. They may also agree on the dates and times for subsequent sittings and the language to be used in the proceedings. This practice aligns with the Nigerian appellate jurisprudence. In **STABILINI VISINONI LTD v. MALLINSON & PARTNERS LTD**[134] the Court of Appeal underscored the importance of early procedural direction in arbitration. Where any disagreement arises at this preliminary stage, the arbitral tribunal has the authority to determine the issue. In doing so, the tribunal must take into account considerations such as cost, availability of facilities, and the convenience of the parties and their witnesses, as provided under **Section 32(3) of the Arbitration and Mediation Act 2023**. Similarly, **Article 17(2) of the Arbitration Rules** provides that, as soon as practicable after its constitution and after

---

[134] 2014] 12 NWLR (Pt 1420) 134

consulting the parties, the arbitral tribunal shall establish a provisional timetable for the arbitration, which may be revised as circumstances or party agreement require.

The parties should also determine whether they wish to be represented by counsel during the proceedings. At this preliminary stage, they are expected to agree on the timelines for the submission of their respective statements of claim and defence. Where the parties are unable to reach an agreement, the arbitral tribunal has the power to fix such timelines and give any other necessary procedural directions.

In line with the principles of fairness and equality of treatment, all communications addressed to the arbitral tribunal including statements of claim, statements of defense, and any supporting documents - must be simultaneously communicated by the submitting party to all other parties. This ensures transparency and prevents any party from obtaining an unfair advantage.

This procedural framework is supported by **Sections 30 and 38(3) of the Arbitration and Mediation Act 2023**, which require equal treatment of parties and proper notice of all proceedings, as well as **Article 3(1) of the Arbitration Rules**, which provides that any written communication shall be delivered to all parties. The Nigerian Supreme Court in **M.V. LUPEX v. NIGERIAN OVERSEAS CHARTERING AND SHIPPING LTD**[135] emphasized that arbitral proceedings must be conducted in accordance with the rules of natural justice, ensuring that each party is given full opportunity to present its case and respond to the other's. Similarly, in **BAKER MARINE (NIG.) LTD v. CHEVRON (NIG.) LTD**[136], the Court of Appeal underscored that fairness and proper communication between parties are fundamental to the arbitral process. The arbitral tribunal may, at the request of

[135] (2003) 15 NWLR (Pt 844) 469 (SC)
[136] (2000) 12 NWLR (Pt 681) 393 (CA)

any party, permit one or more third persons to be joined in the arbitration as parties, in accordance with **Section 40 of the Arbitration and Mediation Act 2023**. Such joinder is permissible only where the person sought to be joined is a party to the arbitration agreement. However, the tribunal retains the discretion to refuse joinder if, after giving all affected parties — including the proposed additional party — an opportunity to be heard, it determines that such joinder would cause prejudice to any of the parties.

Pursuant to **Article 17(5) of the Arbitration Rules**, the arbitral tribunal may render either a single award or separate awards in respect of all parties involved in the arbitration. This provision promotes procedural efficiency while safeguarding the principles of fairness and equality of treatment among all parties to the proceedings.

In **SHELL (NIG.) EXPLORATION & PRODUCTION CO. LTD v. FEDERAL INLAND REVENUE SERVICE**[137], the Supreme Court affirmed that joinder in quasi-judicial and arbitral-type proceedings must not prejudice existing parties and must be based on a demonstrable connection to the subject matter in dispute.

5.3 WRITTEN AND ORAL PROCEEDINGS

Section 38 of the Act provides-

1. **Subject to a contrary agreement by the parties, the arbitral tribunal shall decide whether the arbitral proceedings shall be conducted:**

a. **By holding oral hearings for the presentation of evidence or for oral arguments;**

b. **On the basis of documents and other material; or**

---

[137] (2021) LPELR-53049(SC)

c. **By a combination of the methods described in paragraph (a) and (b), and, unless the parties have agreed that no hearing be held, the arbitral tribunal shall hold such hearings at an appropriate stage of the proceedings if so requested by any party.**

2. **The arbitral tribunal shall give the parties sufficient advance notice of any hearing and meeting of the arbitral tribunal, held for the purpose of inspection of documents, goods, or other property.**

3. **Except on the application for preliminary order under Section 22 of this Act, every statement, document or other information supplied to the arbitral tribunal or other authority by one party shall be communicated to the other party.**

4. **Any expert report or evidentiary document on which the arbitral tribunal may rely in making its decision shall be communicated to the parties.**

5. **Unless otherwise agreed by the parties, the arbitral tribunal may, for the purpose of the arbitral proceedings concerned-**

a. **Direct that a party to an arbitration agreement or a witness who gives evidence in proceedings before the arbitral tribunal be examined on oath or on affirmation; and**

b. **Administer oaths or affirmations for the purposes of the examination.**

Where an oral hearing is to be held, the arbitral tribunal must give the parties adequate advance notice of the date, time, and venue of the hearing, in accordance with **Article 29 of the Arbitration Rules**. During such hearings, witnesses including expert witnesses may be heard under the conditions and examined in the manner determined by the arbitral tribunal.

The Rules provide that arbitral proceedings should generally follow procedures similar to those adopted in civil actions before a court of law. Thus, the claimant in arbitration occupies the position of a plaintiff, while the respondent stands in the position of a defendant. Each party may conduct its case personally or be represented by counsel or a lay representative. However, the arbitral tribunal has no power to restrict legal representation unless the parties have expressly or impliedly agreed otherwise.

Arbitration is a private process and proceedings are held in camera, unless the parties agree otherwise. The tribunal may request that witnesses including expert witnesses withdraw from the hearing after giving evidence. Members of the public are not entitled to attend unless all parties and the tribunal consent. Those entitled to be present include the parties themselves, persons claiming through them, and individuals assisting them in presenting their case. Where such persons are excluded without good cause, and the exclusion results in prejudice, the award may be set aside.

This principle was articulated by **Tunner LJ** in ***Haigh v Haigh***[138]. who stated thus:

> ***I certainly do not mean to lay it down that an arbitrator is bound to submit to insults from those who attend him, but I think that before he excludes anyone from attending on behalf of any of the parties interested, he is bound to ascertain that there is good ground for the exclusion, and to take the best care he can that the party who is affected by the exclusion is not prejudiced by it.***

---

[138] (1861) 31 L.J. Ch. 420

In the Haigh Case, the arbitrator wrongfully excluded the claimant's son who was familiar with the business accounts and a shorthand writer from the hearing. The Court held that their exclusion without sufficient cause entitled the aggrieved party to have the award set aside, regardless of its substantive fairness.

Article 29 further provides that the tribunal may permit witnesses, including expert witnesses, to give evidence through technological means such as video conferencing or telecommunication, eliminating the need for physical presence at the hearing.

Additionally, **Section 35 of the Arbitration and Mediation Act 2023** give the parties autonomy to agree on the language or languages to be used during the arbitral proceedings. In the absence of such an agreement, the default language is English. The chosen language shall apply to all written statements, hearings, awards, and other communications unless otherwise determined by the parties or the tribunal. The tribunal may also require that any documentary evidence be accompanied by a certified translation into the agreed or designated language.

These provisions collectively promote procedural flexibility, fairness, and respect for party autonomy, while maintaining the confidentiality and efficiency characteristic of arbitral proceedings.

5.4 POWER OF THE ARBITRAL TRIBUNAL AS TO REMEDIES

Section 37 of the Arbitration and Mediation Act 2023 (formerly Section 29 of the Arbitration and Conciliation Act, Cap A18, LFN 2004) provides that the parties may agree on the powers exercisable by the arbitral tribunal with respect to remedies.

In the absence of such agreement, the arbitral tribunal has wide discretionary powers to grant reliefs similar to those available to a court of law.

Unless otherwise agreed by the parties, the arbitral tribunal may:

a. **Make a declaration** as to any matter determined in the proceedings;

b. **Order the payment of a sum of money**, in any currency claimed by a party; and

c. Exercise powers similar to those of the court to:

i. Order a party to do or refrain from doing any act;

ii. Order **specific performance** of a contract (other than a contract relating to land); and

iii. Order the **rectification, setting aside, or cancellation** of a deed or other document.

These powers ensure that arbitral tribunals in Nigeria are not merely limited to awarding damages but may also grant equitable and declaratory reliefs, provided such remedies are within the scope of the arbitration agreement and the reference made by the parties.

In **BAKER MARINE (NIG.) LTD v. CHEVRON (NIG.) LTD**[139], the Court of Appeal recognized the tribunal's competence to make binding awards that mirror the remedies available in court, provided the tribunal acts within its jurisdiction.

Similarly, in **M.V. LUPEX v. N.O.C. LTD**[140], the Supreme Court affirmed that arbitration is a substitute for litigation and that an arbitral tribunal can grant effective remedies that finally settle disputes between the parties.

5.5 CONSOLIDATION AND CONCURRENT HEARING

Section 39 of the Arbitration and Mediation Act 2023 provides for the consolidation of ongoing arbitral proceedings, including those

[139] (2000) 12 NWLR (Pt. 681) 393 (CA)
[140] (2003) 15 NWLR (Pt. 844) 469 (SC)

involving different parties. It also allows for concurrent hearings to be held.

However, the decision to consolidate proceedings or conduct concurrent hearings lies solely with the parties. The arbitral tribunal cannot order consolidation or concurrent hearings on its own initiative without the consent of all parties involved.

The purpose of allowing such procedures is to promote efficiency and economy in arbitration. Consolidated or concurrent hearings help to save time, cost, and resources, while reducing the duplication of arbitral efforts. This approach also minimizes the burden on the courts, especially where parties later seek interim reliefs or judicial review of arbitral awards.

5.6 PROCEEDING EX PARTE

Under Section 41 of the Arbitration and Mediation Act 2023 (AMA), an arbitral tribunal is empowered to proceed *ex parte* that is, in the absence of one of the parties *for good cause*. This authority arises both from the nature of arbitral proceedings and from express statutory provision. Section 41 provides that where, without showing sufficient cause, a party fails to appear at a hearing or fails to produce documentary evidence, the arbitral tribunal may continue the proceedings and make the award based on the evidence before it.

This principle reflects the position in **WOOD V. LEAKE**[141], where it was held that an arbitrator may properly proceed in the absence of a party who has been duly notified but refuses or neglects to attend. The rationale is to prevent a party from frustrating the arbitral process by deliberate absence or delay. However, the arbitrator must ensure that the absent party had adequate notice of the proceedings

---

[141] Supra

and a reasonable opportunity to be heard, in line with the principle of natural justice.

Section 41 is replicated hereof verbatim:

(1) Unless otherwise agreed to by the parties, if, without showing sufficient cause-

a. ***The claimant fails to state the claim as required under section 36(1) of this Act, the arbitral tribunal shall terminate the proceedings provided that where a respondent has a counterclaim and has evinced an intention to file same, the proceedings shall not be terminated.***

b. ***The respondent fails to state the defence as required under section 36(1) of this Act, the arbitral tribunal shall continue the proceedings without treating the failure in itself as an admission of the claimant's allegation; or***

c. ***Any party that fails to appear at a hearing or to produce documentary evidence, the arbitral tribunal may continue the proceedings and make an award on the evidence before it.***

Proceeding *ex parte* in arbitration occurs where a party, though duly notified of the hearing, fails to attend without sufficient cause. Under **Section 41(1) of the Arbitration and Mediation Act 2023 (AMA)**, the arbitral tribunal may, having regard to all the circumstances, proceed in that party's absence if it is satisfied that the failure to appear is without good reason and is intended to delay or frustrate the proceedings. This power is not to be exercised lightly. It is a serious procedural step, and the arbitrator must ensure that adequate written notice of the hearing was given to the absenting party, clearly stating the date, time, and place of the meeting and the intention to proceed *ex parte* if the party fails to attend. A notice marked "peremptory" is generally sufficient to show that the tribunal intends to proceed regardless of attendance. If the arbitrator fails to give proper notice, the award may be set aside for misconduct or breach of fair hearing, as due process is a fundamental principle of arbitration.

If the tribunal, after a first peremptory notice, grants another appointment, it must also mark the second appointment as peremptory before it can validly proceed *ex parte* at that sitting.

Where a party absents himself on the ground of alleged bias or distrust of the tribunal, the tribunal may nonetheless proceed in that party's absence, particularly where the allegations are unfounded. However, it remains good practice to notify the absenting party of subsequent meetings, giving them the opportunity to rejoin the proceedings if they wish.

5.7 DEFAULT AND DELAY

Under Section 41(3) AMA, where a claimant, after submitting a claim, is guilty of inordinate and inexcusable delay, the tribunal may make an award dismissing the claim if the delay:

a. creates a substantial risk that a fair resolution of the dispute may not be possible, or

b. has caused or is likely to cause serious prejudice to the respondent.

Similarly, under Section 41(4), if a party fails to comply with the tribunal's orders or directions, the tribunal may issue a peremptory order prescribing a deadline for compliance. Failure to comply with a peremptory order to provide security for costs, for instance, empowers the tribunal to dismiss the claim under Section 41(5).

5.8 PRINCIPLES OF FAIR HEARING AND NEUTRALITY

Except where justified by the circumstances, arbitration proceedings should be conducted in the presence of both parties. The tribunal must not receive evidence or communications from one party in the absence of the other, as this would breach the principle of audi alteram partem (hear the other side) and may result in the setting aside of the award.

In **HAIGH v. HAIGH**[142], the court held that:

> ***an award was properly set aside where the arbitrator excluded a party's assistant and shorthand writer without sufficient cause, as this amounted to procedural unfairness.***

This principle has been adopted by Nigerian courts in construing the duty of fairness in arbitral proceedings.

Similarly, in **BAKER MARINE (NIG.) LTD v. CHEVRON (NIG.) LTD**[143], the Supreme Court emphasized that:

> ***arbitrators must adhere strictly to procedural fairness and the terms of the reference; failure to do so renders the award vulnerable to being set aside for misconduct.***

In **M.V. LUPEX v. NIGERIAN OVERSEAS CHARTERING & SHIPPING LTD**[144], the Court reiterated that:

> ***parties who choose arbitration must abide by the rules and procedure governing the reference.***

The tribunal's power to proceed *ex parte* where a party fails to attend was implicitly recognized, provided such power is exercised in good faith and with due notice.

5.9 TERMINATION OF PROCEEDINGS AND FINALITY

---

[142] Supra
[143] Supra
[144] Supra

Under Section 48(2) AMA, arbitral proceedings terminate when:

ι. a final award is made;

ιι. the claimant withdraws the claim;

ιιι. the parties agree to terminate the proceedings; or

ιϖ. the tribunal determines that continuation has become unnecessary or impossible.

Once terminated, the tribunal's mandate ceases under Section 48(3), and it becomes *functus officio*, meaning it cannot take any further action in relation to the dispute.

Furthermore, under Section 63 AMA, a party who fails to raise a timely objection to any procedural irregularity during the proceedings is deemed to have waived the right to object later. This was affirmed in **NIGER GATE LTD v. NIGER STATE GOVERNMENT**[145], where the Court of Appeal held that a party who knowingly participates in an arbitration but withholds objections until after the award cannot later challenge the process.

The tribunal's power to proceed *ex parte* ensures that arbitration is not frustrated by the deliberate absence of a party. However, this power must be exercised cautiously and consistently with the principles of fair hearing, procedural fairness, and party equality. Appellate Court decisions such as **BAKER MARINE, M.V. LUPEX**[146]**, AND NIGER GATE LTD v. NIGER STATE GOVERNMENT**[147], have underscored the balance between tribunal efficiency and procedural justice, reflecting both the letter and spirit of the **Arbitration and Mediation Act 2023**.

5.10 EVIDENCE IN ARBITRATION

Evidence in arbitral proceedings may be oral or documentary. It may also include maps, charts, and diagrams illustrating the subject

---

[145] (2008) 13 NWLR (Pt. 1103) 111 (CA)

[146] Supra

[147] Supra

matter of the dispute, such as property boundaries, building layouts, or site plans. The provisions of the Evidence Act do not apply to arbitral proceedings in Nigeria. This principle was affirmed in several judicial authorities including **BAKER MARINE (NIG.) LTD v. CHEVRON (NIG.) LTD**[148], where the Court of Appeal held that an arbitrator is not bound by technical rules of evidence applicable in regular courts.

By virtue of Section 31(1) of the Arbitration and Mediation Act, 2023, parties are at liberty to choose the applicable rules to their arbitral proceedings, however where parties have no agreement, then arbitral proceedings shall be conducted in accordance with the Arbitration Rules contained in the First Schedule to the Act. Where the Rules are silent on any procedural issue, the arbitral tribunal may, subject to the Act, conduct the proceedings in such a manner as it considers appropriate, provided that each party is given a fair hearing and equal opportunity to present its case.

This discretion includes the power to determine the admissibility, relevance, materiality, and weight of any evidence presented before it. Accordingly, the arbitral tribunal may admit evidence that would ordinarily be inadmissible in court, if such evidence assists in achieving a fair and efficient resolution of the dispute; or reject evidence that, although admissible under strict legal rules, would cause undue delay or is otherwise unhelpful to the arbitral process.

This flexibility is not absolute. The tribunal must not admit evidence that is manifestly unreliable, fabricated, or prejudicial to the integrity of the proceedings. Doing so may constitute legal misconduct, rendering the award liable to be set aside under Section 55(3)(a)(iii), (vi), or (vii) of the Act.

---

[148] Supra

As was emphasized in **TAYLOR WOODROW (NIG.) LTD v. ETINA WERRO & SONS LTD**[149], an arbitrator's discretion must be exercised judicially and fairly, ensuring that justice is done between the parties.

Under Section 43 of the Arbitration and Mediation Act, 2023, unless otherwise agreed by the parties, the arbitral tribunal has the power to administer oaths or affirmations to parties and witnesses appearing before it.

Additionally, any party to an arbitral proceeding may apply to the Court or a Judge in Chambers for judicial assistance in securing attendance or production of evidence. The Court may:

a. Issue a writ of subpoena ad testificandum to compel a witness to appear and give evidence before the tribunal;
b. Issue a writ of subpoena duces tecum to compel a witness to produce relevant documents or materials; and
c. Order the issuance of a writ of habeas corpus ad testificandum to bring a prisoner before the tribunal for examination.

5.11 POWER OF ARBITRAL TRIBUNAL TO APPOINT EXPERTS

Under Section 42 of the Arbitration and Mediation Act 2023 (AMA), the arbitral tribunal has express powers to appoint one or more experts to assist in determining specific technical or factual issues arising in the dispute. Statutory Provision Section 42(1) provides that, unless otherwise agreed by the parties, the tribunal may:

i. appoint one or more experts to report on a specific issue to be determined by the tribunal; and

---

[149] (1993) 3 NWLR (Pt. 282) 127

ii. require a party subject to any applicable legal privilege to provide the expert with any relevant information, documents, goods, or other property necessary for inspection.

This provision ensures that the tribunal has the benefit of independent and specialized technical knowledge where matters in dispute fall outside its expertise.

Section 42(2) further provides that, unless otherwise agreed, where a party so requests or the tribunal considers it necessary the appointed expert must participate in a hearing after submitting their written or oral report. At such a hearing, the parties have the opportunity to:

a. put questions to the expert; and

b. present their own expert witnesses to testify on the same issues.

This ensures transparency, fairness, and compliance with the principles of natural justice, as each party is given an opportunity to challenge the expert's findings or provide counter-opinions. Expert evidence is particularly important in technical or specialized disputes, such as those involving valuation, facility or project management, engineering, construction, oil and gas, maritime operations, or accounting matters. The tribunal's ability to appoint an expert helps prevent undue delay, simplifies complex evidence, and promotes informed and balanced decision-making. In **NIGERIAN PORTS AUTHORITY v. CONSTRUCTION GENERAL FILLI & ANOR** [150], the Court affirmed that:

> ***experts may be relied upon by arbitrators to interpret technical data, provided the evidence is made available for the other party's scrutiny and challenge.***

---

[150] (1974) 1 All NLR (Pt. 2) 463

A simple example showing the relevance of an Estate Surveyor and Valuer as an expert in an arbitration where the subject of the dispute is compensation for compulsory acquisition of land by the Government. In such case, for the arbitral tribunal to effectively determine the most appropriate compensation payable under the award, the tribunal will need to retain an Estate Valuer who will then inspect, value the land and then tender its valuation report which he may be summoned by the tribunal to adopt the said valuation report while all parties, particularly the opposing party will examine or question the Estate Valuer vis a viz his report with a view to discrediting either his competence or the correctness of his valuation report.

5.12 INTERIM MEASURES AND PROVISIONAL RELIEF

Section 20 of AMA provides as follows:

1. **Unless otherwise agreed to by the parties, the arbitral tribunal may, at the request of a party, grant interim measures.**

2. **An interim measure is a temporary measure, whether in the form of an award or in another form, which, at any time before the award which decides the dispute is issued, the arbitral tribunal orders a party to:**

a. **Maintain or restore the status quo pending determination of the dispute;**

b. **Take action that may prevent, or refrain from taking action that is likely to cause, current or imminent harm or prejudice to the arbitral process itself;**

c. **Provide a means of preserving assets out of which a subsequent award may be satisfied.**

d. **Preserve evidence that may be relevant and material to the resolution of the dispute or preserve the subject matter of the arbitration itself.**

The Arbitration and Mediation Act (AMA) confers on the arbitral tribunal the power to grant interim measures such as directing the parties to maintain or restore the *status quo* pending the determination of the dispute, to preserve the subject matter of the arbitration or any evidence that may be relevant and material to its resolution, and to provide means for securing assets from which a subsequent award may be satisfied. These powers may also include the grant of preliminary orders, unless otherwise agreed by the parties. The purpose of an interim measure, as the name implies, is to protect the property or rights in dispute. It ensures that the property retains its status and value during the pendency of the proceedings so that it remains relevant and beneficial to the parties once the dispute is resolved. Such measures may include the sale of perishable property, the deposit of disputed property with a third party, the maintenance of machinery or works, or the continuation of certain phases of construction to prevent irreparable harm. The arbitral tribunal may also require any party to provide security for the costs of implementing these measures.

The Act provides a clear framework for the enforcement of interim measures and preliminary orders, including those made without notice to the other party, i.e. Ex parte. The tribunal may modify, suspend, or terminate an interim measure or preliminary order upon the application of a party or in exceptional circumstances. Furthermore, the arbitral tribunal may require an applicant for an interim measure to provide security and may hold such an applicant liable for any costs or damages caused to the other party as a result of the measure or order.

Decisions of the arbitral tribunal granting interim measures are binding on the parties. In **NIGERIAN AGIP OIL CO. LTD v. KEMMER**[151], the Court of Appeal affirmed that interim measures

[151] (2001) 8 NWLR (Pt. 715) 659

are essential to safeguard the subject matter of arbitration and prevent the frustration of the arbitral process.

It is clear that Courts have the power to grant interim reliefs as part of their inherent jurisdiction, though such powers are usually supported by statute. Under the now repealed **Arbitration and Conciliation Act (ACA)**, Courts could make orders necessary to preserve the subject matter of a dispute for example, granting a stay of proceedings or issuing a subpoena *duces tecum*.

However, **Section 19 of the Arbitration and Mediation Act (AMA)** has expanded this power. Courts in Nigeria can now grant interim measures in connection with both domestic and international arbitrations, ensuring that the subject matter of the dispute is protected. Importantly, the court is required to consider and decide any such application within 15 days, in line with the Arbitration Rules.

CHAPTER 6

THE ARBITRAL AWARD

6.1 ARBITRAL AWARD

Neither the Arbitration and Mediation Act, 2023 nor the Arbitration Rules defines the term *"award."* Indeed, there is no universally accepted definition of the term, and even the Convention on the Recognition and Enforcement of Foreign Arbitral Awards (New York Convention, 1958) refrains from providing one. The Convention merely clarifies in Article I(2) that the term *"arbitral awards"* includes awards made by permanent arbitral bodies as well as those made by arbitrators appointed for individual cases.

This definition captures both the substantive and procedural essence of an arbitral award as a final, binding determination of the issues submitted to arbitration, whether or not it results in monetary compensation. It underscores the judicial character of arbitral decisions while preserving their distinct private-law foundation.

The nearest the New York Convention comes to a definition is found in Article I(2), which provides that:

> **The term 'arbitral awards' shall include not only awards made by arbitrators appointed for each case but also those made by permanent arbitral bodies to which the parties have submitted.**[152]

Prof. Fabian Ajogwu, SAN, provides one of the most precise and widely accepted definitions of an arbitral award. He defines an award as:

---

[152] Convention on the Recognition and Enforcement of Foreign Arbitral Awards (New York, adopted 10 June 1958, entered into force 7 June 1959) 330 UNTS 38

> **A determination on the merits by an arbitral tribunal in an arbitral proceeding, and is analogous to a judgment in a Court of law. It is referred to as an award even where the claimant's claim fails in its entirety (and thus no money needs to be paid by either party), or the award is of a non-monetary nature.**[153]

Ajogwu's definition appears to exclude awards that are not strictly based on the merits such as procedural awards, interim awards, consent awards and even default awards now under section 45. Modern arbitration law, including the **Arbitration and Mediation Act 2023** recognizes that an arbitral award may resolve procedural, jurisdictional, or interim matters without determining substantive rights. Hence, by focusing narrowly on "determination on the merits," the definition may be unduly restrictive.

One of the principal difficulties in formulating an acceptable definition of an *arbitral award* is that there are many kinds of awards within the arbitral process. The question thus arises: should a definition of "award" encompass all these different categories, or should it distinguish between them?

During the drafting of the **UNCITRAL Model Law on International Commercial Arbitration**, a proposal was in fact made to adopt a definition of "award." This proposal underscored the complexity of identifying a formulation broad enough to include final, partial, and interim awards some of which dispose of the entire dispute, while others determine only certain issues. The proposed definition read as follows:

> ***Award means the final award which disposes of all issues submitted to the arbitral tribunal and any***

---

[153] Fabian Ajogwu, *Commercial Arbitration in Nigeria: Law and Practice* (3rd edn, Centre for Commercial Law Development 2020) 330.

> ***other decision of the arbitral tribunal which finally determines any question of substance or the question of its competence or any other question of procedure but, in the latter case, only if the arbitral tribunal terms its decision an award.***

This draft definition reveals the core challenge distinguishing between awards that are final in nature and those that are interim or procedural. The drafters ultimately decided not to adopt this definition, precisely because it risked creating confusion over what decisions of an arbitral tribunal should be treated as "awards" for purposes such as recognition, enforcement, and challenge.

Under Nigerian law, and from the context of the Arbitration and Mediation Act 2023, the term *"award"* can reasonably be inferred to refer to the final, binding decision of the arbitral tribunal that conclusively settles the dispute between the parties. This understanding is consistent with the structure and wording of **Sections 45-49 of the Act**, which collectively deals with the **form, contents, delivery, and effects of arbitral awards**.

Thus, after hearing the parties and receiving their evidence, the arbitral tribunal deliberates on the issues and records its decision in writing in the form of an award. Such an award, once rendered, represents the culmination of the arbitral process the final and binding determination of the rights and obligations of the parties in respect of the matters submitted to arbitration.

In **RAS PAL GAZI CONSTRUCTION CO. LTD v. F.C.D.A** [154] The Court of Appeal defined an award as a formal expression of the decision reached by an arbitral tribunal on matters submitted to it, intended to settle the dispute between the parties. Similarly, in **KANO STATE URBAN DEVELOPMENT BOARD v. FANZ**

[154] (2001) 10 NWLR (Pt. 722) 559 (CA)

CONSTRUCTION CO. LTD[155] the Supreme Court Per **Karibi-Whyte, J.S.C. held that:**

> **An award is a decision of an arbitrator or umpire upon the matters referred to him. It is the equivalent of a judgment of a Court of law and is binding upon the parties once published.**

6.2 MAKING OF AN AWARD

Neither the Arbitration and Mediation Act nor the Arbitration Rules sets a fixed time within which an arbitral award must be delivered after proceedings begin. However, the parties are free to agree on a time limit in their arbitration agreement. When such a time frame is provided, the arbitral tribunal is expected to give its award within that period.

If, for any reason, the tribunal cannot meet that deadline, it may extend the time - but only with the *consent of the parties*. This extension can even be made *after the original time has expired.* Where no time limit is agreed upon, the tribunal can rely on **Section 66 of the Arbitration and Mediation Act, 2023**, which gives it the power to extend any time period it considers necessary for carrying out its duties under the Act.

That said, the absence of a specific deadline does not mean the tribunal can take as long as it wishes. It still has a duty to make its award *within a reasonable time*, taking into account the nature and circumstances of the case. If there is an *unjustified or excessive delay* in delivering the award, either party may take steps to *terminate the tribunal's mandate* under **Section 10 of the Act**.

Under **Section 44(1)** of the **Arbitration and Mediation Act**, any decision of an arbitral tribunal consisting of more than one arbitrator including its final award must be made by a majority of all its members, unless the parties have agreed otherwise.

[155] Supra

In practice, however, it may sometimes be difficult to secure a majority decision. For example, in a three-member tribunal, it is possible that two arbitrators may not agree on the outcome of the case. Some jurisdictions address this problem by allowing the presiding arbitrator to make a decision if the tribunal cannot reach a majority.

The Act takes a more limited approach. Under Section 44(2), the presiding arbitrator may, with the authorization of the parties or all members of the tribunal, make decisions only on procedural matters that is, on how the arbitration is to be conducted. This means that where the tribunal cannot reach a majority decision, the presiding arbitrator cannot unilaterally make the award; they can only decide procedural questions, provided they have the required consent.

When making its award, the arbitral tribunal must consider several factors many of which are statutory. The way the tribunal addresses these factors is crucial, as it may ultimately affect the validity or enforceability of the award.

6.3 FEATURES OF A VALID AWARD

This is going to be discussed under two major sub-headings: Formal and Substantive Requisites:

a. FORMAL REQUISITES

Apart from the requirements set out under the various subsections of Section 47 of the Arbitration and Mediation Act, 2023, there is no special form prescribed for writing an arbitral award unless the parties have specifically agreed to one in their arbitration agreement.

However, to minimize ambiguities and to avoid future disputes over interpretation, arbitral awards are usually divided into two main parts:

i. **The Recitals**, and

ii. **The Operative Part**.

i. The Recitals

It is entirely at the discretion of the arbitrator whether or not to include introductory recitals in the award. Although recitals are not essential to the validity of an award, they are often helpful, particularly where the nature of the dispute or the reasoning behind the decision may not be clear without some preliminary background.

When recitals are included, they should be clear, accurate, and consistent with the operative part of the award. They should provide a logical introduction that leads naturally to the final decision.

Typically, recitals may refer to the following matters:

a. The agreement or order of reference to arbitration.

b. The subject matter of the arbitration that is, the existence and nature of the dispute between the parties.

c. The appointment and authority conferred on the arbitrator or arbitral tribunal.

d. Any special powers, conditions, or issues arising during the proceedings that are specifically determined in the award.

Errors or omissions in the recitals do not invalidate the award. Nonetheless, inaccuracies can create ambiguity or lead to misinterpretation, so care should be taken to ensure that the recitals are precise and reliable.

Some examples of inaccurate recitals that have been held not to vitiate an award include:

a. Where the arbitrator fails to set out the exact source of their authority or omits to note that the time for making the award had been extended.

b. Where a mistake is made in the Christian name of one of the arbitrators.

c. Where an error occurs in stating the number of arbitrators who signed or executed the award.

In each of these cases, the Courts have held that such errors were mere irregularities and did not affect the substance or validity of the award itself.

In **BAKER MARINE (NIG.) LTD v. CHEVRON (NIG.) LTD**[156] it was held that An arbitral award will not be set aside for mere procedural or clerical errors, so long as the tribunal acted within its powers and the award reflects its genuine decision on the issues referred.

ii. **The Operative Part**

This is the heart of the award the part that contains the tribunal's actual findings and final decision on the issues in dispute. It is the only essential part of the award, and even if there were no recitals, this section alone would still amount to a valid award. The main responsibility of the arbitral tribunal is to reach and clearly express its decision on the matters submitted to it. Once that decision is communicated in clear and definite terms, the specific choice of words or structure is not what really matters.

That said, the Arbitration and Mediation Act requires the tribunal to state the reasons for its decision, unless the parties have agreed that no reasons should be given. Where the award is made on agreed terms under Section 45 of the Act,

---

[156] Supra

the tribunal must say so in the award and in that situation, no further explanation is needed.

This rule in Section 47(3)(a) represents a real improvement over the old arbitration laws. In the past, arbitrators were not required to give reasons for their awards. But if they did, and those reasons revealed an error in law, the Courts could set aside the award for showing an error of law on its face. The modern approach recognizes that decision-making is not an instinctive act; it's a process of thought and reasoning. For that reason, parties deserve to know how and why the tribunal reached its conclusion.

Across the world, the trend now strongly favours giving reasons for arbitral awards unless the parties expressly agree otherwise. This is reflected in Article 31(2) of the UNCITRAL Model Law, which states:

> **The award shall state the reasons upon which it is based, unless the parties have agreed that no reasons are to be given, or the award is an award on agreed terms.**

The same approach is taken by the Washington Convention (ICSID), which requires every arbitral award to include reasons, and by the ICC Court of Arbitration, which considers an award defective in form if it is not properly reasoned.

Finally, under Section 47(1) of the Act, every arbitral award must be in writing and signed by the arbitrator or arbitrators. This is a mandatory legal requirement. The award must also follow any form or formalities that the parties have agreed upon. An arbitrator cannot delegate the decision making function, as that is personal and central to the arbitral mandate.

However, it is entirely proper for the arbitrator to employ a legal adviser, draftsman, or secretary to help draft, type, or formalize the award, so long as the final decision and approval rest solely with the arbitrator.

iii. **Execution**

The award must be *signed by the arbitrator or arbitrators***.** Where the arbitral tribunal is composed of three arbitrators, the *signature of the majority* is sufficient to render the award valid, **provided** that the reason for the absence of any signature is clearly stated on the face of the award.

A practical question often arises: must all the arbitrators sign the award at the same time and in the same place for it to be valid? Under the old common law rule, the answer was yes. The traditional position was that:

> **In the case of an award by more than one arbitrator, all the arbitrators making the award should execute it at the same time and in the presence of each other.**

However, this rule has been relaxed in modern practice. In **EUROPEAN GRAIN AND SHIPPING LTD v. JOHNSTON** [157], **Lord Denning MR** observed that with the advent of modern means of communication such as the telephone, typewriter, and other electronic methods strict adherence to simultaneous signing is no longer necessary. What truly matters is that the arbitrators **communicate with one another and agree on the content of the award**, whether that agreement is reached in person, by telephone, or in writing.

The authors align with this modern view expounded by Lord Denning. What is essential is that the arbitrators are *ad idem*, i.e. in complete agreement as to the decision embodied in the award. Whether they sign the document together at the same time or

---

[157] [1982] 2 Lloyd's Rep 431,

separately at different times should not affect the validity of the award, so long as their **collective intention and agreement** are clearly established.

In **NIGERIAN NATIONAL PETROLEUM CORPORATION (NNPC) v. CLIFCO NIGERIA LTD**[158] the Supreme Court reiterated that Courts must respect arbitral autonomy and not invalidate awards for procedural imperfections, so long as the fundamental requirements of the law are met. This reinforces that non-simultaneous signing would not render an award void if the signatures reflect genuine agreement.

Although no Nigerian Court has specifically decided whether all arbitrators must sign an award at the same time and in the same place, the overall position under Nigerian law is quite clear.

Reading Section 47(1) of the Arbitration and Mediation Act 2023 together with the reasoning in the NNPC case cited above and the persuasive English case of **EUROPEAN GRAIN & SHIPPING LTD v. JOHNSTON**[159], it shows that Nigerian law now takes a practical, modern approach to this issue.

iv. Date and place of the Award

The date and place of the award must also be stated on the award as provided for in Sections 47(3) (b) and (c) of the Act.

v. Delivery and Publication

The arbitral tribunal is required by the Act to deliver a copy of the signed and dated award to each party. This delivery constitutes publication. For publishing the award to the outside world, it seems that the consent of the parties must be secured. Once an arbitrator (or arbitrators as the case may be)

---

[158] (2011) 10 NWLR (Pt. 1255) 209 (SC)
[159] Supra

has executed his award, he becomes *functus officio*, this is to say, his powers entirely cease, save for the powers given to him under section 49 of the Act to correct and interpret the award or to make additional award.

b. SUBSTANTIVE REQUISITES

For an arbitral award to be valid, it must be certain, consistent, possible, unambiguous, non-contradictory, unconditional, and unimpeachable. In essence, the award must conclusively resolve the matters that were submitted to arbitration and no more.

While there is no need for technical or ceremonial language, an arbitrator must ensure that the award is precise and clearly expressed, as arbitral decisions often determine valuable rights and obligations, sometimes permanently.

Although Nigerian Courts generally adopt a pro-arbitration stance and are inclined to uphold the validity of awards where possible, this presumption does not extend to questions of jurisdiction. As the Courts have emphasized, the legal maxim omnia praesumuntur rite esse acta ("all things are presumed to have been duly done") does not apply to arbitral proceedings or to other inferior tribunals. Thus, where there is any doubt as to whether an arbitrator acted within the scope of their authority, the Courts will not presume regularity but will carefully examine the jurisdictional foundation of the award.

This approach was affirmed in **BAKER MARINE (NIG.) LTD v. CHEVRON (NIG.) LTD**[160], where the Court of Appeal held that an arbitral award would not be interfered with merely because it appears unsatisfactory, but that an award made outside the arbitrator's jurisdiction or one that is ambiguous, uncertain, or inconsistent may be set aside. Similarly, in **NNPC v. CLIFCO NIGERIA LTD**[161]the Supreme Court reaffirmed that while Courts are reluctant to upset arbitral awards, jurisdictional defects

---

[160] Supra
[161] Supra

or procedural irregularities affecting the fairness of the proceedings will not be overlooked.

The requirement of certainty and finality was also underscored in **FANZ CONSTRUCTION LTD v. FCDA**[162], where the Court of Appeal held that an award must be clear and definite in its terms so as to be enforceable. Ambiguity or contradiction in the operative part of an award may render it unenforceable, as it prevents the Court from ascertaining the rights and obligations determined by the arbitrator

In the case of **UNITED NIGERIA INSURANCE CO. LTD v. STOCCO**[163]. In this case the Court held that:

> ***It is the duty of a Court to construe an award so as to make it, if possible, certain and final, and an award will be sustained even though the arbitrator has omitted to mention some claim or other matter submitted by a party, if, according to the fair interpretation of the award, it is to be presumed that the claim or matter has been taken into consideration. Where an award purports to be made concerning the matters submitted, the presumption is that the arbitrator intended to dispose finally of all the matters in difference, and the award is good notwithstanding that the arbitrator has not made a distinct adjudication on each or any of the several distinct matters submitted to him, provided it does not appear that he has excluded any. An award which is clear and unambiguous in its terms and deals with the only issue in controversy must be deemed to have impliedly***

---

[162] Supra

[163] (1973) N.S.C.C. Vol. 8, 246

disposed of all matters referred to the arbitrator and all the points of claim and defence submitted to him.

i. The Award Must Be Final

An award, in order to be binding, must settle all points raised under the arbitration agreement, so that the parties to the dispute will be enabled to know their position without having to resort to further judicial inquiry. Where there is and in order to avoid rendering the award bad from want of finality, the arbitrator can make an interim award, that is, an award dealing with certain matters referred to him, to be followed later by a decision on the remaining points.

An award will not be invalid for lack of finality simply because the parties failed to present all their disputes before the arbitrator, so long as the arbitrator has effectively decided all the issues that were actually submitted to him. What matters is that the arbitrator has dealt with every point raised for determination within the scope of the reference.

An award may also be expressed in the alternative and still remain final and binding. This occurs where the award directs one of two possible actions to be taken and even if one of those alternatives turns out to be uncertain or impossible, the award will still be valid and final if the other alternative is clear, certain, and capable of performance. In such a case, the party concerned is bound to perform the second, certain alternative.

However, an award will lack finality if the arbitrator fails to give the necessary directions to give effect to his decision, leaving the award incomplete or uncertain. Likewise, an award will be bad for want of finality where the arbitrator improperly reserves or delegates his judicial authority that is, where he leaves substantive matters to be decided later or by someone else.

That said, an arbitrator may validly reserve or delegate a purely ministerial act such as the calculation of figures or the mechanical execution of a decision to himself or to another person, even after the time for making the award has expired. What he cannot do is delegate or postpone judgment on any matter submitted for adjudication.

Ultimately, any award that fails to finally determine the matters in dispute either by incompleteness, uncertainty, or improper delegation of authority will be set aside by the Court for want of finality.

In **UNITED NIGERIA INSURANCE CO. LTD v. STOCCO**[164] A dispute arose between United Nigeria Insurance Co. Ltd and Stocco concerning a claim under an insurance policy. The matter was referred to arbitration. After the arbitrator made his award, one of the parties challenged it on the ground that it was uncertain and not final arguing that the arbitrator had failed to address every specific claim raised before him. The Court held that

> ***an award will not be invalid for want of finality merely because the arbitrator did not specifically mention or rule on every single claim, provided it can be fairly inferred that he took all matters submitted into consideration and intended his award to dispose of them finally.***

ii. The Award Must Be Certain

An award must be expressed in such a clear language that no reasonable doubt can arise upon its face as to the meaning of

---

[164] Supra

its provisions, or as to the nature and extent of the duties imposed by it on the parties. If there is any doubt as to whether the award has decided the dispute or the question referred, the award will be invalid.

If the arbitrator does not specify a sum of money but gives a rule for computing the amount, the award is sufficiently certain, in accordance with the maxim *id certum est quod certum redid potest* (That which can be made certain is certain). Therefore, some awards, although they may appear to lack certainty will not be bad if they contain sufficient indications of the intention of the arbitrator(s) to enable a decision of certainty to be deduced. Certain situations have been recognized in which an arbitral award will be declared void for uncertainty, because it fails to make clear what exactly is to be done or by whom. For example:

a. Where the award provides that "A or B" shall do a specified act, the award is void for uncertainty, since it is unclear who among the two persons is obliged to perform the act. The lack of precision as to the responsible party renders the award ambiguous and unenforceable.

b. Where the award directs a party to replace certain fixtures that had been removed, but fails to specify the value, quantity, or nature of the fixtures to be provided, the award will likewise be held invalid for uncertainty. Without such particulars, the obligation imposed cannot be meaningfully or fairly carried out.

iii. **The Award Must Be Consistent**

An award must be consistent in all its parts and must not be ambiguous or self-contradictory. This rule is essentially a corollary to the requirement of certainty. It becomes particularly important in cases where several issues have been referred to arbitration, or where the award directs that certain acts, terms, or conditions be performed.

In such situations, the arbitrator must ensure that the findings and directions in the award are coherent and compatible with one another, and that they align with the overall intent and reasoning of the decision. Any internal inconsistency or contradiction within the award can render it defective or open to challenge.

A clear illustration of inconsistency can be seen in an arbitration where the issue was whether a party had committed fraud. The arbitrator expressly found that the accused party was *not guilty of fraud*, yet nevertheless decided the case against him. The Court set aside the award, with Park J. remarking:

> ***The conclusion to which the arbitrator has come in this case is absurd. He says, 'I think he is innocent,' and then awards against him.***[165]

This example highlights that an award must speak with one voice the reasoning and the conclusion must point in the same direction. Where an arbitrator's findings contradict the ultimate decision, the award will not stand.

iv. The Award Must Be Legal and Capable of Performance

This means that award must be physically possible for the parties to perform the award and to perform it without

[165] e Hall and Hinds (1841) 2 M. & G. 847; 133 ER

contravening the law. The rule is similar to the rule of the Law of Contract, which requires all contracts to be capable of performance and to be legal and not contrary to public policy.

An arbitrator awarded that the defendant, in an action which had been referred to him, should repair a weir at the eastern bank of a river. The eastern bank of the river was not the property of the defendant, and he had no right to go on to it to execute the repairs. It was held that the arbitrators had no power to order an act which would amount to a trespass, and the award was not binding. This must however be distinguished from a case where the award directs one of the parties to pay a sum of money which is beyond his means. This would not be regarded as a legal impossibility. Similarly, where an act directed by an award is possible at the time the award is made, but later becomes impossible due to the conduct of one of the parties or even a third party, the party bound by the award is not thereby discharged from performing it. The subsequent impossibility does not excuse non-compliance, since the obligation to perform arose at a time when performance was still possible.

In **DAWSON v. FITZGERALD**[166], the parties submitted a dispute to arbitration. The arbitrator made an award directing one party to perform a specific act which, at the time of the award, was perfectly possible to carry out. However, after the award was made, the act became impossible due to the actions of a third party. The party bound to perform the act argued that the impossibility excused them from complying with the award. The Court held that

---

[166] (1876) 1 Ex. D. 257

the party was not discharged from the obligation. If the act was possible at the time the award was made, the party is bound to perform it, and any subsequent impossibility whether caused by the party's own act or by that of a stranger does not excuse non-performance.

v. The Award Must Be Directed to All Matters Referred.

For an arbitral award to be valid, it must fully resolve all the issues that the parties agreed to submit to arbitration. If the arbitrator leaves out any of those issues, the award is considered incomplete and cannot be enforced.

At the same time, an award will also be invalid if the arbitrator decides matters that were never part of the agreement of reference. The arbitrator's authority comes strictly from what the parties agreed to refer; anything beyond that is outside their jurisdiction. However, if the part of the award that goes beyond the reference can be separated from the part that properly falls within it, the valid portion may still stand, while only the excess will be set aside.

In practice, the Court usually assumes that the arbitrator stayed within the scope of their authority and decided only the issues that were properly referred. Anyone who challenges the award has the burden of proving otherwise that the arbitrator either went beyond the matters submitted or failed to decide some of them[167].

6.4 CATEGORIES OF AWARDS

Earlier in this work, the difficulty of defining an award was highlighted. This difficulty partly stems from the fact that there are

---

[167] See Baker Marine (Nig.) Ltd v. Chevron (Nig.) Ltd (2000) 12 NWLR (Pt. 681) 393 (CA)

various kinds of award which may be made in arbitral processes. Some of these awards recognized internationally and locally are examined hereunder:

i. Final Award

In a sense all awards may be said to be "final" in that (subject to the possibility of challenge in the Courts) they dispose of one or more of the issues in dispute between the parties. For instance, an interim (or a preliminary award) by the arbitral tribunal to the effect that it does have jurisdiction to determine the dispute before it is a final decision on the issue of jurisdiction, subject of course to any appeal to the Court.

However, the term "final award" is customarily reserved for an award which completes the mission of the arbitral tribunal. The handing down of a final award normally renders the arbitral tribunal *functus officio*. It ceases to have any further jurisdiction over the dispute; and the special relationship that exists between the arbitral tribunal and the parties during the currency of the arbitration stops. This has significant consequences. An arbitral tribunal should not issue a final award until it is satisfied that its mission has actually been completed. If there are outstanding matters to be determined, such as questions relating to costs or interest, or further directions to be given relating to the disposal of property, the arbitral tribunal should issue an award which is expressly designated as an interim award.

ii. Interim Award

An interim award or preliminary award, as it is sometimes called, is an award which disposes of a preliminary question, such as the issue of the jurisdiction of the arbitral tribunal. Alan Redfern and Martin Hunter have described the *interim award* as:

***a useful weapon in determining matters which are susceptible of determination during the course of the proceedings and which, once determined, may save considerable time and money for all involved.*[168]**"

According to them, where the arbitral tribunal lacks jurisdiction to deal with a dispute, it is in the interest of all parties that such a decision be made in the form of an award at an early stage, rather than after a lengthy process only to discover that the tribunal had no jurisdiction from the outset.

Such an award, though dealing with jurisdiction and therefore capable of being classified as an interim award, is nonetheless a *final award* on the issue of jurisdiction. This is because, upon deciding that it lacks jurisdiction, the arbitral tribunal effectively ceases to exist, having concluded its mandate in that respect.

The power of an arbitral tribunal to issue an interim award may arise either from the arbitration agreement itself or from the applicable arbitration law or rules. However, doubts may arise where neither the arbitration agreement, the applicable institutional rules, nor the governing law expressly or implicitly confers such authority on the tribunal.

A further instance where an interim award is particularly useful is in *international arbitration* where a dispute exists between the parties as to the *applicable law* governing the merits of the case. Unless resolved early, each party may be compelled to argue its case under different legal systems, possibly relying on expert evidence from lawyers qualified in

---

[168] Alan Redfern, Martin Hunter, Nigel Blackaby and Constantine Partasides, *Redfern and Hunter on International Arbitration* (6th edn, Oxford University Press 2015) 416–419.

each jurisdiction. In such circumstances, it is often pragmatic for the arbitral tribunal to make a preliminary determination on the applicable law. When this is done, it is customary though not obligatory for the decision to take the form of an interim award.

Similarly, it is often desirable to issue a preliminary or interim award where the issue of liability can conveniently be separated from that of *quantum*. In such cases, once liability is determined, the parties (or their accountants) may be able to agree on the amount of damages without further arbitral involvement. Hence, the tribunal may issue an interim award on liability, reserving issues of quantum for later determination.

Nevertheless, a major disadvantage of interim awards whether they concern jurisdiction, applicable law, or substantive claims is that they may open the door to judicial intervention. This may occur where a dissatisfied party seeks to set aside the interim award, thus creating an additional avenue for Court review and potential delay in the arbitral process. It is, however, commendable that the drafters of the *Arbitration and Mediation Act 2023* (AMA) have sought to mitigate such delays. The Act now provides that, in order to prevent the delays inherent in the public Court system from impeding the efficient conduct of arbitration, an arbitral tribunal may commence or continue proceedings and may even deliver an award pending the hearing and determination of any application before a Court.[169]This provision underscores the legislature's commitment to ensuring that arbitration in Nigeria remains an expeditious and effective mechanism for dispute resolution, largely insulated from unnecessary judicial interference.

---

[169] *Arbitration and Mediation Act 2023* (Nigeria), s 5(2).

iii. Partial Award

It is not always easy to distinguish between an *interim award* and a *partial award,* as the two terms are often used interchangeably in arbitral practice. However, a conceptual distinction can be observed, particularly in civil law jurisdictions, where the term *partial award* is generally used to describe an award that finally disposes of one or more of the substantive or monetary issues between the parties, while leaving other issues for later determination. By contrast, an *interim award* usually deals with a preliminary or procedural matter which does not finally determine any substantive right of the parties.[170]

Under Nigerian law, the *Arbitration and Mediation Act 2023* through the Arbitration Rules adopts an inclusive approach by recognising both *interim* and *partial* awards within its procedural framework. Article 42(1) of the rules provide that the arbitral tribunal may make separate awards on different issues at different times.[171] This means that, regardless of their nomenclature, both interim and partial awards are capable of recognition and enforcement as arbitral awards under the Act. The practical implication is that a tribunal sitting in Nigeria may issue an award resolving part of the dispute (for instance, liability or jurisdiction) without having to wait until all issues, including quantum, are ready for determination.

iv. Default Award

In some cases, commercial arbitrations are conducted in which one of the parties usually the respondent either fails to participate in the proceedings *ab initio* or withdraws midway through the process. When this occurs, the *Arbitration and*

---

[170] Redfern and Hunter, **op. cit.** 418-419
[171] Arbitration and Mediation Act, op.cit

Mediation Act 2023 empowers the arbitral tribunal to proceed with the arbitration and render its award notwithstanding such default.

According to Section 41 of the Act, unless otherwise agreed by the parties, if, without showing sufficient cause:

a. The claimant fails to state the claim as required under Section 36(1) of the Act, the arbitral tribunal shall terminate the proceedings, provided that where the respondent has a counterclaim and has evinced an intention to file same, the proceedings shall not be terminated;

b. The respondent fails to state the defence as required under Section 36(1), the arbitral tribunal shall continue the proceedings without treating the failure in itself as an admission of the claimant's allegations; or

c. any party fails to appear at a hearing or to produce documentary evidence, the arbitral tribunal may continue the proceedings and make an award on the evidence before it.

The award referred to in this context is known technically as a *default award.* A default award is therefore an award rendered by the arbitral tribunal when it has proceeded *ex parte*. Even in such circumstances, it is essential that the arbitral tribunal affords the defaulting party an opportunity to present its case. Where the tribunal ultimately makes an award in favour of the participating party, it must ensure that the award is both procedurally and substantively defensible. To this end, the tribunal should ensure that the award records in sufficient detail the procedure adopted, as well as the efforts made to communicate the claimant's case to the defaulting party, thereby demonstrating that the party was given every opportunity to be heard.

Furthermore, the reasons stated in the award should reflect that the tribunal genuinely considered the merits of the dispute. This approach not only enhances the legitimacy of the arbitral process but also strengthens the enforceability of the resulting award under Nigerian law and international standards.[172]

v. Consent Award

As in litigation, parties to an arbitration may arrive at a settlement of dispute during the course of the proceedings. If this happens the arbitral tribunal terminates the proceedings and if the parties so request and the request is accepted by the arbitral tribunal, the terms of the settlement shall be recorded as the terms of the arbitral award on agreed terms. This type of award is recognized by the Act. Section 45 provides as follows:

a. Where, during the arbitral proceedings, the parties settle the dispute, the arbitral tribunal shall terminate the arbitral proceedings, and shall, if requested by the parties and not objected to by the arbitral tribunal, record the settlement in the form of an arbitral award on agreed terms.

b. An award on agreed terms recorded under Subsection (1) of this Section shall:

i. Be in accordance with the provisions of Section 47 of this Act and state that it is such an award; and

[172] Redfern and Hunter, **op. cit.** 421-422

ii. Have the same status and effect as any other award on the merits of the case.

The advantage of recording the terms of settlement as a consent award is that it is easier to enforce performance of such agreement as an arbitral award. If it is not so recorded, it will be an ordinary agreement, the enforcement of which will be only by action, making it more expensive and time consuming.

vi. Interlocutory Award

This type of decision refers to a determination made by the arbitral tribunal on a purely procedural question. The better view, however, is that such decisions should not properly be regarded as *awards* but rather as *procedural orders*. Alan Redfern and Martin Hunter have explained the distinction as follows:

> **The term 'award' should be reserved for decisions by the arbitral tribunal which finally determine the issues with which they deal. This involves distinguishing between awards (which are concerned with issues) and procedural orders and directions (which are concerned with the conduct of the arbitration). Procedural orders and directions help to move the arbitration forward they deal with such matters as the exchange of written evidence, the production of documents and the arrangements for the conduct of the hearing. They do not have the status of awards and they may perhaps be called into question after the final award has been made.**[173]

[173] Redfern and Hunter, **op. cit.** 415

In essence, while awards determine the substantive rights or obligations of the parties and are final and binding in respect of those matters, *procedural orders* merely regulate the manner in which the arbitral proceedings are conducted. Procedural orders therefore lack the finality and enforceability that attach to arbitral awards. They remain within the control of the tribunal and may be varied, amended, or reconsidered in the course of the proceedings. This distinction is important because only *awards* whether interim, partial, or final are subject to recognition and enforcement under the *Arbitration and Mediation Act 2023*, whereas *procedural orders* are not

vii. Additional Award

An additional award is one that an arbitral tribunal makes to address claims that were properly presented during the arbitration but accidentally left out of the final award. Normally, once the tribunal gives its final award, it becomes functus officio meaning its work is done and its authority over the case has come to an end. However, Section 49(4) of the Arbitration and Mediation Act 2023 allows for a narrow exception. If a party notices that a particular claim was presented but not decided, that party may, within thirty days of receiving the award, ask the tribunal to make an additional award covering the omitted issue.

Section 49(5) further states that the rules on the form and content of arbitral awards in section 47 also apply to additional awards. This means an additional award must meet the same standards as any other award it must be signed, dated, reasoned, and formally delivered to the parties.

The key question, though, is whether an additional award stands alone as a separate category of award, or whether it simply forms part of the existing final award. In our respectful view, an additional award cannot properly stand on its own. It is best understood as a continuation or extension of the final award, intended not to introduce new determinations but to remedy an omission in the tribunal's original decision. Its purpose is simply to ensure that all claims submitted for arbitration are fully addressed. Once made, the additional award merges with and becomes part of the final award, thereby completing the tribunal's adjudicatory task. Accordingly, it should not be regarded as a separate or independent category of arbitral award.

6.5 CORRECTION AND INTERPRETATION OF AWARD

Section 49 of the Act provides as follows:

(1) Unless another period has been agreed upon by the parties, a party may, within 30 days of the receipt of an award and with notice to the other party, request the arbitral tribunal-

a. To correct in the award any errors in computation, any clerical or typographical errors or any errors of a similar nature;

b. To give an interpretation of a specific point or part of the award.

(2) If the arbitral tribunal considers any request made under subsection (1) of this section to be justified, it shall within 30 days of the receipt of the request, make the correction or give the interpretation, and such correction or interpretation shall form part of the award.

(3) The arbitral tribunal may, on its own volition and within 30 days from the date of the award, correct any error of the type referred to in subsection (1) (a) of this Section."

At common law the arbitral tribunal could not alter the award in any way whatsoever. Indeed, it could not even correct any type of errors or mistakes whether clerical or typographical. It must be noted that the type of correction permissible is only as provided in the Act under this section. The provision is not intended to correct the errors or mistakes of the arbitral tribunal itself. In other words, the provision is not designed to be employed by the arbitral tribunal to impeach its own award. Such was the issue in the case of **SUTHERLAND v. HANNEVING BROTHERS LTD**[174]**.** In this case, an umpire made an award and afterwards delivered an amended award, making an alteration with respect to costs. The Court having come to the conclusion that the umpire had written down what he intended to write in the original award and not omitted anything by accident, held that he had no power to alter it and the original award must stand.

The Act also empowers the arbitral tribunal to make an additional award if some claims presented in the arbitral proceedings were inadvertently omitted from the award. Where this is the case, any of the parties to the arbitral proceedings may apply within 30 days of receipt of the award to the arbitral tribunal to make additional award to cover the omitted claims or reliefs sought.

The Section 55(5) and (6) of the **Arbitration and Mediation Act 2023** provides for the severance and remittance of an arbitral award in cases where the award includes decisions on matters that fall outside the scope of the parties' submission to arbitration. In such cases, the Court may set aside only the portion of the award that

---

[174] (1921) IKB.336.

deals with matters not submitted to arbitration, so long as the valid parts of the award can be clearly separated from the invalid ones.

This principle reflects the position in **SUTHERLAND v. HANNEVIG BROTHERS LTD**[175] where the Court held that an award which covers issues beyond the reference is bad to that extent, but the valid portion can still stand if it can be distinguished from the rest.

[175] Supra

CHAPTER 7

CHALLENGES AND POST-AWARD PROCEEDINGS

7.1 GROUNDS FOR SETTING ASIDE AN AWARD

When an award is set aside, it is reduced to a nullity, and the parties are left in the same position as they were before the reference. This state of affairs is a matter of serious concern to the parties or to some of them. Because of this, the cases in which an award will be set aside by the Court are limited in number.

7.1.1 Application for Setting Aside Arbitral Award

Section 55 of the **Arbitration and Mediation Act 2023 (AMA 2023)** provides the exclusive grounds and procedure for challenging an arbitral award before the courts. The Act expressly limits judicial interference with arbitral awards and affirms the principle of finality in arbitration by stating that recourse to court may be made *only* through an application for setting aside in accordance with subsections (3) and (4).

Sub-section (2) further reinforces this finality by providing that an award cannot be challenged on the ground of an error on its face, or on any other basis not expressly stated in Subsection (3). In other words, mere mistakes of law or fact by the arbitral tribunal do not justify judicial intervention.

Under Subsection (3), the court may set aside an arbitral award only where specific and serious defects are proven. These include:

a. that a party lacked legal capacity;

b. that the arbitration agreement was invalid;

c. that proper notice of the proceedings or appointment of an arbitrator was not given;

d. that a party was unable to present its case;

e. that the award went beyond the terms of submission to arbitration;

f. that the composition of the tribunal or procedure was irregular; or

g. that the dispute itself was not arbitrable or the award contravenes Nigerian public policy.

Importantly, Subsections (4) to (6) introduce procedural safeguards to balance fairness and efficiency. An application for setting aside must be brought within three months from receipt of the award, ensuring that challenges are made promptly. Where a defect is found, the court may, under Subsection (5), either remit the award to the arbitral tribunal for reconsideration or set it aside in whole or in part, depending on the extent of the irregularity.

Furthermore, Subsection (6) empowers the court, upon request by a party, to suspend setting-aside proceedings temporarily. This allows the arbitral tribunal to resume the proceedings or take corrective action to remove the defect that prompted the challenge. The purpose of this mechanism borrowed from Article 34(4) of the **UNCITRAL Model Law** is to preserve the arbitral process and avoid unnecessary annulment of awards that can be remedied.

Two of the most significant grounds for setting aside, as provided in **Section 55(3)(a)(iv)** and **(v)**, relate to jurisdiction. An arbitral award may be set aside if it deals with disputes not contemplated by, or falling outside, the scope of the submission to arbitration, or if it contains decisions on matters beyond that scope. In essence, these provisions recognise that where an arbitral tribunal acts without jurisdiction, its award is a nullity.

The rules developed by Nigerian courts over the years are now clearly reflected in Section 55 of the Arbitration and Mediation Act 2023. Courts have consistently held that arbitral awards should be final and binding, and that they will only interfere in exceptional situations — for example, where the tribunal had no jurisdiction, where there was misconduct, or where a party was denied a fair hearing. Cases like **BAKER MARINE v. CHEVRON**[176], **KANO STATE URBAN DEVELOPMENT BOARD v. FANZ CONSTRUCTION CO. LTD**[177], **AND NNPC v. KLIFCO (NIG.) LTD**[178] all show that mere errors of law or fact are not enough to set aside an award.

Section 55(3) now puts these principles into law by listing the specific grounds for setting aside an award, such as lack of jurisdiction, invalid arbitration agreement, unfair hearing, or conflict with public policy. The Act also allows the court, under Subsections (5) and (6), to send the award back to the tribunal or pause proceedings so that minor issues can be corrected instead of cancelling the entire award. This approach supports fairness while still protecting the finality and efficiency that arbitration is meant to provide.

7.1.2 The Issue of Jurisdiction

The issue of jurisdiction is central to the proper understanding of this section and must therefore be discussed in details. An arbitral tribunal owes its jurisdiction to the agreement of the parties. This is the only source from which that jurisdiction can come. If the arbitral tribunal lacks jurisdiction, its acts are null and void. In particular, if it makes an award when it has no jurisdiction to do so, that award will be a nullity. Lack of jurisdiction is therefore a ground for setting aside awards.

---

[176] Supra
[177] Supra
[178] Suprs

In **ARBICO (NIG.) LTD v. NNPC**[179] The court held that the arbitrator exceeded his jurisdiction when he decided issues not submitted to him by the parties. This decision aligns directly with **Section 55(3)(a)(iv) and (v), AMA**, which deal with jurisdictional overreach.

Three kinds of lack of jurisdiction:

i. Awards may be made in the absence of jurisdiction.

ii. Awards may be made in excess of jurisdiction (*extra petita*)

iii. Awards may be made without dealing with all the matters referred (*infra petita).*

i. Award Made in The Absence of Jurisdiction

Section 55(3)(iv) of the Arbitration and Mediation Act (AMA) allows a party to ask the court to cancel an arbitral award if the arbitral tribunal had no jurisdiction to make it. In other words, the party must show that the tribunal decided a dispute that was not covered by the arbitration agreement or went beyond what the parties had agreed to submit to arbitration.

However, as explained in Russell on Arbitration[180], if the problem is that the entire arbitration was invalid because the tribunal never had jurisdiction at all, then applying to set aside the award is not the right procedure. This is because if there was no valid arbitration agreement, then there was no real arbitration and no valid award for the court to set aside.

In such a case, the right thing to do is either to wait until someone tries to enforce the award and then challenge it, or to go to court and ask for a declaration that the award is invalid.

---

[179] (2004) 2 NWLR (Pt. 858) 288 (CA)

[180] *Russell on Arbitration* (24th edn, Sweet & Maxwell 2015) para 8–060

ii. Awards Made in Excess of Jurisdiction

The Supreme Court in **BAKER MARINE (NIG.) LTD v. CHEVRON (NIG.) LTD**[181] held that "An arbitrator has jurisdiction to decide only what has been submitted to him by the parties for determination. If he decides something else, he will be acting outside his authority, and consequently the whole of the arbitration proceeding, including the award, will be null and void and of no effect."

Where an arbitral tribunal goes beyond the matters submitted to it and deals with issues outside its mandate, the resulting award may be set aside by the court upon the application of any party to the arbitration agreement. Similarly, Lord Denning LJ in **ZERVOS v. DORCHESTER HOTEL LTD**[182], observed that making an award of damages based on an illegal contract amounts to an excess of jurisdiction, thereby empowering the court to set the award aside.

The jurisdiction of an arbitrator arises solely from the agreement of the parties. This means that the arbitrator's authority is confined strictly to the disputes referred to him. He has no power to investigate or decide on other issues outside that scope. The only exception is where both parties, under a common mistake, have treated certain matters as being within the reference and have presented their cases accordingly. In that limited situation, the arbitrator's award on those matters may still be valid. In **ARBICO (NIGERIA) LTD v. NIGERIAN MACHINE TOOLS LTD**[183] The Court of Appeal held that where both parties voluntarily submit a dispute to arbitration, even if that dispute was not expressly covered by the arbitration clause, they are bound by the resulting award. The court reasoned that the parties' joint conduct amounted

---

[181] Supra
[182] [1955] 3 All ER 330 (CA)
[183] Supra

to an extension of the reference, and the arbitrator had jurisdiction over the matters so submitted.

However, where an arbitrator clearly exceeds his authority, the award will not bind the parties to the extent that it deals with matters outside the arbitration agreement. In **TRIANA LTD v. UNIVERSAL INSURANCE CO LTD**[184] The Court of Appeal emphasized that an arbitrator must confine himself strictly to the issues submitted for determination. Where he goes beyond those issues, the award to that extent is unenforceable.

Importantly, Section 55(3)(iv) of the Arbitration and Mediation Act 2023 provides a safeguard known as the doctrine of severance. Under this doctrine, if the parts of the award that relate to matters within the arbitration agreement can be separated from those that do not, the valid portion will be upheld while the invalid portion will be struck out. But this is only possible if the valid and invalid parts are clearly distinguishable.

This principle is a useful mechanism for preserving arbitral awards, ensuring that only the offending portions are removed while the legitimate parts remain binding on the parties. In many cases, what a dissatisfied party seeks to challenge is a minor or separable error, and severance allows the court to save the rest of the award from total nullity.

iii. Awards Made Infra Petita:

A fundamental question that sometimes arises in arbitration is what happens when an arbitral tribunal fails to deal with all the issues referred to it for determination. Does such an omission render the entire award invalid, or is the award still valid in respect of the issues that were actually determined?

---

[184] (2021) 10 NWLR (Pt 1784) 139 (CA).

Some learned authors argue that an award should remain valid in respect of the matters actually decided, since there can be no doubt that the arbitral tribunal had jurisdiction to deal with those matters. In their view, the omission merely leaves certain issues undetermined, without affecting the validity of the rest of the award.[185]

In **UNIVERSITY OF LAGOS v. AIGORO**[186] The Supreme Court held that *a decision is perverse where a tribunal fails to consider all the issues properly raised before it.* Every issue submitted by the parties must be fully and fairly considered before a valid decision can be reached. Again, in **MOGAJI v. ODOFIN**[187]

The Supreme Court held that a proper evaluation and consideration of all issues and evidence is fundamental to justice. Any decision made without considering all material issues and evidence cannot stand.

The authors herein dissent respectfully the view of the learned authors cited above and align instead with the Supreme Court's position. We submit that even though Section 55 of the Arbitration and Mediation Act 2023 does not expressly cover this scenario, an award made in such circumstances cannot be sustained. The failure of the tribunal to address all the issues submitted to it undermines the finality of the award, rendering it defective.

---

[185] *Russell on Arbitration* (24th edn, Sweet & Maxwell 2015) paras 8-059–8-060; Sir Michael Mustill and Stewart C Boyd, *Commercial Arbitration* (2nd edn, Butterworths 1989) 405–406; Nigel Blackaby and Constantine Partasides, *Redfern and Hunter on International Arbitration* (6th edn, OUP 2015) paras 9.96–9.98; Akinseye-George, *Arbitration Law in Nigeria: Practice and Procedure* (MIJ Professional Publishers 2019) 214–215.

[186] (1985) 1 NWLR (Pt 1) 143 (SC).

[187] (1978) 4 SC 91.

Furthermore, judicial authorities recognise that if an arbitral tribunal deliberately refuses to determine certain matters referred to it, the award may be set aside for misconduct.

Accordingly, a distinction should be drawn between:

a. Cases where the tribunal inadvertently fails to determine all the issues in which case the award is bad for want of finality; and
b. Cases where the tribunal refuses or neglects to deal with certain issues - in which case the award may be set aside for misconduct.

This principle finds support in **TAYLOR WOODROW (NIG.) LTD v. S.E. GMBH**[188] and **BAKER MARINE (NIG.) LTD v. CHEVRON (NIG.) LTD**[189] where the courts emphasized that arbitral tribunals must act within the scope of the submission and determine all matters properly before them, otherwise their awards are vulnerable to challenge.

7.1.3 Remittance to the Arbitral Tribunal for Reconsideration

Sub-sections (5) and (6) of Section 55 AMA 2023 reintroduces an important procedural innovation - remittance of the award to the arbitral tribunal for reconsideration.

Under Sub-section (5), if the court finds that one or more of the grounds in Sub-section (3) have been proved and that it has caused or will cause substantial injustice, the court may remit the award to the arbitral tribunal, in whole or in part, for reconsideration, or may set it aside in whole or in part.

Sub-section (6) goes further by allowing the other party, when faced with an application to set aside the award, to request that the court suspend the setting-aside proceedings and remit the matter to the

---

188 Supra
189 Supra

arbitral tribunal for correction. The tribunal is then empowered to resume the proceedings or take such other action as will eliminate the grounds for setting aside.

This provision demonstrates a deliberate legislative policy to preserve arbitration awards wherever possible, rather than destroy them for correctable procedural defects. It enhances the efficiency of arbitration and promotes confidence in the process.

The remittance mechanism complements Section 49 AMA 2023, which allows the arbitral tribunal to correct clerical, typographical, or computation errors, provide interpretations, or issue an additional award.

7.2 SETTING ASIDE (IMPEACHMENT) OF AWARDS

An award given in a reference pursuant to an arbitration agreement is final and conclusive between the parties upon all points which have been raised and decided in the arbitration. Thus, it was held that "An award operates as a final and conclusive judgement unless there is an express contrary provision in the arbitration submission or the award is an interim award". See **UNITED NIGERIA INSURANCE CO LTD v. STOCCO**[190]

Parties resort to arbitration in order to resolve their disputes through a private avenue other than the Court of law. In every arbitration agreement therefore, there is an implied term that the parties shall abide by the decision of the arbitral tribunal and carry out the terms of the award. Thus Article 42(2) of Arbitration Rules provides as follows: "All awards shall be made in writing and shall be final and binding on the parties. The parties undertake to carry out the award without delay."

The Court, when asked to set aside an arbitral award, may, where appropriate and so requested by a party, suspend the setting aside

---

[190] Supra

proceedings for a period it determines, to give the arbitral tribunal an opportunity to resume the arbitral proceedings or take such other action as may eliminate the grounds for setting aside the award. Section 55(6) of the Act empowers the Court, when an application is made to set aside an award, to suspend the setting-aside proceedings rather than immediately nullifying the award. The purpose of this mechanism is to preserve the effectiveness and finality of arbitration by allowing minor or curable defects to be remedied without the need to start the entire process afresh. It reflects the principle of minimal Court intervention and promotes the efficiency and autonomy of arbitral proceedings.

7.3 AWARD REVIEW TRIBUNAL

Section 56 of the Arbitration and Mediation Act 2023 introduces an innovative feature known as the Award Review Tribunal (ART). This mechanism allows parties to agree, in their arbitration agreement, that any challenge to an arbitral award will first be reviewed by a separate tribunal the ART before going to court. This is a major step toward making arbitration more self-contained and efficient.

For an ART to be validly constituted, the parties must have expressly agreed to it in their arbitration agreement. Once a party wishes to challenge an arbitral award, it must send a Notice of Challenge to the other party within the three-month time limit provided under Section 55(4). This notice must include key documents such as the award itself, the arbitration agreement, and, if necessary, certified English translations of both.

Unless the parties agree otherwise, the ART must have the same number of arbitrators as the original tribunal (known as the *First Instance Tribunal*). The ART is required to render its decision, in the form of an award, within 60 days of its constitution, and the provisions of the Act apply to it *mutatis mutandis* (that is, with necessary modifications).

A significant innovation under Section 56 is that the court retains a supervisory role. Where the ART sets aside an award, a party can apply to the court for a review of that decision. If the court finds that the ART's reasoning is "unsupportable," it may reinstate the original award, either wholly or partly. Conversely, where the ART upholds the award, any further challenge to the court is limited to only two grounds:

(i) that the subject matter of the dispute is not arbitrable under Nigerian law, or

(ii) that the award is contrary to public policy in Nigeria.

This dual-layer review system shows the legislature's intention to strengthen confidence in arbitration by providing a built-in corrective mechanism within the arbitral process itself. It helps prevent the unnecessary annulment of awards for correctable errors, thus promoting arbitration as a final and reliable alternative dispute resolution mechanism.

7.4 TIME LIMITS, PROCEDURE, AND APPEAL RESTRICTIONS

Section 55 of the Arbitration and Mediation Act 2023 (AMA) embodies one of the most decisive pro-finality features of modern arbitration law: the imposition of a strict time limit for setting aside an arbitral award. The provision stipulates that an application to set aside an award must be brought within three months from the date on which the party making the application received the award (or, where applicable, from the date of disposal of a request for correction or interpretation under Section 49). This is supported by a plethora of decided cases.[191]

---

[191] See; City Engineering (Nig.) Ltd v Federal Housing Authority (1997) 9 NWLR (Pt 520) 224 (SC); Kano State Urban Development Board v Fanz Construction Ltd (1990) 4 NWLR (Pt 142) 1 (SC); Taylor Woodrow (Nig.) Ltd v S.E. GMBH (1993) 4 NWLR (Pt 286) 127 (CA).

7.4.1 The Three-Month Limitation Period

The three-month period is not a mere procedural guideline; it is a substantive statutory condition precedent to the court's jurisdiction. Once the time lapses, the right to apply for setting aside is extinguished. The language of the statute is mandatory, and significantly, the AMA contains no express provision permitting extension of time.

The legal consequence is clear:

a. An application filed outside the three-month period is incompetent.

b. The court lacks jurisdiction to entertain it.

c. The defect cannot be cured by consent of parties or by invocation of general powers of enlargement under rules of court.

This strictness reflects Nigeria's adoption of the UNCITRAL Model Law framework, particularly Article 34(3), which similarly prescribes a non-extendable three-month limitation period. The objective is to promote certainty, stability of awards, and commercial predictability.

7.4.2 Rationale for the Strict Time Bar

The limitation serves several doctrinal and policy objectives:

a. **Finality of Awards.** Arbitration is premised on finality. Allowing indefinite challenges would defeat the essence of the arbitral process.

b. **Commercial Certainty**. Parties must know within a defined timeframe whether an award will stand or be challenged.

c. **Prevention of Tactical Delay**. A losing party should not be permitted to "keep the award under suspense" while exploring enforcement vulnerabilities or negotiation leverage.

d. **Alignment with International Practice**. The time limit harmonises Nigeria's arbitration regime with global best practices under the Model Law and the New York Convention system.

7.4.3 Jurisdictional Nature of the Time Limit

Although the AMA does not expressly use the word "jurisdictional," Nigerian courts have historically treated statutory time bars affecting rights of action as jurisdictional where the statute creates the right and prescribes the manner and timeframe for its enforcement.

Under this reasoning:

a. The right to challenge an arbitral award exists solely by virtue of Section 55.

b. The same provision conditions that right upon compliance with the three-month period.

c. Failure to comply removes the legal foundation upon which the court may act.

Thus, the limitation is not merely procedural; it extinguishes the statutory remedy itself.

7.4.4 Debate in Nigerian Judicial Circles

The strictness of the three-month rule has generated debate. Some practitioners have argued that, in the absence of express prohibition, general procedural rules allowing extension of time should apply. Others contend that because arbitration is consensual and statutory, enlargement would undermine legislative intent.

However, the prevailing judicial and academic view remains that:

a. The three-month period is mandatory;

b. Courts lack discretion to extend it;

c. Arbitration law must be interpreted in favour of finality.

This interpretation strengthens Nigeria's pro-arbitration reputation and discourages dilatory post-award litigation.

7.4.5 Interaction with Correction and Interpretation Requests

Where a party invokes Section 49 to seek correction, interpretation, or an additional award, the three-month period runs from the date of disposal of that request. This ensures procedural fairness by preventing premature limitation while post-award clarifications are pending.

However, once the Section 49 process concludes, the clock begins to run with full force.

7.4.6 Appeal Restrictions and Limited Judicial Intervention

The AMA reinforces the time-bar regime with a broader principle: court intervention is strictly limited. Recourse against an award may be made only through the setting-aside mechanism provided under Section 55. There is no general right of appeal on the merits.

This restriction is consistent with long-standing Nigerian jurisprudence affirming that courts will not sit as appellate bodies over arbitral tribunals. Errors of law or fact are not grounds for challenge unless they fall within the statutory categories such as jurisdictional excess, procedural irregularity, or public policy.

The combined effect of:

a. A strict three-month limitation period,

b. Exhaustive statutory grounds for challenge,

c. Absence of merit appeals,

creates a tightly controlled supervisory framework that prioritises arbitral autonomy and commercial finality.

7.4.7 Comparative Perspective

The Nigerian approach mirrors:

a. Article 34(3) UNCITRAL Model Law
b. Section 70(3) UK Arbitration Act 1996 (28 days, even stricter)
c. International best practice in Model Law jurisdictions

CHAPTER 8

RECOGNITION AND ENFORCEMENT OF AWARDS

8.1 AWARD ENFORCEMENT

When the losing party accepts the decision and quickly complies with the terms of an arbitral award, the matter ends smoothly. But often, the losing party is unhappy with the outcome and refuses to obey the award. In such a case, the winning party has no choice but to take steps to enforce it.

Because an arbitral award is not automatically a court judgment, the successful party cannot immediately seize or sell the losing party's property to satisfy the award. Before doing that, the award must first be recognized by a court, so that it becomes as enforceable as a judgment of that court. This process is known as the recognition and enforcement of an arbitral award, and it gives the award the same legal weight as a court decision. Once this is done, the successful party can then use the normal enforcement procedures available under Nigerian law to recover what is due. He can do this through one of the following ways.

8.2 DOMESTIC ENFORCEMENT MECHANISMS

The domestic enforcement of arbitral awards in Nigeria proceeds from the settled position that arbitration, though private in origin, is intended to culminate in public enforceability where voluntary compliance fails. Under the Arbitration and Mediation Act 2023 (AMA), an arbitral award, while final and binding between the parties, does not by itself operate as a judgment of court. Rather, enforceability is activated through judicial recognition and the grant of leave to enforce[192].

This interposition of the court is not an invitation to re-examine the merits of the dispute, but a statutory mechanism for clothing the award with the coercive authority of the State.

At the enforcement stage, the court's function is deliberately confined. The court is not concerned with the correctness of the tribunal's reasoning, nor with the weight of evidence evaluated by the arbitrators. Its inquiry is limited to ascertaining whether a valid award exists and whether any of the exclusive statutory grounds for refusal under the Act have been established.[193] Nigerian appellate courts have repeatedly affirmed that enforcement proceedings are not an appellate forum and that dissatisfaction with the substance, reasoning, or conclusions of an arbitral award does not justify judicial interference.[194]

As enshrined in Section 57(3), once leave to enforce is granted, the award becomes executable in the same manner as a judgment or order of court. This does not entail a re-characterisation of the arbitral award as a judicial determination on the merits; rather, it signifies that the court has authorised the deployment of its enforcement machinery in support of the tribunal's dispositive orders. This position is consistent with the decision of the Court of Appeal in **EBOKAN v. EKWENIBE & SONS TRADING CO LTD**[195], where it was emphasised that an arbitral award is binding between the parties unless and until it is set aside in accordance with the law, and that enforcement proceedings do not invite a rehearing of the dispute. The enforcement regime therefore reflects a careful

---

[192] Arbitration and Mediation Act 2023, ss 57(1), 57(3).
[193] Arbitration and Mediation Act 2023, s 58; New York Convention 1958, art V.
[194] See; IPCO (Nigeria) Ltd v Nigerian National Petroleum Corporation (2015) 6 NWLR (Pt 1454) 279 (CA).
[195] (1999) 10 NWLR (Pt 622) 242 (CA).

institutional balance: arbitral tribunals finally determine rights and obligations, while courts ensure that those determinations are not rendered ineffective by non-compliance. This balance was further affirmed by the Supreme Court in **NIGERIAN NATIONAL PETROLEUM CORPORATION v. FUNG TAI ENGINEERING CO LTD**[196], which clarified that the court's role at the enforcement stage is not to revisit the substance of the dispute but to give effect to the award within the framework prescribed by the arbitration statute. In this way, domestic enforcement under the AMA reinforces arbitral finality while preserving the limited and supportive role of the judiciary.

8.3 INTERNATIONAL ENFORCEMENT UNDER THE NEW YORK CONVENTION

Foreign awards are enforceable in Nigeria subject to the New York Convention (1958) and the applicable provisions of the Arbitration and Mediation Act, 2023. Enforcement may be refused only on the recognised statutory grounds, including invalid arbitration agreement, denial of fair hearing, excess of mandate, or public policy.

Mustill and Boyd explained the legal foundation for enforcing an arbitral award in court when they stated:

> ***Parties to an arbitration agreement impliedly promise to perform a valid award. If the award is not performed, the successful claimant can proceed by action in the ordinary courts for breach of this implied promise and obtain a judgment giving effect to the award. The court may give judgment for the amount of the award, or damages for failure to perform the award. It may also, in appropriate cases, decree specific performance of the award,***

---

[196] (2023) 15 NWLR (Pt 1906) 117 (SC).

> ***grant an injunction preventing the losing party from disobeying the award, or make a declaration that the award is valid, or as to its construction and effect.***[197]

This means that every arbitration agreement carries an implied obligation on both parties to comply with the final award. If either party fails to do so, that failure amounts to a breach of the arbitration agreement, and the successful party may bring an action in court to enforce the award and obtain judgment in its terms.

To succeed in such an action, the claimant must prove the following:

i. That there was a valid arbitration agreement;

ii. That a dispute arose within the scope of that agreement;

iii. That the arbitrator(s) were properly appointed in line with the agreement;

iv. That a valid award was made; and

v. That the losing party has failed to comply with the award.

Since the presumption *omnia praesumuntur rite esse acta* (all things are presumed to have been duly done) does not apply to arbitration proceedings, the claimant must establish each of these elements affirmatively. If the award does not involve payment of money but requires the losing party to perform a specific act, and monetary damages would not provide adequate compensation, the court may order specific performance of the award. However, being an equitable remedy, specific performance will not be granted where:

a. Full relief cannot be granted to both parties;

b. The award and arbitration agreement together amount to an unreasonable or unworkable arrangement;

---

[197] Mustill and Boyd, *Commercial Arbitration op cit. 397-398*

c. There has been unreasonable delay in seeking enforcement; or

d. The award is unenforceable at law by reason of the Statute of Frauds.

8.4 REQUIREMENTS FOR RECOGNITION AND ENFORCEMENT

Section 57(1) of the Arbitration and Mediation Act 2023 provides that

> **an arbitral award shall, irrespective of the country or state in which it is made, be recognized as binding, and upon a written application to the Court, be enforced by the Court subject to the provisions of this section and Section 58 of this Act.**

In simple terms, this means that an arbitral award whether made in Nigeria or abroad is treated as final and binding, and can be enforced through the courts once certain formal requirements are met. A party seeking to enforce an award only needs to apply to the High Court and submit the following documents:

a. The original arbitral award or a certified copy of it;

b. The original arbitration agreement or a certified copy of it; and

c. If either the award or the arbitration agreement is in a language other than English, a certified English translation.

Once these documents are filed, the court may recognize and enforce the award as if it were a judgment of the court. However, the opposing party may also apply to the court to resist enforcement or seek refusal of recognition, relying on specific grounds permitted under the Act.

8.4.1 Summary Procedure of Enforcement of an Award

Section 57(3) of the Arbitration and Mediation Act 2023 provides that:

> **An award may, by leave of the Court or a judge, be enforced in the same manner as a judgment or order to the same effect.**

This provision offers an inexpensive and straightforward method for enforcing an arbitral award. It allows the successful party to apply directly to the court for permission known as *leave* - to enforce the award without the need for a full trial. This process saves time and costs, provided the validity of the award is not in dispute.

However, where there is a serious doubt about the validity of the award, and that doubt cannot be resolved without a full hearing, the court will refuse to grant leave. In such a case, the applicant must instead bring a formal action on the award that is, file a regular court case seeking judgment based on the award.

The application for leave to enforce should be made by originating motion, supported by an affidavit that:

i. Verifies the existence of the arbitration agreement;

ii. Attaches the duly authenticated original award or a certified copy of it;

iii. States the names and addresses (or last known places of business) of both the applicant and the respondent; and

iv. Confirms whether the award has been performed, or to what extent it has been performed.

Once leave is granted, the successful party is placed in the same position as a judgment creditor. This means that they can use normal enforcement procedures such as a writ of fieri facias (to seize and sell the debtor's property) or garnishee proceedings (to attach debts owed to the debtor by third parties) to recover the award.

However, courts[198] have identified several situations where this summary procedure for enforcement is not available, including:

a. Where the original arbitration agreement was oral;

b. Where the award is purely declaratory;

c. Where the award lacks clarity;

d. Where the award is a foreign award;

e. Where it is not possible for the court to give a judgment or order "to the same effect" as the award;

f. Where there are genuine grounds for doubting the validity of the award; and

g. Where the award arises under a statutory arbitration rather than a consensual one.

In such situations, the proper course is to pursue enforcement through a regular court action rather than the summary procedure.

8.5 GROUNDS FOR REFUSAL OF RECOGNITION

Section 58 of the Arbitration and Mediation Act 2023 sets out the grounds on which a court in Nigeria may refuse to recognize or enforce an arbitral award. They include:

i. Any party to an arbitration agreement may ask the court not to recognize or enforce the arbitral award.

---

[198] See M.V. Lupex v. Nigerian Overseas Chartering & Shipping Ltd (2003) 15 NWLR (Pt. 844) 469 at 492–493; S*tatoil (Nig.) Ltd v. NNPC* (2013) 14 NWLR (Pt. 1373) 1 (CA

ii. Regardless of the country where the award was made, the court can only refuse recognition or enforcement in the following situations:

a. At the request of the party against whom the award is being enforced, if that party is able to prove that:

i. One of the parties to the arbitration agreement was incapacitated;

ii. The arbitration agreement is invalid under the law chosen by the parties, or under the law of the country where the award was made;

iii. The party against whom the award is enforced was not properly notified of the appointment of the arbitrator or the arbitration proceedings, or was otherwise unable to present their case;

iv. The award deals with a dispute that was not contemplated by or does not fall within the terms of the arbitration agreement;

v. The award contains decisions on issues outside the scope of the arbitration agreement, except that any separable parts of the award that relate to matters properly submitted to arbitration may still be recognized and enforced;

vi. The composition of the arbitral tribunal or the procedure used did not comply with the parties' agreement;

vii. Where there was no agreement on the tribunal's composition or procedure, these were not in accordance with the law of the country where the arbitration took place; or

viii. The award has not yet become binding on the parties, or it has been set aside or suspended by a court in the country where it was made or under whose law it was made.

b. The Court itself may also refuse recognition or enforcement if it finds that:

i. The subject matter of the dispute cannot be settled by arbitration under Nigerian law; or

ii. The award is contrary to the public policy of Nigeria.

Iii. Where an application has been made in a foreign court to set aside or suspend the award, the Nigerian court may postpone its decision on whether to recognize or enforce the award. It may also, if the party seeking enforcement requests it, order the other party to provide security (for example, a financial guarantee) while the foreign proceedings are ongoing.

The courts have repeatedly affirmed that they will not sit as an appellate body over arbitral awards, and that enforcement will be denied only when one of the statutory grounds is clearly established. In **IPCO (NIGERIA) LTD v. NIGERIAN NATIONAL PETROLEUM CORPORATION (NNPC)**[199], the Court of Appeal emphasized that the court's role at the enforcement stage is limited to verifying the existence of a valid award and determining whether any of the grounds for refusal under the Act apply.

Similarly, in **EBOKAN v. EKWENIBE & SONS TRADING CO. LTD**[200], the Court of Appeal held that an arbitral award is binding between the parties unless and until set aside in accordance with the law. The court noted that mere dissatisfaction with the reasoning or conclusions of the arbitrator is not a valid ground for refusing enforcement.

---

[199] (2015) LPELR-24891(CA)

[200] (1999) 10 NWLR (Part 622) 242

On the question of public policy, Nigerian courts have adopted a narrow interpretation consistent with international best practice. In **M. V. LUPEX v. N.O.C. LTD**[201], the Supreme Court warned that public policy should not be used as a "catch-all" excuse to undermine arbitration, stressing that only awards that violate Nigeria's fundamental notions of justice or morality should be refused enforcement.

8.6 EFFECT AND CONSEQUENCES OF ENFORCEMENT ORDERS (RECOGNITION, LEAVE AND THE POST-AWARD "JUDGMENT" REGIME UNDER THE AMA 2023)

8.6.1 Conceptual foundation: recognition/enforcement as a post-award judicial function, not a rehearing of the merits

Under the Arbitration and Mediation Act 2023 (AMA), the court's role at the enforcement stage is deliberately ancillary and enforcement-oriented. The court is not invited to re-determine the underlying dispute; rather, it is asked to recognise the award as binding and where sought grant leave to enforce so that the coercive machinery of the State may be deployed against a recalcitrant award-debtor. Section 57(1) provides the statutory hinge: an arbitral award shall be recognised as binding, and on application in writing be enforced subject to section 58 of the Act.[202]

This conception aligns with the international enforcement philosophy of the New York Convention (as domesticated) that enforcement proceedings should be summary, limited, and pro-finality, with resistance confined to enumerated grounds.[203] It also resonates with the long-standing Nigerian judicial attitude that

[201] Supra

[202] Arbitration and Mediation Act 2023 (Nigeria) s 57(1).

[203] Convention on the Recognition and Enforcement of Foreign Arbitral Awards (New York, 1958) art V; see also AMA 2023 s 58 (grounds for refusal).

courts should support, not suffocate, the arbitral process by merits review disguised as enforcement objections.[204]

8.6.2 The statutory "conversion": once leave is granted, the award becomes enforceable "as a judgment"

The central practical effect of an enforcement order is that the award (while remaining an arbitral award) becomes executable in the same manner as a judgment or order of court. Section 57(3) states the operative consequence in direct terms: "An award may, by leave of the Court, be enforced in the same manner as a judgment or order to the same effect."

Two points are doctrinally important:

a. The award is not metamorphosed into a fresh adjudication on the merits. The court does not "convert" the arbitral reasoning into a judicial judgment; rather, it grants leave that attaches the State's enforcement apparatus to the award's dispositive commands. Enforcement, in this sense, is a post-determination procedure.

b. The enforceability is to "the same effect", meaning that the court treats the award's operative parts (damages, declarations, specific performance directives, interest, costs, etc.) as though they were contained in a judgment of the court, capable of attracting the ordinary incidents of judgment execution.

This functional equivalence is not new; it is continuous with the earlier Arbitration and Conciliation Act regime, but the AMA 2023

[204] See generally Baker Marine (Nig) Ltd v Chevron (Nig) Ltd (2006) (Supreme Court, Nigeria) (authority on limited grounds and refusal to enforce awards tainted by recognised defects).

modernises the ecosystem and (significantly) strengthens the pro-enforcement posture by refining procedure and reaffirming the narrow refusal grounds.[205]

8.6.3 Jurisdictional breadth in enforcement proceedings and the non-dependence on subject-matter jurisdiction

A major practical issue in Nigeria has been whether a particular High Court can recognise and enforce an award where the underlying transaction would ordinarily fall outside that court's constitutional subject-matter jurisdiction. The Supreme Court has now provided decisive clarity: the jurisdiction to recognise and enforce an arbitral award is not determined by the subject-matter jurisdictional allocation that governs the trial of substantive causes. In Nigerian National Petroleum Corporation v Fung Tai Engineering Co Ltd[206], the Supreme Court held (under the predecessor statutory definition of "court", materially replicated in the AMA's definition) that:

> ***the courts listed by the arbitration statute have jurisdiction to enforce arbitral awards without importing subject-matter limitations not expressed in the statute.***

The implication for enforcement orders and their consequences is profound. An enforcement order is treated as a special statutory post-award proceeding. The enforcing court is not adjudicating the underlying cause of action; it is enabling execution of an already-determined award. In that sense, enforcement is better understood as the judicial supervision of arbitral finality, not a constitutional trial of a cause.

---

[205] Arbitration and Conciliation Act (Cap A18 LFN 2004) (repealed) s 31 (prior enforcement framework); AMA 2023 ss 57–58 (current framework).
[206] 2023) 15 NWLR (Pt 1906) 117 (SC).

8.6.4 Procedural and evidential consequences: what the enforcement order authorises the award-creditor to do

Once leave is granted under Section 57(3), the award-creditor can invoke the ordinary judgment-enforcement procedures available under Nigerian law and rules of court, including (depending on the relief and the debtor's asset profile) Writs of fieri facias against movable property, attachment and sale (where permitted by the rules of court and enforcement statutes), garnishee proceedings to attach debts owed to the judgment-debtor (commonly bank accounts), judgment summons / committal mechanisms for non-payment in appropriate circumstances subject to constitutional and procedural safeguards, charging orders or other proprietary execution devices subject to the rules of Court, orders of possession or delivery (where the award's effect is analogous to such relief), injunction-backed compliance for arbitral orders of specific performance (bearing in mind the court's discretion and the nature of the relief). The key is that the enforcement order grants the award executory life within the procedural architecture that ordinarily serves judgments.

8.6.5 Consequential orders: the court's ancillary powers to make enforcement effective

The provision in the Act that "the court may also make such consequential orders as are necessary to give practical effect to enforcement" captures a crucial reality of Nigerian enforcement practice. An order granting leave to enforce is often insufficient by itself unless paired with ancillary directions designed to prevent frustration and to operationalise the award.

There are three principal legal sources for consequential orders in this context:

i. Express statutory levers within the AMA 2023 itself

Even within the recognition/enforcement framework, the AMA contemplates supportive judicial measures. For example, where there is a pending set-aside or suspension application in the country of origin, Section 58(3) empowers the Nigerian court to adjourn the decision on recognition/enforcement and, critically, "order the other party to provide appropriate security." That is a paradigmatic consequential order which preserves the award-creditor's position and mitigates asset-dissipation risk while the challenge is determined elsewhere.

Likewise, the AMA's broader architecture in Section 58(3) (including provisions on interim measures and security in aid of arbitration) reflects a policy that judicial power may be used supportively to prevent arbitral outcomes from being rendered nugatory. In practice, once enforcement proceedings are commenced, the same pro-efficacy policy supports tailored consequential orders consistent with the statute and rules of court.

ii. Nigerian superior courts possess inherent powers to make orders necessary to prevent abuse of process and to ensure that their decisions are not rendered ineffectual. While this is frequently discussed in the context of judgment enforcement generally, the logic applies with equal force once an arbitral award has been clothed with enforceability "as a judgment."[207] Consequential orders may therefore include directions as to asset disclosure, timelines for compliance, modes of execution, and other case-management orders that ensure enforcement is real rather than symbolic always

[207] Constitution of the Federal Republic of Nigeria 1999 (as amended) s 6(6) on judicial powers and inherent powers doctrine.

within the bounds of procedural fairness and statutory limits.

iii. The rules of court governing execution and post-judgment procedure. Enforcement is practically carried out through the rules of the enforcing court. Once the award is enforceable as a judgment, the award-creditor is entitled to deploy those rules; correspondingly, the court is empowered to make ancillary orders contemplated by them (for example, in garnishee proceedings, third-party debt attachment, or protective orders around execution).

8.6.6 What "consequential orders" commonly look like in award enforcement practice

In Nigerian practice, consequential orders flowing from an enforcement order may include Orders for interest and computation. Where an award grants interest or where post-award/post-judgment interest becomes relevant under applicable rules; the court may give directions on rates, periods, and computation, particularly for clarity in execution.

Where the award is in foreign currency, the court may make directions necessary to enable execution against naira-denominated assets (while respecting the award's terms and applicable monetary rules). Enforcement proceedings generate costs; Nigerian courts often exercise discretion to award costs against an award-debtor that unreasonably resists enforcement on grounds that do not fall within Section 58. It is fundamental to emphasise that the AMA explicitly provides security in the adjournment scenario; courts may also, where procedurally appropriate, structure interim protection to prevent the enforcement process from being stultified. Orders binding third parties in execution such as garnishee orders nisi/absolute against banks or debtors of the award-debtor are procedurally distinct from recognition, but a direct consequence of the award becoming executable. The controlling principle is proportionality to the enforcement purpose. Consequential orders must implement, not expand, the award; they should not rewrite the tribunal's dispositive relief but should ensure that the award, as recognised, can be realised in fact.

8.6.7 Judicial attitude to resistance: Section 58 grounds are exclusive; "creative" objections are discouraged

Under the AMA 2023, refusal of recognition/enforcement is tightly controlled by Section 58, which substantially tracks the Model Law/New York Convention refusal grounds. Where an award-debtor attempts to resist enforcement by arguments that amount to a merits appeal (or by dressing procedural dissatisfaction as "public policy"), Nigerian courts have shown increasing willingness to insist on the statutory limits of resistance. A recent illustration of this discipline appears in **ARMADA SHIP MANAGEMENT (S) PTE LTD v. SCHISTE OIL & GAS NIGERIA LTD**[208] where the court considered the award-debtor's attempt to deploy "incapacity" in a manner that effectively excused a wilful refusal to participate in the arbitration; the analysis reinforces that Section 58 grounds are not elastic devices for avoiding enforcement where due process was available but ignored.

The practical consequence for enforcement orders is that, where the debtor's opposition is weak or tactical, the court is more likely not only to grant leave but also to issue robust consequential directions that prevent further dilatory conduct.

8.6.8 Finality and systemic consequences: enforcement orders protect arbitral integrity and commercial certainty

The enforcement order, once made, performs a systemic function: it signals that Nigeria treats arbitral awards as meaningful instruments, not mere moral victories. The combination of Section 57(1) (recognition), Section 57(3) (execution as judgment), and section 58 (limited refusal grounds) makes the court's enforcement order the

[208] Unreported Case. Federal High Court, Lagos; Suit No FHC/L/CS/2322/2023)

bridge between private adjudication and public coercion. This is why the consequences of enforcement orders extend beyond the immediate parties. It creates room for commercial certainty so that parties contract on the assumption that awards will be enforceable.

CHAPTER 9

COSTS AND ANCILLARY MATTERS IN ARBITRATION

9.1 COSTS IN ARBITRATION

Costs are the hidden constitution of arbitration. They determine whether arbitral justice is practically accessible, whether procedural efficiency is rewarded, and whether abusive tactics are deterred. In Nigeria, the Arbitration and Mediation Act 2023 ("AMA") treats costs not as an incidental footnote, but as a core part of the tribunal's mandate and the post-award legal order. The statute in Sections 50, 51, and 54 requires the tribunal to fix costs in its award, broadens the heads of recoverable costs to reflect modern practice (including third-party funding costs), regulates the reasonableness of arbitrators' fees, provides for deposits to sustain proceedings, and recognises a statutory lien that protects tribunals and institutions from strategic non-payment.

The normative architecture is deliberate. Arbitration depends on party autonomy for its origin, but it depends on juridical discipline for its legitimacy. That discipline is threatened if costs are allowed to become excessive and arbitrary, or parties can weaponize costs by starving the process of funds, multiplying interlocutory skirmishes, or forcing a successful party to incur enforcement expenses that are disproportionate and unrecoverable. The AMA responds by combining managerial powers (deposits, interim measures) with remedial powers (allocation, reasonableness assessment) and protective powers (lien, security, court-assisted enforcement).

9.2 NATURE AND COMPONENTS OF ARBITRATION COSTS

9.2.1 Statutory definition: what counts as "costs of arbitration"

The AMA requires that the arbitral tribunal "shall fix" the costs of arbitration in its award and defines "costs" expansively.[209] The heads include:

a. arbitrators' fees;
b. arbitrators' travel and expenses;
c. costs of expert advice and assistance required by the tribunal;
d. party/witness/expert expenses to the extent approved as reasonable;
e. legal representation and assistance costs of the successful party (where claimed and only to the extent reasonable);
f. administrative costs (institutional or appointing authority charges; venue; sitting; correspondence);
g. the costs of obtaining third-party funding; and
h. other costs approved by the tribunal.

This definition matters for three reasons; namely:

First, it pushes arbitration away from the court model of token cost recovery and towards a commercial model of meaningful reimbursement subject to reasonableness.

Second, it enables tribunals to address the "real" cost drivers of arbitration (experts, hearing logistics, document management, institutional fees).

Third, it recognises contemporary financing realities. Third-party funding is not treated as an alien phenomenon but as a potential cost incident of proceedings.

---

[209] Arbitration and Mediation Act 2023 (Nigeria) s 50(1)(a)–(h).

9.2.2 Analytical classification: tribunal-centred and party-centred costs

For doctrinal clarity and practical decision-making, arbitration costs may be classified into:

i. Tribunal-centred costs: arbitrators' fees and expenses; tribunal-appointed expert costs; administrative/ institutional charges. These are necessary to keep the arbitral system operational and, accordingly, are closely connected to deposit regimes and lien protection.

ii. Party-centred costs: party legal fees; party experts; witnesses; translations; travel; document services; and (where claimed and reasonable) third-party funding costs. These costs require proportionality scrutiny because they are the easiest to inflate and the most prone to becoming punitive.

9.2.3 The controlling standard: "reasonableness"

The AMA in Section 50(2) insists that arbitrators' fees must be reasonable, having regard to factors such as the amount in dispute, complexity, time spent, and other relevant circumstances. Even where the Act does not repeat the word "reasonable" for every head, reasonableness is structurally embedded: (i) some heads are recoverable only to the extent "approved" and "reasonable"; (ii) legal fees are recoverable only to the extent the tribunal deems reasonable; and (iii) the tribunal's allocation discretion is review-resilient only where exercised judicially and explained.[210]

The consequences for pleadings and evidence are immediate: if a party wishes to recover a cost head (especially legal fees and funding costs), it must be claimed in the arbitration and supported

[210] Arbitration and Mediation Act 2023 (Nigeria) s 50(1)(d)–(e).

with sufficiently intelligible evidence to enable a reasonableness assessment.

9.3 ALLOCATION AND APPORTIONMENT OF COSTS

9.3.1 Duty to Fix Costs in the Award: Finality and the Anti-Satellite Policy

Section 50(1) mandates that the arbitral tribunal shall fix costs *"in its award."* This requirement reflects a deliberate anti-satellite policy. Disputes over costs are not intended to outlive the substantive determination of the dispute or mutate into a secondary arena of contention after the award has been rendered.

The statutory duty to quantify and determine costs within the award itself serves several interlocking objectives. First, it promotes finality, ensuring that the arbitral award brings the dispute to a complete close, inclusive of its financial consequences. Arbitration is designed to deliver a conclusive resolution, and unresolved costs would undermine that objective by leaving a residual controversy outstanding.

Secondly, it enhances enforcement clarity. A costs order that is fixed and quantified within the award allows the successful party to enforce the award as a single, coherent instrument, without recourse to further applications or interpretive disputes as to quantum. An unquantified or deferred costs determination would frustrate enforcement and dilute the commercial utility of the award.

Thirdly, it reinforces procedural discipline. Knowing that costs will be conclusively determined and potentially shifted at the end of the proceedings incentivises parties to prosecute and defend their cases responsibly, to calibrate their procedural choices, and to cost their positions realistically. The tribunal's obligation to fix costs thus operates not merely as a remedial mechanism, but as a behavioral regulator throughout the arbitral process.

9.3.2 The Default Rule and the Power to Depart

The AMA starts from a clear and familiar position: costs follow the event. In simple terms, the party who wins the case is ordinarily entitled to recover its costs. This default rule promotes predictability and allows parties to assess risk before and during the arbitration.

However, the Act does not treat this rule as rigid. It gives the tribunal discretion to depart from it where fairness demands, and it requires the tribunal to give reasons for doing so. This combination reflects best international practice: a stable default rule, tempered by equitable flexibility to address the realities of how the case was actually conducted.

Departure from the default rule is commonly justified where:

a. success is partial or mixed, with each party winning on different issues;

b. the "successful" party engaged in disproportionate or wasteful conduct;

c. there was non-compliance with procedural directions;

d. costs were inflated by unnecessary experts or duplication of counsel; or

e. a party unreasonably refused realistic settlement opportunities, subject to the applicable rules on admissibility of settlement communications.

In buttressing this point, consider a scenario for a construction arbitration in Abuja where the Claimant seeks ₦500 million for alleged delays and defects from the Defendant/ Contractor. After hearing the case, the tribunal awards only ₦120 million, rejecting most of the claims. On paper, the Claimant has "won".

However, the tribunal notes that:

i. the claimant insisted on calling three experts when one would have sufficed;

ii. large portions of the hearing were spent on claims that were ultimately abandoned; and

iii. the respondent had earlier offered ₦150 million in settlement, which was unreasonably rejected.

In these circumstances, applying the default rule mechanically would be unjust. The tribunal may therefore order that each party bears its own costs, or that the claimant recovers only a reduced proportion of its costs, and the tribunal must explain its reasoning in the award.

9.3.3 The doctrinal limits: costs allocation must not be a disguised merits rehearing

A tribunal's decision on costs must, of course, remain anchored in procedural fairness and within the scope of its statutory mandate. Once an arbitral award is made, however, Nigerian courts have consistently resisted attempts to reopen the dispute through statutory challenges disguised as complaints about costs.

This approach is firmly rooted in the Supreme Court's decision in **BAKER MARINE NIGERIA LTD v. CHEVRON NIGERIA LTD**.[211] In that case, the Court emphatically held that:

> ***an arbitral award is final and binding on the parties, and that courts are not permitted to re-examine the merits of the dispute merely because one party is dissatisfied with the outcome.***

The Court made clear that arbitration would be undermined if losing parties were allowed to invite judicial reconsideration of the tribunal's reasoning under the guise of statutory intervention.

---

[211] (SC 374/2001) [2006] NGSC 105 (8 June 2006) (SC).

Although *Baker Marine* was decided in the context of setting aside and enforcement, the principle it establishes applies with equal force to costs. Dissatisfaction with the scale, allocation, or reasoning of a costs award does not, without more, open the door to judicial reconstruction. Courts are concerned with legality and jurisdiction, not with substituting their own view for that of the tribunal.

This policy stance is most sharply reflected in enforcement proceedings. There, the court's task is not to re-decide the dispute, but to apply the statutory rules governing recognition and enforcement of arbitral awards. The costs component, being an integral part of the award, therefore travels on the same rails of finality as the substantive reliefs granted by the tribunal.

9.4 SECURITY FOR COSTS, DEPOSITS, AND FINANCIAL CONTINUITY

9.4.1 Deposits and Advances under Section 51: the Funding Spine of the Process

Section 51 empowers the tribunal to request the parties to pay deposits (typically equal) to cover anticipated expenses of arbitration. Where a party fails to pay within the statutory time frame, the tribunal may invite the other party to pay; failing that, the tribunal may suspend or terminate proceedings. Indeed, this is not merely administrative; it is an anti-sabotage device. Arbitration is consensual, but it cannot function if one party can unilaterally render it financially impossible. Section 51 therefore aligns arbitral autonomy with procedural viability. Ideally tribunals should use Section 51 proactively (case management conferences; staged deposits; transparent budgeting) because deposit disputes are a major source of delay and cost inflation.

9.4.2 Security for Costs: Protective, Exceptional, and Proportionate

Deposits protect the tribunal; security for costs protects the opposing party against non-recoverability. The AMA's modernization discourse expressly recognizes security for costs as part of the toolkit of contemporary arbitration in Nigeria. The tribunal should treat security as exceptional, but legitimate where evidence demonstrates:

i. a real risk that an adverse costs order will be unrecoverable; and

ii. that ordering security will not stifle a genuine claim.

In any event, the principle is that proportionality security should neutralise identified risk, not serve as a weapon to choke the claim.

9.5 LEGAL FEES, TRIBUNAL FEES, ADMINISTRATIVE CHARGES, AND THE TRIBUNAL'S LIEN

9.5.1 Legal Fees: Recoverability Depends on Claim, Proof, and Reasonableness

Legal representation costs are recoverable where claimed during the arbitration and only to the extent the tribunal determines them to be reasonable. This structure has three consequences:

a. Pleading consequence: costs must be claimed, not assumed.

b. Evidential consequence: the tribunal needs intelligible material (bills, time records, schedules, expert invoices) to assess reasonableness.

c. Managerial consequence: tribunals should discourage "cost ambush" by ordering costs schedules and submissions early enough to enable fair response.

9.5.2 Tribunal Fees and Administrative Charges: Legitimacy through Reasonableness

Section 50(2) requires arbitrators' fees to be reasonable, assessed by reference to objective factors such as the amount in dispute, complexity, and time spent. This is normatively crucial for Nigeria's arbitration ecosystem: the perception that arbitration is expensive is often driven by fee opacity and lack of proportionality. Section 50(2) provides a statutory anchor for proportional fee discipline.

9.5.3 The Statutory Lien: Section 54 and Why It Matters

Section 54 gives an arbitral tribunal (or arbitral institution) a statutory lien over the award. In practical terms, this means the tribunal is entitled to withhold the release of the award until its fees and expenses have been paid.

The purpose of this rule is straightforward and systemic. It protects arbitrators and institutions from strategic non-payment, particularly by a losing party that might otherwise try to delay or frustrate the process by refusing to pay fees while still demanding the award. Without such a lien, parties could weaponize the timing of award delivery and undermine the integrity of the arbitral process.

In Nigeria, the courts have developed strong jurisprudence in favour of enforcement, finality, and non-intervention in arbitration. However, there is relatively little reported appellate authority that directly addresses disputes over the quantum of arbitrators' fees arising from the exercise of a lien, especially in publicly available law reports.

For this reason, a sound and disciplined analytical approach is to proceed as follows. First, the tribunal's right to assert a lien should be firmly grounded in Section 54 itself, which provides clear statutory authority. Secondly, it should be recognised that court oversight may arise in exceptional cases, particularly where a party alleges that the lien has been exercised unreasonably or abusively. Thirdly, and most importantly, detailed disputes about the amount of arbitrators' fees are generally resolved outside the courts, by reference to the parties' agreement, applicable institutional rules, and overarching principles of reasonableness.

9.6 COSTS AS SANCTIONS FOR PROCEDURAL MISCONDUCT

9.6.1 Juridical Rationale: Arbitration must be Protected against Abuse

Arbitration cannot rely on contempt powers in the same way as courts; its primary coercive tool is the authority to shape procedural consequences, especially through costs. The AMA's wide cost definition and the tribunal's discretion to allocate costs provide the juridical basis for cost sanctions targeted at misconduct.[212]

9.6.2 Typical Misconduct and Cost Consequences

Tribunals in Nigeria commonly confront misconduct that increases costs and undermines efficiency. A mature costs regime demands that such misconduct attracts consequences. The most frequent categories include:

a. Dilatory tactics: repeated adjournments; late pleadings; tactical medical excuses; delays in witness statements.

   Cost response: wasted costs orders; shifting hearing-day costs; adverse allocation of tribunal time costs.

b. Non-compliance with procedural directions: refusal to comply with timetables; non-production of ordered documents; late production that forces extra hearing days.
   Cost response: costs "thrown away"; disallowance of costs for unnecessary steps; indemnity-leaning cost allocation in extreme cases.

c. Jurisdictional gamesmanship: raising jurisdiction late after substantive participation (contrary to the policy of timely objections).

---

[212] Arbitration and Mediation Act 2023 (Nigeria) s 50(1)(h).

Cost response: adverse costs on jurisdictional objections; refusal of costs for avoidable applications.

d. Unmeritorious inflation: exaggerated claims, unnecessary experts, duplication of counsel beyond the needs of the dispute.

   Cost response: disallowance or reduction of claimed party costs; partial costs recovery even for the "successful" party where inflation is proved.

9.6.3 Due Process Safeguard: Sanctions must be Reasoned and Proportionate

Because costs decisions can become challenge points, sanctions must be reasoned. The tribunal should identify the misconduct, explain causation (how it increased costs), and justify proportionality. This reduces the risk of post-award arguments framed as denial of fair hearing or public policy.

9.7 INTEREST ON COSTS

9.7.1 Costs as a Monetary Obligation Capable of Attracting Interest

Once fixed in an award, costs become part of the award's monetary obligations. Where the tribunal awards interest on costs, that interest is enforceable along with the award. The AMA's enforcement logic awards are recognized as binding and, by leave, enforceable "as a judgment… to the same effect" means the costs component does not have a separate enforcement identity; it is part of the award as a whole.[213]

As a matter of best practice, tribunals should state expressly whether costs attract interest, the rate of interest, the start date, and whether the interest is simple or compound. Leaving these matters unstated creates uncertainty.

---

[213] Arbitration and Mediation Act 2023 (Nigeria) s 57(3).

Silence on interest often shifts the dispute to the enforcement stage, where parties argue over how the award should be interpreted rather than simply enforced. In practice, this leads to additional applications, delay, and higher legal costs, undermining the efficiency arbitration is meant to deliver.

Nigerian enforcement experience shows that even where the merits are settled, ambiguous financial terms in an award can trigger expensive post-award skirmishes. Clear treatment of interest in the award avoids this friction and preserves finality.

9.8 COSTS OF ENFORCEMENT PROCEEDINGS

9.8.1 The Enforcement Pathway and Why It often Multiplies Costs

Arbitral tribunals do not execute awards; courts do. Section 57 provides that awards are recognised as binding and enforced by the court; and by leave, enforceable as judgments "to the same effect". Consequently, enforcement proceedings can generate significant additional cost burdens: legal fees; affidavit evidence; applications for stay; adjournments; security motions; and sometimes parallel proceedings (set-aside, enforcement, anti-suit maneuvers).

9.8.2 Supreme Court Clarification Reducing "Technical" Cost Inflation: NNPC v. Fung Tai

Historically, one of the biggest drivers of cost and delay at the enforcement stage has been jurisdictional technicality parties fighting over which court is entitled to enforce an arbitral award.

The Supreme Court addressed this problem directly in **Nigerian National Petroleum Corporation v. Fung Tai Engineering Co Ltd**[214]. The Court clarified that:

> ***the Federal High Court has jurisdiction to recognise and enforce arbitral awards under the arbitration***

[214] (2023) 15 NWLR (Pt 1906) 117 (SC).

statute, and that this enforcement jurisdiction is not constrained by the constitutional subject-matter limits that apply to substantive trial jurisdiction.

In practical terms, this means that enforcement proceedings are treated differently from the original dispute. The court is not being asked to determine liability in, for example, aviation, maritime, or oil and gas matters; it is simply being asked to recognise and enforce an arbitral award.

The consequence is significant. An arbitral award arising from an aviation-related dispute may be enforced in a State High Court, notwithstanding Section 251 of the Constitution, which reserves aviation matters to the exclusive jurisdiction of the Federal High Court for substantive trials. Enforcement is procedural, not substantive, and jurisdictional objections based on subject matter should not be allowed to derail it.

9.8.3 Enforcement Resistance and Statutory Discipline: the "Incapacity"Argument under AMA 2023

Recent enforcement disputes under the AMA show that Nigerian courts are increasingly firm that refusal grounds are not flexible escape routes for losing parties. There are narrow statutory exceptions, not tools for delay or avoidance.

This approach is illustrated by **ARMADA SHIP MANAGEMENT (S) PTE LTD v. SCHISTE OIL & GAS NIGERIA LTD[215].** In that case, the court reportedly clarified the meaning of "incapacity" under Section 58(1)–(2)(a)(i) of the AMA. The court rejected attempts to treat wilful non-participation or deliberate refusal to engage in the arbitration as "incapacity". In essence, a party cannot

[215] (Federal High Court, Lagos Judicial Division, Suit No FHC/L/CS/2322/2023, unreported).

sit out the proceedings by choice and later rely on that choice to resist enforcement.

The cost consequence of this strict approach is significant. When courts interpret refusal grounds narrowly and in line with the statute's pro-enforcement policy, they reduce the incentive for speculative or tactical opposition to enforcement. This, in turn, lowers enforcement-stage legal costs and shortens timelines.

In large commercial arbitration, this matters greatly. The financial loss caused by enforcement delay through legal fees and the time-value of money often exceeds the tribunal's costs themselves. By closing the door to artificial resistance, the courts help preserve both the economic efficiency and finality of arbitration.

9.8.4 Allocation of enforcement costs: court discretion and deterrence

Enforcement costs are governed by court rules and cost discretion. A party that unreasonably resists enforcement risks adverse costs orders. In practice, this is essential to arbitration's credibility: if an award debtor can impose large enforcement costs without consequence, arbitration becomes merely the first stage of a longer and more expensive litigation arc.

9.9 COSTS OF AWARD REVIEW AND AWARD CHALLENGE (COURT SET-ASIDE; AWARD REVIEW TRIBUNAL)

The AMA creates dual post-award review pathways: the traditional court-based set-aside mechanism under Section 55 and, where the parties so agree, an Award Review Tribunal (ART) under Section 56. This design transforms the choice of review mechanism into a cost-architecture decision rather than a purely procedural one. Court set-aside proceedings typically involve formal motion practice, substantial counsel fees, the risk of appeals, delay, applications for security, and sometimes parallel enforcement skirmishes, all of which can significantly inflate post-award costs. By contrast, ART review entails additional arbitrator fees, deposits, and party costs, but may offer a more specialist and streamlined review depending on the parties' agreement and applicable rules. Scholarly and practitioner commentary on the AMA therefore emphasizes that the ART's effectiveness is highly sensitive to disciplined drafting of scope, timetable, and cost consequences, without which it risks becoming a second and unnecessary cost layer.[216] In either pathway, costs perform a deterrent function: they should discourage speculative or abusive challenges that undermine arbitral finality. This deterrent rationale is reinforced by Nigerian Supreme Court jurisprudence, which consistently affirms the principles of finality and limited curial intervention and rejects attempts to relitigate arbitral outcomes under the guise of statutory challenge.[217] Courts' insistence on narrow intervention grounds provides the policy foundation for robust cost consequences against unmeritorious award challenges, ensuring that post-award review does not become a strategic continuation of the dispute.[218]

---

[216] Glory Utazi, 'Appraisal of the Award Review Tribunal under the Nigerian Regulatory Arbitration Framework' (SSRN, 17 May 2024) https://ssrn.com/abstract=5141771 accessed 10 February 2026; Templars (Dispute Resolution Team), 'Revolutionising Arbitration: The Impact and Global Alignment of Nigeria's Award Review Tribunals (ARTs) under the Arbitration and Mediation Act 2023' (Templars, 27 August 2024) https://www.templars-law.com/app/uploads/2024/08/Revolutionising-Arbitration.pdf accessed 10 February 2026.

[217] Baker Marine Nigeria Ltd v Chevron Nigeria Ltd (Supreme Court, SC 374/2001, 8 June 2006).

[218] Nigerian National Petroleum Corporation v Fung Tai Engineering Co Ltd (2023) 15 NWLR (Pt 1906) 117 (SC).

CHAPTER TEN

INTERNATIONAL ARBITRATION

10.1 MEANING OF INTERNATIONAL ARBITRATION

International arbitration is a private way of settling disputes where parties from different countries agree to allow neutral arbitrators decide their case. It is used when a business relationship or investment crosses national borders.

By the provisions of Article 1 of the UNCITRAL Model Law on International Arbitration[219], a dispute is considered "international" when there is any foreign element, for example:

a. The companies involved are from different countries.

b. The contract was performed in more than one country.

c. The seat (legal home) of the arbitration is outside the parties' home states.

d. The subject matter of the contract is international.

Example: Where a Nigerian oil company signs a gas supply contract with a company from Italy and the parties agree that any dispute will be resolved by arbitration in Iraq. This is an international arbitration because the parties are from different states and the seat is in another country.

International arbitration is regulated by a combination of:

i. **National laws** – e.g., Nigeria's Arbitration and Mediation Act 2023[220], or the law of the chosen seat.

---

[219] United Nations Commission on International Trade Law, *UNCITRAL Model Law on International Commercial Arbitration 1985, with amendments as adopted in 2006.*

ii. **International treaties** – especially the New York Convention (1958)[221], which Nigeria has ratified.

iii. **Arbitration rules** – like ICC Rules[222], LCIA Rules[223], or UNCITRAL Arbitration Rules and soon the College of Arbitration Nigeria Rules (COAN)

These laws and rules help ensure fairness, neutrality, and enforceability of awards.

The major advantages of International Arbitration are that:

a. It is flexible; hence parties can design the procedure they want. This is supported also by Article 19(1) UNCITRAL Model Law

b. It is confidential unlike public court trials. Article 30 of the LCIA Arbitration Rules imposes confidentiality obligations on parties, arbitrators, and the LCIA itself.

c. It is neutral. In this sense, Article 18 of the UNCITRAL Model Law guarantees equal treatment of the parties and full opportunity to present their case

d. The final decision (award) is easy to enforce internationally under the New York Convention which has a global enforcement network. Articles III–V require contracting states to recognize and enforce foreign arbitral awards with very limited grounds for refusal. Nigeria in Section 60 of the AMA 2023 complied with

---

220 Arbitration and Mediation Act 2023 (Nigeria).
221 Convention on the Recognition and Enforcement of Foreign Arbitral Awards (adopted 10 June 1958, entered into force 7 June 1959)
222 International Chamber of Commerce, *ICC Arbitration Rules* (in force 1 January 2021).
223 London Court of International Arbitration, *LCIA Arbitration Rules* (in force 1 October 2020).

the New York Convention in recognising international awards.

10.2 SCOPE OF INTERNATIONAL ARBITRATION

International arbitration is used in many types of cross-border disputes. The main areas include:

a. International Commercial Disputes

These are business disputes between companies in different countries. Common examples include:

i. Influencer/Content Creator Agreement

A Nigerian content creator (living in Lagos) signs a product promotion or ambassadorial contract with Geely, a car-manufacturing company from China. Disputes arise and the influencer claims Geely failed to pay the agreed promotional fee. Geely also claims that the influencer did not meet the content delivery requirement of 80 Instagram posts per day. Consequently, Geely simply blocks and cuts off communication with the Nigerian content creator. There is disagreement about whether the contract was properly terminated.

Why this is an international commercial dispute?

a. The parties are from different countries (Nigeria and China).

b. The promotional content will target audiences in several countries especially across Africa.

c. Payment may be processed internationally from Bank of China to Zenith Bank Nigeria

d. The contract likely contains a foreign governing law and arbitration clause.

This dispute can be submitted to international arbitration, for example under ICC, LCIA, or UNCITRAL Rules.

ii. International Trade or Shipping

An Onitsha Main Market importer buys used "Okirika" clothes from his Chinese supplier, but the goods arrive faded and unmerchantable or late.

This situation which involves international parties will likely have an arbitration clause specifying a neutral forum such as London.

iii. Cross-Border Technology Supply

A London fintech company buys specialized software from an Enugu based tech firm. If the software fails, both sides may disagree about refunds or liability. Rather than travel from London to the High Court of Enugu State, or from Enugu State to the High Court in London, parties may consider international arbitration.

b. Investment Arbitration (Foreign Investor vs. Government)

This occurs when a foreign investor sues a government under a bilateral investment treaty or investment contract.

PROCESS & INDUSTRIAL DEVELOPMENTS LTD v. FEDERAL REPUBLIC OF NIGERIA[224] is one of the most famous international arbitration cases involving Nigeria.

In 2010, Nigeria's Ministry of Petroleum Resources signed a Gas Supply and Processing Agreement with P&ID, a company based in the British Virgin Islands (a foreign investor). By the said agreement, Nigeria was supposed to

224 [2023] EWHC 2638 (Comm)

supply natural gas to P&ID for 20 years. P&ID in turn undertook to build and operate a gas-processing plant in Cross River State such that after processing the gas, P&ID would return the clean/processed gas to Nigeria to use for power generation. Unfortunately, the project never took off. Both sides failed to fulfil certain parts of the contract. P&ID later claimed that Nigeria breached the agreement by failing to provide the gas and failing to prepare the project site. Because the contract contained an arbitration clause, the dispute was taken to international arbitration in London, instead of being heard in Nigerian courts.

In 2017, the arbitral tribunal ruled in favour of P&ID and awarded them about US$6.6 billion, plus interest which grew to over US$10 billion

The Federal Republic of Nigeria challenged the award in the courts of England and Wales. During the challenge, Nigeria argued that the award was obtained by fraud, bribery, corruption, concealment of evidence, and lack of transparency in the arbitration process. In 2023, the English High Court agreed that the award was tainted by fraud and set it aside[225].

c. Disputes Involving Governments or State-Owned Enterprises

Disputes involving Nigerian governments or state-owned enterprises frequently go to international arbitration because Government bodies like the Federal Ministry of Works, NNPC, amongst other regularly partner with foreign firms to achieve infrastructure projects.

---

[225] The Federal Republic of Nigeria v Process & Industrial Developments Ltd [2023] EWHC 2638 (Comm).

Large-scale infrastructure projects in Nigeria often involve foreign contractors, international experts, and state or federal governments. Because such projects require massive capital and long-term commitments, they commonly contain international arbitration clauses to protect foreign participants from political changes or unexpected government decisions.

A good example is the Lagos - Calabar Coastal Highway Project, one of the most expensive road projects in Nigeria's history. It has generated wide public debate and political disagreement due to its high cost, environmental concerns, and the displacement of businesses and communities. The reality therefore is that if there are foreign participants on this project and the government of the day changes, they might abruptly suspend the project leading to a termination of obligations with the foreign participants. Although the project is in Lagos and with the Nigerian Government, the foreign participants will rather than seek remedy in the Nigerian Courts, invoke the jurisdiction of the International Arbitral Tribunal usually contained in their contract. This way, neutrality and protection for foreign participants is guaranteed.

10.3 DISTINCTIONS BETWEEN DOMESTIC AND INTERNATIONAL ARBITRATION

Although similar in structure, international arbitration differs from domestic arbitration in several key respects:

a. Cross-Border Elements:

International arbitration involves parties from different jurisdictions or transactions spanning multiple countries. Domestic arbitration is confined to one state.

In **Statoil (Nig.) Ltd v. NNPC**[226] there was a Production Sharing Contract (PSC) between Statoil, a Norwegian oil company, and NNPC. When a dispute arose over cost recovery and profit, Statoil sought to refer the matter to international arbitration as provided in the contract. NNPC resisted, arguing that the dispute should not go to arbitration. The Court of Appeal held that the PSC had clear cross-border elements, since it involved a foreign company, international oil operations, and obligations performed both inside and outside Nigeria. It was also held that the arbitration clause was valid and enforceable, and parties must be bound by the terms they freely agreed to. NNPC's status as a government-controlled corporation did not exempt it from international arbitration. The dispute was properly referable to international arbitration under the contract.

b. **Legal Framework:**

International arbitration is shaped by international conventions (e.g., the New York Convention) and the UNCITRAL Model Law. Domestic arbitration usually relies solely on national statutes.

c. **Enforcement of Awards:**

International awards benefit from broad enforceability under international treaties. Awards made outside Nigeria or awards considered "international" under Section 60 AMA can be enforced in Nigerian courts with relative ease through the instrumentality of the New York Convention. Likewise, Nigerian international awards benefit from the same global structure and can be enforced abroad with fewer hurdles. Domestic awards may face more limited recognition outside the seat country.

---

[226] (2013) 14 NWLR (Pt. 1373) 1,

d. **Procedural Flexibility:**

International proceedings are less formal and adapt to varied legal traditions. Domestic arbitration often follows local procedural norms.

e. **Neutrality:**

Parties in international arbitration prioritise neutral arbitrators, venues, and governing laws to avoid perceived home-court advantage.

f. **Language and Culture:**

International arbitration frequently requires multilingual and cross-cultural competence.

10.4 SOURCES OF INTERNATIONAL ARBITRATION LAW

International arbitration is regulated by a complex framework comprising national laws, treaties, conventions, and institutional rules. The primary sources include the following:

i. **United Nations Commission on International Trade Law (UNCITRAL) Model Law**

The Model Law, adopted in 1985 and amended in 2006, serves as the most influential template for national arbitration legislation. It harmonises arbitration laws across jurisdictions by standardising principles such as party autonomy, limited court intervention, enforcement of agreements, interim measures, and setting aside procedures. Many countries have enacted Model Law-based statutes, thereby facilitating predictability and uniformity in international arbitration. Before 2023, Nigeria used the Arbitration and Conciliation Act 1988, which was based partly on the 1985 Model Law. The Arbitration and Mediation Act 2023 fully incorporates key provisions of the 1985 Model La1, integrates the 2006 amendments on interim measures, and brings Nigeria in line with global best practices. This makes Nigeria a Model Law jurisdiction, ensuring predictability and international confidence in its arbitration framework.

ii. New York Convention (1958)

Formally known as the Convention on the Recognition and Enforcement of Foreign Arbitral Awards, it is the backbone of international arbitration and enforcement of Awards. The Convention obliges contracting states to respect arbitration agreements, recognize foreign arbitral awards, and enforce them with minimal delay. Grounds for refusing enforcement are defined and they include incapacity to contract ab initio, invalid arbitration agreement, due process violations, excess of jurisdiction, irregular composition of the tribunal, and public policy. Section 60 of the AMA makes the New York Convention the principal treaty for the enforcement of foreign awards in Nigeria.

iii. ICSID Convention (1965)

The International Centre for Settlement of Investment Disputes (ICSID) Convention establishes an autonomous and self-contained system for resolving investment disputes between sovereign states and foreign investors. Nigeria, a contracting state since 1967, treats ICSID awards as equivalent to final judgments of the Supreme Court under the ICSID (Enforcement) Act[227]. Consequently, Nigerian courts have no power to review, vary, or set aside ICSID awards, and their role is limited to registration and enforcement. The Convention enhances investor confidence by guaranteeing neutral, depoliticised dispute resolution and safeguarding foreign investors against unfair treatment, expropriation, and discriminatory state conduct under

[227] International Centre for Settlement of Investment Disputes (Enforcement of Awards) Act, Cap I20 Laws of the Federation of Nigeria 2004.

Nigeria's bilateral and multilateral investment treaties. This framework strengthens Nigeria's credibility as an investment destination while ensuring that State obligations to foreign investors are governed by international legal standards rather than domestic judicial discretion.

iii. Institutional Rules (ICC, LCIA, SIAC, etc.)

Many international arbitrations proceed under institutional rules issued by reputable arbitral bodies such as:

- **ICC (International Chamber of Commerce)**
- **LCIA (London Court of International Arbitration)**
- **SIAC (Singapore International Arbitration Centre)**
- **HKIAC (Hong Kong International Arbitration Centre)**
- **ICSID** for investor-state disputes
- **Lagos Court of Arbitration (LCA)**
- **Lagos Chamber of Commerce International Arbitration Centre (LACIAC)**
- **College of Arbitrators Nigeria (Draft rules, forthcoming)**

These rules provide detailed procedural frameworks on appointment of arbitrators, emergency arbitration, document production, hearings, costs, and award issuance.

10.5 PARTY AUTONOMY IN INTERNATIONAL ARBITRATION

Party autonomy is the foundation of international arbitration and is firmly recognised in Nigeria, especially under the Arbitration and Mediation Act 2023 (AMA 2023). It allows Nigerian parties and their foreign counterparts to decide the key elements of the arbitration process. This includes choosing the governing substantive law such as Nigerian law for an oil and gas contract, or English law for an offshore financing agreement as well as selecting the seat of arbitration, which may be Lagos, Abuja, London, Dubai, or Paris depending on what the parties consider neutral and convenient. Parties are also free to adopt institutional rules, for example the LCA or LACIAC Rules for a Lagos-seated arbitration, or the ICC or LCIA Rules for an arbitration seated in London. They may determine the number and qualifications of arbitrators, appointing, for instance, a Nigerian construction expert for a building dispute or a foreign maritime arbitrator for an offshore vessel contract. They may also specify procedural rules, choose Igbo as the language of proceedings, and agree to confidentiality which is often crucial in sensitive sectors such as oil and gas, banking, and telecoms.

However, as in all Model Law jurisdictions, party autonomy in Nigeria is not unlimited. The parties' choices must comply with the mandatory provisions of the law of the seat. For example, if Enugu is the seat, the AMA 2023 requires equal treatment of parties and sets out mandatory grounds for challenging arbitrators and setting aside awards. Similarly, international public policy places boundaries such that Nigerian courts will not enforce an agreement that permits bribery, money laundering, or arbitrations conducted in a manner contrary to natural justice. Thus, while Nigerian law strongly upholds the parties' freedom to design their arbitration process, this autonomy exists within safeguards intended to preserve fairness, legality, and the integrity of the arbitral system.

In **NIGERIAN NATIONAL PETROLEUM CORPORATION (NNPC) v. LUTIN INVESTMENT LTD**[228]**.** The Court reinforced that courts cannot rewrite arbitration agreements. It held that whatever procedural framework the parties select whether number

[228] (2006) 2 NWLR (Pt. 965) 506

of arbitrators, appointment method, or applicable rules must be honoured.

In **SOLEL BONEH INTERNATIONAL LTD v. GOVERNOR OF CROSS RIVER STATE** [229], the Court of Appeal affirmed that although party autonomy is a central pillar of arbitration in Nigeria, it is not absolute. Parties cannot, through procedural agreements, exclude or restrict the court's supervisory jurisdiction under the Arbitration and Conciliation Act (now the Arbitration and Mediation Act 2023). Mandatory legal safeguards such as fair hearing, impartiality, and statutory grounds for setting aside awards override any contrary procedural agreement. The case thus illustrates that party autonomy operates only within the boundaries of Nigerian public policy and the mandatory provisions of the law of the seat.

In **CUKUROVA FINANCE INTERNATIONAL LTD v. ALFA TELECOM TURKEY LTD**[230] the Court found that while parties may design their own arbitral procedures, such autonomy cannot undermine the fundamental right to be heard. The English Court of Appeal held that procedural agreements cannot authorise decisions that deny a party a fair opportunity to present its case.

10.6 APPOINTMENT OF ARBITRATORS IN INTERNATIONAL DISPUTES

The appointment of arbitrators in international arbitration is shaped by the arbitration agreement and reinforced by established frameworks such as the UNCITRAL Arbitration Rules, the Regional Centre for International Commercial Arbitration (RCICA) Lagos Rules, and the Nigerian Arbitration Rules 2023 made under

---

[229] *(2018) 4 NWLR (Pt. 1608) 289*

[230] (2017) EWCA Civ 1392

the Arbitration and Mediation Act 2023 (AMA 2023). Under all three regimes, the number of arbitrators is governed by default rule that parties are at liberty to choose in the first instance. Article 7 UNCITRAL Rules and Article 8.1 RCICA provide that the tribunal shall consist of three arbitrators unless otherwise agreed, while section 6(2) AMA 2023 presumes a sole arbitrator where the parties fail to specify. As to party participation, the standard model for three-member tribunals where each party appoints one arbitrator and both appointees select the presiding arbitrator is expressly set out in Articles 9–10 UNCITRAL Rules, Article 10 RCICA, and section 7(3) AMA 2023. All three frameworks also emphasise independence and impartiality. Arbitrators must disclose circumstances that may raise doubts about their neutrality. This duty appears in Article 11 UNCITRAL, Article 12 RCICA, and section 8 AMA 2023. Where a party defaults in making an appointment or where the arbitrators cannot agree on a chairperson, default mechanisms ensure continuity of proceedings. Articles 8 UNCITRAL empower the designated appointing authority to step in; Article 9 RCICA gives appointment power to the Director of the RCICA; and Section 7(4) AMA 2023 allows the court where the parties and any designated authority are unable to appoint arbitrator to constitute the tribunal where necessary.

Under the UNCITRAL Arbitration Rules 2021, while there is no explicit provision that mandates "special technical expertise," appointing authorities are required to consider independence and impartiality under Art 6(7), and parties remain free to agree their own requirements. Similarly, under Nigeria's Arbitration and Mediation Act 2023, Section 7(5) requires the appointing authority to "have due regard to the qualification required of an arbitrator in the arbitration agreement," thereby allowing parties to specify expertise (e.g., in energy, construction, maritime law, or international trade) so that the tribunal's competence aligns with the technical complexity of the dispute.

10.7 CONDUCT OF INTERNATIONAL ARBITRAL PROCEEDINGS

International arbitration proceedings are designed to promote efficiency, neutrality, and procedural fairness, and these objectives are clearly reflected in both the UNCITRAL Arbitration Rules and the RCICAL Arbitration Rules 2008. The UNCITRAL Rules establish a structured framework for written submissions, beginning with the statement of claim in Article 20 and the statement of defence in Article 21. The RCICAL Rules adopt a similar approach, making corresponding provision for the written statement of claim and defence in Articles 20 and 21 respectively.

The management and exchange of evidence form a central component of arbitral proceedings. Under the UNCITRAL Rules, the tribunal's authority over evidence is set out in Article 27, which empowers it to require the production of documents, exhibits, and other forms of evidence. The RCICAL Rules contain an equivalent provision in Article 27, enabling the tribunal to direct parties to produce documents or other evidentiary materials within a specified time. This alignment underscores the importance both regimes place on controlled, tribunal-supervised document production rather than unrestricted disclosure.

Hearings are similarly regulated in both sets of rules. The UNCITRAL Rules address oral hearings in Article 28, affirming the tribunal's power to hold hearings for witness examination, submissions, or other oral presentations, unless the parties agree to a documents-only procedure. The RCICAL Rules mirror this in Article 28, which provides for oral hearings-whether physical or remote—where parties may present evidence, examine witnesses, and make oral submissions. This ensures that, unless otherwise agreed, the opportunity for an oral hearing remains a fundamental safeguard of procedural fairness.

Interim and conservatory measures are another essential feature of international arbitration practice. Under the UNCITRAL Rules, Article 26 authorises the tribunal to grant interim measures such as asset preservation, maintenance of the status quo, or protection of evidence. The RCICAL Rules contain an analogous provision in Article 29, which empowers the tribunal to grant provisional or protective measures, including orders relating to the preservation of property or the provision of security. These mechanisms serve to protect the integrity of the proceedings and prevent frustration of the award.

Case-management powers are central to the tribunal's ability to conduct proceedings efficiently. Under the UNCITRAL Rules, Article 17 grants the tribunal broad authority to conduct the arbitration in a manner it considers appropriate, provided the parties are treated with equality and given a full opportunity to present their case. The RCICAL Rules include an equivalent guarantee in Article 18, which not only affirms equal treatment but also empowers the tribunal to organise procedural conferences, set timelines, and formulate provisional timetables in consultation with the parties. These provisions emphasise proactive case-management as a hallmark of modern arbitration.

Both regimes expressly recognise the use of experts as a means of resolving technically complex disputes. The UNCITRAL Rules permit the appointment of tribunal-appointed experts under Article 29, granting parties the right to comment on expert reports and to question the expert at a hearing. The RCICAL Rules adopt the same structure in Article 30, enabling the tribunal to appoint independent experts and ensuring that parties may participate fully in the expert process. This promotes procedural transparency and technical accuracy.

A key area where the two regimes diverge is confidentiality. The UNCITRAL Rules do not impose automatic confidentiality; instead, confidentiality depends on party agreement or tribunal direction under its general procedural powers. The RCICAL Rules take a different approach by expressly imposing confidentiality obligations under Article 4, which requires parties, their representatives, and the tribunal to maintain the confidentiality of the proceedings, documents, and deliberations. This textual inclusion reflects the policy preference of the Lagos regime for stronger confidentiality protections.

Finally, both sets of rules adopt a firm commitment to due process and fairness. While Article 17(1) of the UNCITRAL Rules expressly requires the tribunal to ensure the equal treatment of the parties and to give each party a full opportunity to present its case, the RCICAL Rules embed these guarantees within the tribunal's general procedural powers rather than in a standalone article. Under the RCICAL framework, Article 18(1) the tribunal must conduct the proceedings in a manner that ensures fairness and respects each party's right to be heard, even as it exercises broad discretion to manage the procedure efficiently. This shared commitment functions as a foundational safeguard, ensuring that procedural flexibility and efficiency never compromise fundamental fairness.

Overall, while the UNCITRAL Arbitration Rules and the RCICAL Arbitration Rules differ in certain structural or policy details such as confidentiality they are fundamentally aligned in their commitment to procedural fairness, efficiency, and tribunal-centred case management. Together, they reflect the global best practices that continue to shape contemporary international arbitration.

10.8 RECOGNITION AND ENFORCEMENT OF INTERNATIONAL AWARDS

The enforcement of arbitral awards is the ultimate objective of international arbitration, and the New York Convention (1958) provides the central legal framework. Article III obliges contracting states to recognise and enforce foreign arbitral awards in the same manner as domestic judgments. Refusal of enforcement is strictly limited to the grounds listed in Article V(1)–(2), which include incapacity or invalidity of the arbitration agreement, Article V(1)(a); lack of proper notice or inability to present one's case, Article V(1)(b)); the tribunal exceeding its jurisdiction Article V(1)(c); irregularity in the composition of the tribunal or arbitral procedure that contradicts the parties' agreement, Article V(1)(d); and the award not yet being binding or having been set aside at the seat of arbitration Article V(1)(e). Additionally, enforcement may be refused if it would violate the public policy of the enforcing state under Article V(2)(b). Courts worldwide including Nigerian courts adopt a pro-enforcement bias, applying these exceptions narrowly to support the Convention's objective of facilitating international trade and investment.

By contrast, awards rendered under the ICSID Convention benefit from an even stronger enforcement regime. Under Article 54 ICSID Convention, an ICSID award is enforceable in every contracting state as if it were a final judgment of that state's courts, and domestic courts cannot review or set aside the award, since annulment is handled exclusively within the ICSID system.

The question whether a foreign arbitral award may be set aside by a Nigerian court has been a recurring source of confusion for practitioners and commercial parties. The Court of Appeal provided authoritative clarification in **LIMAK/SAHELIAN ENERGY**[231] case where it firmly rejected the notion that Nigerian courts may annul foreign awards. The decisions reaffirm the territoriality principle embedded in international arbitration and the New York Convention framework.

[231] Limak Yatırım Enerji Üretim İşletme Hizmetleri ve İnşaat A. S & Ors v Sahelian Energy & Integrated Services Ltd, Court of Appeal, Abuja Division, Civil Appeal Nos CA/A/CV/795/2020 & CA/A/CV/796/2020

In these appeals, the applicants sought to challenge a foreign award rendered outside Nigeria by inviting the Nigerian courts to set it aside. The Court of Appeal held that such an application is fundamentally misconceived because Nigeria lacks supervisory jurisdiction over awards made in a foreign seat. The Court emphasised that only the courts of the seat of arbitration - the "primary jurisdiction"- may exercise supervisory powers such as annulment, correction, or revision of an award. Nigerian courts, by contrast, function solely as a "secondary jurisdiction" under the New York Convention, with powers limited to recognising and enforcing foreign awards or refusing enforcement on the narrow grounds set out in the Convention.

The Court explained that Article V(1)(e) of the New York Convention clearly envisages that set-aside applications can only be made before "the competent authority of the country in which, or under the law of which, the award was made." This wording reflects the global consensus that the validity of an award is governed by the procedural law of the seat. Accordingly, Nigerian law whether under the former Arbitration and Conciliation Act or the current Arbitration and Mediation Act 2023 contains no provision authorising Nigerian courts to annul foreign awards.

Consequently, parties aggrieved by a foreign award must challenge it before the courts of the seat of arbitration. Their only remedy in Nigeria is to resist enforcement by raising one or more of the limited Convention defences, such as incapacity, procedural irregularity, lack of jurisdiction, or public policy. The *Limak/Sahelian* decisions therefore provide much-needed doctrinal clarity: Nigerian courts may enforce or refuse enforcement of foreign awards, but they possess no jurisdiction to set them aside.

10.9 SOVEREIGN IMMUNITY AND STATE PARTIES

When a State or State-owned entity participates in international arbitration, questions of sovereign immunity arise at two distinct stages:

a. **Immunity from Jurisdiction**

b. **Immunity from Execution**

a. Immunity from Jurisdiction

Sovereign immunity ordinarily shields a State from being sued before foreign domestic courts. However, in international arbitration, the position is different. When a State signs an arbitration agreement, most legal systems and arbitral frameworks treat this as a waiver of immunity from jurisdiction, although it does not automatically waive immunity from execution. This distinction is fundamental in public international law and comparative arbitration law.

Article 1(1) of the UNCITRAL Arbitration Rules reinforces this approach by providing that the Rules apply to disputes arising out of a "defined legal relationship … whether contractual or not." This broad formulation allows the Rules to govern not only commercial disputes but also treaty-based and public-law disputes, including those involving States.

UNCITRAL's official explanatory materials confirm that the UNCITRAL Arbitration Rules are used in commercial arbitration, investor-State arbitration, and State-to-State arbitration, where the parties, including States, have consented to their application."[232] Furthermore, the revised Article 1(4) further supports this reality by

[232] United Nations Commission on International Trade Law, *UNCITRAL Arbitration Rules (as revised in 2010), with new article 1, paragraph 4, as adopted in 2013* (United Nations 2013) Introductory Note https://uncitral.un.org/sites/uncitral.un.org/files/media-documents/uncitral/en/uncitral-arbitration-rules-2013-e.pdf accessed 19 November 2025.

incorporating the UNCITRAL Rules on Transparency into treaty-based investor-State disputes, thereby expressly contemplating the participation of sovereign parties.

This means that consent to apply the UNCITRAL Arbitration Rules operates as a waiver of jurisdictional immunity. Once consent is validly given whether via an investment treaty, contract, legislation, or other binding instrument a State stands before the arbitral tribunal on an equal procedural footing with the private party.

Additionally, Articles 3 and 7 of the UNCITRAL Rules, which govern the commencement of arbitration and the constitution of the arbitral tribunal, presuppose the procedural equality of the parties. They provide no special procedural status for States. It is therefore right to submit that once an arbitration is commenced under Articles 3 and 7, and the State has consented to arbitration through Article 1(1), a State cannot subsequently invoke jurisdictional immunity to escape arbitral proceedings. The waiver is inherent in the act of agreeing to arbitration.

Under the Regional Centre for International Commercial Arbitration (RCICA) Lagos Rules, Articles 1 & 4 provide that the Rules explicitly apply to disputes involving States, State entities, and intergovernmental organisations, provided they have consented to arbitration.

Similarly, under the ICSID Convention, Article 25(1) provides that Consent of the State and investor confers exclusive ICSID jurisdiction on an arbitral tribunal. Once given, consent cannot be withdrawn, and the State cannot claim immunity from ICSID proceedings.

In SOUFRAKI v. UAE[233], the tribunal clarified the effect of a State's consent to ICSID arbitration under the ICSID Convention. Although the case ultimately turned on the claimant's failure to prove Italian nationality, the tribunal took the opportunity to reaffirm a broader procedural principle that when a State gives its consent to ICSID arbitration whether through a treaty, contract, or investment legislation it effectively waives any claim to jurisdictional immunity before the tribunal. In **STATOIL (NIG.) LTD v. NNPC**[234], the Court of Appeal reaffirmed the principle that a state entity which freely enters into an arbitration agreement is bound by its terms in the same manner as a private commercial actor. The Court rejected the argument that the Nigerian National Petroleum Corporation (NNPC), as a state-controlled entity, could invoke sovereign immunity to avoid or obstruct arbitral proceedings arising from its contractual commitments. By signing the relevant petroleum agreement which contained a clear arbitration clause NNPC had unequivocally waived any claim to immunity in respect of arbitral jurisdiction.

b. Immunity from Execution

A waiver of jurisdictional immunity does not automatically waive immunity from execution. After an award is issued, a distinction is made between:

i. Sovereign (Non-Commercial) Assets

These remain immune from seizure, such as:

- Central Bank reserves
- Embassy property
- Military equipment
- Government ministries and buildings

---

[233] Hussein Nuaman Soufraki v United Arab Emirates (Award) ICSID Case No ARB/02/7 (7 July 2004).

[234] Supra

iii. Commercial Assets

Assets "used for or intended for commercial purposes" *may* be attachable, depending on national law.[235]

Article 34(2) of the UNCITRAL Arbitration Rules provides that an arbitral award is final and binding on the parties, meaning they must comply with it. However, the Rules do not themselves create an enforcement mechanism. Instead, the actual process of enforcing the award such as attaching assets or seeking recognition depends entirely on the domestic law of the country where enforcement is sought, often through that country's arbitration statute or its adoption of the New York Convention. When the award is sought to be enforced against a State or State entity, the situation becomes more complicated because the enforcement must be subject to the country's immunity laws which will usually preclude attachment of sovereign assets & properties.

Article 40 of the RCICA Lagos Rules provides that Awards are binding, but enforcement must comply with the law of the State where enforcement is sought, including rules on state immunity from execution.

While Article 54(1) of the ICSID Convention provides that ICSID awards are enforceable like final domestic court judgments, Article 55 thereof provides that State immunity from execution remains intact and is determined by each State's domestic law.

NML Capital Ltd v. Argentina[236] , is one of the most influential modern cases on the limits of sovereign immunity

---

[235] See Article 21, United Nations, *Convention on Jurisdictional Immunities of States and Their Property* (adopted 2 December 2004, opened for signature 17 January 2005) UN Doc A/59/508, arts 19–21.

in the enforcement of international awards and judgments. The dispute in this case arose from Argentina's 2001 sovereign debt default, after which certain bondholders including NML Capital refused restructuring terms and pursued full repayment through litigation and enforcement actions worldwide. Although the courts recognised that Argentina had clearly consented to the jurisdiction of foreign courts by issuing sovereign bonds with waiver clauses, the enforcement stage raised the more complex question of whether Argentina's assets abroad could be seized.

In both jurisdictions, the courts drew a firm distinction between sovereign (non-commercial) assets and commercial assets. The US courts, applying the Foreign Sovereign Immunities Act (FSIA), and the UK courts, applying the State Immunity Act 1978, held that assets used for governmental functions remain inviolable. These include Argentina's embassy properties, diplomatic bank accounts, and most importantly central bank reserves held through the Banco Central de la República Argentina (BCRA). Such sovereign property was categorically immune from attachment and execution.

Conversely, the courts affirmed that commercial assets, meaning property used for or intended for commercial activities, are not entitled to execution immunity. Where Argentina or its instrumentalities engaged in commercial dealings such as proceeds from commercial trading entities or revenue-generating state-owned enterprises those assets could, in principle, be targeted by creditors.

---

[236] *699 F 3d 246* (2nd Cir 2012) ; [2011] UKSC 31, [2011] 2 AC 495.

10.10 PUBLIC POLICY IN INTERNATIONAL ARBITRATION

Public policy is a narrowly construed but significant ground for refusing enforcement or setting aside arbitral awards under both Nigerian and international arbitration law. It applies only where an award violates a State's most fundamental legal, moral, or public interests. Such violations include corruption or bribery, breaches of natural justice, illegality in the underlying contract, or conduct that threatens the sovereignty or essential interests of the State. Courts worldwide consistently emphasize that public policy must be interpreted restrictively to preserve the finality and predictability of international arbitration.[237]

Under Nigerian law, Sections 55(3)(b)(ii) and 58(2)(b)(ii) of the Arbitration and Mediation Act 2023 (AMA) allow courts to set aside or refuse enforcement of an award if it is contrary to Nigeria's public policy.[238] These provisions mirror Article V(2)(b) of the New York Convention 1958, which authorizes refusal of enforcement where doing so would be contrary to the enforcing State's public policy. The UNCITRAL Model Law adopts a similar framework in Articles 34(2)(b)(ii) and 36(1)(b)(ii), which the AMA 2023 largely reflects.

Nigerian courts have repeatedly affirmed the narrow scope of public policy in arbitration. In **NNPC v. LUTIN INVESTMENTS LTD**, the Court of Appeal held that public policy should not be expansively interpreted and applies only to violations of fundamental Nigerian values such as illegality or fraud.[239] The Supreme Court reiterated in **MEKWUNYE v. IMOUKHUEDE** that errors of law or fact do not constitute public policy grounds.[240] Similarly, in **NNPC v. CLIFCO NIGERIA LTD**, the court

---

[237] Nigel Blackaby and others, Redfern and Hunter on International Arbitration (7th edn, OUP 2022) 637

[238] Arbitration and Mediation Act 2023, ss 55(3)(b)(ii), 57(2)(b)(ii).

[239] Supra

[240] Supra

confirmed that although illegality may implicate public policy, the doctrine should be sparingly applied to uphold arbitral finality.[241]

English jurisprudence persuasive in Nigerian courts adopts an equally restrictive approach. In **DALLAH REAL ESTATE v. PAKISTAN,** the UK Supreme Court distinguished between jurisdictional review and public policy, holding that respect for the rule of law forms part of public policy and may justify refusal of enforcement where the tribunal acted without jurisdiction[242]

In the international sphere, ICSID tribunals similarly apply a strict standard. In **WORLD DUTY FREE v. KENYA**, the tribunal held that contracts procured through bribery are unenforceable because corruption violates transnational public policy.[243] Likewise, the tribunal in **METAL-TECH v. UZBEKISTAN** dismissed the investor's claims because corruption tainted the investment process, reaffirming the centrality of legality in international arbitration.[244] Public policy thus serves as a limited safeguard, applied only where the award threatens essential legal norms such as the rule of law, fundamental morality, due process, or state sovereignty. It is not a mechanism for re-litigating the merits or correcting errors. Courts in Nigeria and globally interpret the doctrine narrowly to ensure that arbitration remains an effective, final, and reliable method of resolving disputes.

10.11 EMERGING TRENDS IN INTERNATIONAL ARBITRATION

The field continues to evolve dynamically. Notable contemporary trends include:

a. Investment Arbitration

---

[241] Supra
[242] [2010] UKSC 46.
[243] (ICSID Case No ARB/00/7), Award (2006).
[244] (ICSID Case No ARB/10/3), Award (2013)

Investment arbitration is an emerging trend in Nigeria due to the country's increasing participation in bilateral and multilateral investment treaties and the large volume of foreign investment flowing into sectors such as oil and gas, power, and infrastructure. These treaties commonly provide protections against expropriation, discriminatory regulation, and unfair or inequitable treatment, and they often give investors access to arbitration under the ICSID Convention or the UNCITRAL Arbitration Rules. Nigeria has faced several high-profile investment claims illustrating this trend for example, **P&ID v. FEDERAL NIGERIA ICSID**[245] concerning a gas-processing project, **INTEROCEAN OIL DEVELOPMENT v. NIGERIA**[246] involving alleged interference with oil block rights, and **SHELL NIGERIA ULTRA DEEP v. FEDERAL REPUBLIC OF NIGERIA**[247] relating to offshore oil concessions. As Nigeria continues to adopt new regulatory frameworks like the very controversial Nigeria Tax Act 2025, and other related laws, foreign investors are increasingly testing these measures against treaty protections for foreign investors, making investor-state arbitration a growing and significant are of International Arbitration Practise.

Article 25(1) of the ICSID Convention provides that ;

> **The jurisdiction of the Centre shall extend to any legal dispute arising directly out of an investment, between a Contracting State (or any constituent subdivision or agency of a Contracting State designated to the Centre by that State) and a national of**

[245] ICSID Case No. ARB/18/11
[246] (ICSID Case No. ARB/13/20)
[247] (ICSID Case No. ARB/07/18)

another Contracting State, which the parties to the dispute consent in writing to submit to the Centre.

Article 1(1) of the UNCITRAL Arbitration Rules provides that Where parties have agreed that disputes between them in respect of a defined legal relationship, whether contractual or not shall be subject to the rules, then the rules shall apply. Article 1(4) introduces the UNCITRAL Rules on Transparency into the UNCITRAL Arbitration Rules for treaty-based investor–State arbitrations. It provides that when an investor brings a claim against a State under an investment treaty using the UNCITRAL Rules, the transparency rules automatically apply unless the treaty parties or the disputing parties have agreed to opt out. In effect, Article 1(4) ensures that modern UNCITRAL investor–State arbitrations are conducted with greater openness, public access to documents, and stakeholder participation. It also confirms that Investor-State arbitrations are covered by the UNCITRAL Rules.

b. Third-Party Funding

Third-party funding involves an external financier funding the arbitration in exchange for a portion of the award. It raises issues of disclosure, conflict of interest, and cost allocation.

Article 14(1) of the ICSID Arbitration Rules 2022 provides that "A party shall file a written notice disclosing the name and address of any non-party from which the party, its affiliate or its representative has received funds for the pursuit or defense of the proceeding (the 'funder'), including through a donation or grant. The notice shall also indicate whether the funder has undertaken to pay an adverse costs order against the party."

Article 11(7) of the ICC Arbitration Rules 2021 provides that "In order to assist prospective arbitrators and arbitrators in complying with their duties under Articles 11(2) and 11(6), each party must promptly inform the Secretariat, the arbitral tribunal and the other parties, of the existence and identity of any non-party which has entered into an arrangement for the funding of claims or defences and under which it has an economic interest in the outcome of the arbitration."

c. Emergency and Expedited Arbitration

Institutions now offer emergency arbitration and fast-track procedures to respond quickly to urgent commercial needs. The ICC Arbitration Rules (2021) provides in Article 29(1) that A party that needs urgent interim or conservatory measures that cannot await the constitution of an arbitral tribunal ('Emergency Measures') may apply for such measures pursuant to the Emergency Arbitrator Rules in Appendix v. Similarly, Article 9(B) of the LCIA Rules 2020 provides that "In cases of exceptional urgency, any party may apply to the LCIA Court for the immediate appointment of a temporary sole arbitrator ('Emergency Arbitrator') to conduct emergency proceedings."

d. Technology and Virtual Hearings

The COVID-19 era accelerated digital transformation, including virtual hearings, electronic filings, and AI-assisted document review. The UNCITRAL Arbitration Rules (2021), Article 17(3) Gives tribunals power to determine the mode of hearings, including remote hearings. ICC Arbitration Rules (2021), Article 26(1) Allows hearings to be conducted by video conference.

CHAPTER ELEVEN

MEDIATION UNDER THE NEW ADR REGIME

11.1 INTRODUCTION

The Arbitration and Mediation Act, 2023 repealed the Arbitration and Conciliation Act and was enacted to create a unified legal framework for the fair and efficient settlement of commercial disputes by arbitration and mediation. In structural terms, the Act places mediation in Part II, spanning Sections 67 to 87, while Section 90 effects the repeal of the earlier ACA. That architecture matters. It signals that mediation is no longer treated as a side-note to arbitration but as a co-equal dispute-resolution mechanism with its own rules on commencement, confidentiality, limitation, settlement, enforcement and international effect.

Yet the 2023 Act is not innovative because Nigeria previously knew nothing of amicable settlement. The repealed ACA already contained a short Part II on Conciliation and a set of Conciliation Rules in its Third Schedule. The true innovation of the 2023 Act lies elsewhere: it replaces a sparse conciliation framework with a fuller mediation code; it expressly defines "mediation" to include processes called mediation, conciliation or any similar expression; it creates an internal enforcement regime for settlement agreements; and it links Nigerian law to the Singapore Convention for qualifying international settlements. In that sense, Part II is best understood as a focused modernisation rather than a creation ex nihilo.

11.2 FROM CONCILIATION UNDER THE REPEALED ACT TO MEDIATION UNDER THE 2023 ACT

Under the repealed Arbitration and Conciliation Act, Part II provided the legal framework for the settlement of disputes by conciliation. The provisions addressed matters such as the right of parties to resort to conciliation, the request for and commencement of conciliation proceedings, the appointment of conciliators, the conduct of the conciliation process, and the recording of terms of settlement.[248] The Third Schedule to the Act went further by recognising written settlement agreements, imposing obligations of confidentiality, providing for the termination of proceedings, suspending arbitral or judicial proceedings during conciliation, preventing a conciliator from subsequently acting as arbitrator or witness in related proceedings, and rendering settlement discussions inadmissible in subsequent proceedings.[249] In this sense, the repealed statute already contained many of the core elements associated with modern mediation law.

What the Arbitration and Mediation Act 2023 does is to elevate those elements into a more coherent statutory regime. Section 91 defines mediation broadly as a process in which parties request a third person to assist them in reaching an amicable settlement of their dispute without the authority to impose a binding decision. Importantly, the provision states that the process may be described as mediation, conciliation, or "an expression of similar import."[250] This formulation creates a deliberate terminological bridge between the repealed legislation and the new statute. It demonstrates that the 2023 Act does not abolish the logic of conciliation; rather, it absorbs and modernises it under the internationally recognised language of mediation.

The shift introduced by the 2023 Act is therefore both linguistic and substantive. Under the repealed Act, a settlement reached through conciliation became binding upon the parties once signed, but the legislation did not establish a comprehensive enforcement

---

[248] Arbitration and Conciliation Act, Cap A18 Laws of the Federation of Nigeria 2004, pt II.
[249] ibid Third Schedule.
[250] Arbitration and Mediation Act 2023, s 91.

architecture for such settlements. By contrast, the 2023 Act provides a structured framework for the legal effect and enforcement of mediated settlements. Sections 82–87 recognise that a mediated settlement agreement is binding and enforceable and may be relied upon in court as a contract, a consent judgment, or a consent award. The Act further prescribes documentary requirements for reliance on such agreements, identifies grounds upon which enforcement may be refused, recognises the possibility of parallel proceedings, and provides for the enforcement of qualifying international settlement agreements in accordance with the United Nations Convention on International Settlement Agreements Resulting from Mediation.[251] Collectively, these provisions represent one of the most significant innovations introduced by the 2023 statute, situating Nigerian mediation law within the contemporary global framework for the recognition and enforcement of mediated settlements.

11.3 SCOPE, DEFINITIONS AND NORMATIVE STRUCTURE OF PART II

Section 67 of the Arbitration and Mediation Act 2023 adopts a deliberately broad scope of application. The provision extends Part II to international commercial mediation, domestic commercial mediation, and domestic civil mediation, as well as to domestic and international settlement agreements resulting from mediation and concluded in writing to resolve a commercial dispute.[252] It further applies to any dispute in which the parties agree in writing that Part II of the Act should govern their mediation process. The section also clarifies that its application is not dependent on the source of the mediation process; accordingly, Part II applies whether mediation

---

[251] Ibid ss 82–87; United Nations Convention on International Settlement Agreements Resulting from Mediation (adopted 20 December 2018, opened for signature 7 August 2019) UN Doc A/RES/73/198

[252] Arbitration and Mediation Act 2023, s 67.

arises from contract, statute, or a direction or suggestion by a court, arbitral tribunal, or governmental authority.

At the same time, section 67 also makes clear that some situations fall outside the mediation regime created by Part II of the Arbitration and Mediation Act 2023. In simple terms, the section is designed to regulate true mediation processes, and not other forms of dispute resolution that may look similar.

First, the Part does not apply to void settlement agreements. For example, if two parties sign a settlement after mediation but the agreement is illegal or was obtained through fraud, the Act will not treat it as a valid mediated settlement capable of enforcement.

Second, it does not apply where a judge or arbitrator personally conducts settlement discussions during ongoing proceedings, unless the parties agree that the mediation provisions should apply. For instance, during a court case over a property valuation dispute, a judge may encourage the parties to negotiate in chambers. That type of settlement effort is generally treated as part of the judicial process rather than a formal mediation under the Act.

Third, the section excludes arbitral awards and court judgments or court-approved settlements. Once a decision has been formally issued by an arbitral tribunal or a court, it falls within the enforcement framework of arbitration or civil procedure rather than mediation law.

A practical illustration may arise in a property valuation dispute. Suppose a developer and an estate valuer disagree over the valuation of a commercial building. If they appoint an independent mediator to help them negotiate a compromise price and they sign a written settlement, Part II of the Act will apply. However, if the dispute is already before a court and the judge facilitates negotiations that lead to a consent judgment, the outcome is treated as a court judgment, not a mediated settlement under the Act.

The purpose of these exclusions is therefore to maintain clear boundaries between mediation, arbitration and judicial decision-making, while still allowing parties to opt into the mediation framework if they expressly wish to do so.

The wide scope of section 67 of the Arbitration and Mediation Act 2023 shows that Nigeria chose to go beyond the basic structure of the UNCITRAL Model Law on International Commercial Mediation and International Settlement Agreements Resulting from Mediation. The UNCITRAL Model Law mainly focuses on international commercial mediation, that is, disputes involving parties from different countries. The Guide to the Model Law explains that a country may expand the framework to cover domestic disputes simply by removing the word "international"[253].

Nigeria's legislature went further than this. The 2023 Act clearly states that the mediation framework applies not only to international commercial disputes, but also to domestic commercial disputes and ordinary civil disputes within Nigeria. At the same time, the Act retains the international framework where issues arise about the recognition and enforcement of settlement agreements across borders.

A practical example can be seen in valuation or property disputes involving estate surveyors. If a Nigerian developer and a Nigerian estate surveyor disagree over the valuation of a shopping complex in Abuja and submit the dispute to mediation, Part II of the Act will apply, even though the dispute is entirely domestic. Similarly, if two Nigerian firms disagree over compensation for land acquisition based on conflicting valuation reports by surveyors, mediation under the Act can be used to resolve the dispute.

---

[253] UNCITRAL, UNCITRAL Model Law on International Commercial Mediation and International Settlement Agreements Resulting from Mediation 2018 and Guide to Enactment and Use (United Nations 2018)

However, the same framework can also apply to international disputes. For example, if a foreign real estate investment company disputes the valuation of a Nigerian property portfolio prepared by a local firm of estate surveyors, and the parties settle the dispute through mediation, the settlement agreement may be recognised and enforced internationally under the framework influenced by the Singapore Convention on Mediation.

In this way, Part II of the Act is both international in inspiration and local in application. It reflects global mediation standards while also accommodating the kinds of domestic commercial and professional disputes such as valuation disagreements that frequently arise within Nigeria's dispute resolution landscape.

Sections 68 and 69 then establish the interpretative and normative foundation of Part II. Section 68 requires that, in interpreting the provisions of the Part, regard must be had to the need for uniformity in application and the observance of good faith. Section 69, in turn, affirms the principle of party autonomy, allowing parties to vary most provisions of the mediation regime by agreement. However, this autonomy is not absolute. The Act preserves a non-derogable fairness requirement by maintaining the obligation contained in section 73(3) that a mediator must treat the parties with fairness and give each party a reasonable opportunity to present its position. The legislative balance is therefore clear: mediation under the Act remains flexible and party-driven, but it cannot be structured in a way that undermines procedural fairness.

Section 91 defines when mediation is considered "international". It also provides that, when interpreting the Act, courts should take into account its international origin and may consult the *travaux préparatoires* of the UNCITRAL Model Laws where appropriate. This provision encourages Nigerian courts to interpret Part II in line with international mediation instruments and materials, rather than treating the Act as purely domestic legislation.

11.4 COMMENCEMENT OF MEDIATION AND SUSPENSION OF LIMITATION

Section 70 modernises commencement rules in a practical way. Where mediation is required by statute or pre-agreed as a precondition to further proceedings, the initiating party must propose in writing that the other party enter a mediation agreement. If no acceptance arrives within 30 days, or within any other period stated in the invitation, the inviter may treat silence as rejection. The same section also allows mediation to be proposed before, during or after judicial or arbitral proceedings, and permits the body conducting such proceedings to recommend mediation where settlement appears possible. The date of commencement is then fixed by Section 70(5): either the date the parties sign the agreement to mediate, the date of the court's referral, or in any other case the date the mediator takes the first step to begin the process.

This approach is more developed than the position under the repealed Arbitration and Conciliation Act, where conciliation commenced when the request for conciliation was accepted by the other party. It also goes beyond the core text of the UNCITRAL Model Law on International Commercial Mediation and International Settlement Agreements Resulting from Mediation 2018, which treats mediation as commencing from the parties' agreement.[254] The 2018 Guide to Enactment and Use separately suggests the possibility of suspending limitation periods during mediation. Nigeria expressly adopted that approach in Section 71 of the Arbitration and Mediation Act 2023.[255]

---

[254] UNCITRAL Model Law on International Commercial Mediation and International Settlement Agreements Resulting from Mediation 2018 art 3.

[255] UNCITRAL Model Law on International Commercial Mediation and International Settlement Agreements Resulting from Mediation (2018) with Guide to Enactment and Use para 84.

Once mediation commences, the limitation period for the claim is suspended; if the mediation ends without settlement, time begins to run again from the point the mediation ended. This is one of the most commercially practical innovations of Part II, as it reduces the risk that parties might lose their claims by attempting settlement through mediation.

11.5 APPOINTMENT, INDEPENDENCE AND CONDUCT OF THE MEDIATOR

Section 72 adopts the usual default rule that mediation is conducted by a single mediator unless the parties agree otherwise. It encourages the parties to agree on the appointment of the mediator but also allows them to request assistance from a mediation provider. The provider may recommend suitable persons or appoint a mediator directly, and where the provider makes the appointment, that appointment is final and binding. The section further imposes a continuous duty of disclosure on any person approached for appointment and on any appointed mediator where circumstances exist that could give rise to justifiable doubts about the mediator's impartiality or independence. A mediator may only continue despite such circumstances if the parties expressly agree.

A simple example may arise from a joint venture real estate development agreement. Suppose Party A contributes land in Abuja for a residential development while Party B provides the capital and construction expertise. A dispute later arises over profit sharing. The parties may jointly appoint a mediator, such as a construction dispute specialist. If they cannot agree on a mediator, they may request a mediation institution to appoint one. If the mediator previously acted as legal adviser to Party B in another project, that relationship must be disclosed. The mediator may proceed only if both parties consent after the disclosure.

Section 73 forms the operational centre of the mediation process. The parties are free to determine how the mediation will be conducted, either by agreeing on specific procedures or by adopting institutional mediation rules. Regardless of the procedure adopted, the parties must attend and participate in good faith. If no procedural agreement exists, the mediator may conduct the mediation in a manner considered appropriate, taking into account the circumstances of the dispute, the wishes of the parties, and the need to achieve a speedy settlement. Section 73(3), which parties cannot exclude, requires the mediator to treat all parties fairly and give each party equal opportunity to present its position.

Returning to the joint venture example, Party A may insist that the project profits were to be shared equally because the land constitutes the most valuable contribution, while Party B may argue that the financial risk and construction costs justify a larger share. If the parties have not agreed on procedural rules, the mediator may structure the process by allowing each party to present its financial calculations, review the development agreement, and explore settlement options that preserve the commercial relationship. Throughout the process, the mediator must ensure that neither party dominates the discussions or is treated unfairly.

Section 73 also introduces several modern procedural features. The mediator must encourage communication between the parties and facilitate meaningful participation in the process. Mediation sessions may take place electronically, including through video conferencing or similar platforms, provided that the identity of the participants can be verified. The mediator may propose settlement options to assist the parties in reaching agreement but cannot impose a binding solution. In addition, the mediator is entitled to fees and expenses unless the parties agree otherwise.

For example, if Party A resides in Abuja while Party B's directors are based in Lagos or abroad, mediation sessions may be conducted through video conferencing. After reviewing the financial projections of the housing development, the mediator might propose a revised profit-sharing structure or phased reimbursement of construction costs. However, the mediator cannot force the parties to accept that proposal; the final settlement must come from the parties themselves.

Two further provisions elaborate the mediation process. Section 74 allows the mediator to hold joint meetings or separate private meetings (caucuses) with each party. Section 75 permits the mediator to disclose the substance of information received from one party to the other unless the information was provided on an express condition of confidentiality. This reflects the practical reality that mediators often engage in "shuttle diplomacy" between parties while also protecting confidential communications where necessary.

Again, the joint venture dispute illustrates this. During a private caucus, Party B might disclose that it is willing to accept a smaller profit share if it can recover construction costs more quickly. The mediator may convey this general willingness to compromise to Party A to encourage settlement, unless Party B expressly instructs that the information remain confidential. In this way, the law recognises the importance of flexible negotiation techniques while preserving the confidential space that makes mediation effective.

11.6 CONFIDENTIALITY, WITHOUT PREJUDICE PROTECTION AND EVIDENTIARY EXCLUSION

Part II of the Act carefully distinguishes between confidentiality and inadmissibility, two related but separate protections within mediation.

Section 76 establishes the general rule that all information relating to mediation is confidential. Statements, documents, and discussions that occur during the mediation process are not to be disclosed outside the process. However, the section recognises certain exceptions. Disclosure may be permitted where it is required by law, necessary to implement or enforce a settlement agreement, required to prevent or reveal a crime or serious threat, or necessary to protect public order within the limits of the law.

Consider a dispute arising from a commercial supply agreement. A Nigerian pharmaceutical distributor (Party A) enters into a contract with a foreign manufacturer (Party B) to supply medical equipment to hospitals across Nigeria. A dispute later arises when Party A claims that the delivered equipment does not meet the agreed specifications. During mediation, Party B admits that some units may have fallen below the required standard and offers to replace them at a discounted rate. Under section 76, these discussions remain confidential and cannot normally be disclosed outside the mediation process. However, if the parties reach a settlement and later need to enforce that agreement in court, disclosure of the settlement terms may be permitted because it is necessary for enforcement.

Section 77 deals with the evidentiary consequence of mediation communications. It provides that parties, mediators, and persons involved in administering the mediation process cannot rely on or introduce certain mediation communications in arbitral, judicial, or similar proceedings. Courts and tribunals are also prevented from ordering disclosure of such communications, and any evidence introduced contrary to the section is inadmissible.

Returning to the supply dispute, suppose the mediation fails and the parties proceed to arbitration. If Party B had suggested during mediation that it might compensate Party A for some of the defective equipment, Party A cannot later rely on that statement in arbitration as evidence that Party B admitted liability. The law prevents mediation communications such as settlement proposals or admissions made in the course of negotiation from being used against a party in subsequent proceedings.

This distinction between Sections 76 and 77 is important. Confidentiality protects the privacy of the mediation process, ensuring that the discussions remain private. Inadmissibility protects the candour of negotiations, encouraging parties to make proposals and concessions without fear that their statements will later be used as evidence against them.

Section 77 also carefully identifies the types of communications that are protected. These include invitations to mediate, settlement proposals, admissions made during mediation, proposals made by the mediator, expressions of willingness to settle, and documents prepared specifically for the mediation process. The protection applies regardless of the form in which the information is communicated and regardless of whether later proceedings involve the same dispute.

At the same time, the law ensures that mediation cannot be used to conceal otherwise admissible evidence. Section 77(5) clarifies that evidence that is independently admissible does not become inadmissible merely because it was used during mediation. For example, if laboratory reports confirming defects in the medical equipment already existed before the mediation, those reports may still be used in later litigation even if they were discussed during mediation.

Compared with the UNCITRAL Model Law on International Commercial Mediation and International Settlement Agreements Resulting from Mediation 2018[256], the Nigerian Act adopts broadly the same structure. However, Section 76 of the Arbitration and Mediation Act 2023 articulates the exceptions to confidentiality more explicitly, particularly where disclosure is necessary to prevent crime, threats, or harm to public order. This reflects a legislative intention to protect the integrity of mediation while

---

[256] Supra

ensuring that confidentiality does not become a shield for unlawful or dangerous conduct.

11.7 TERMINATION OF MEDIATION AND ITS INTERFACE WITH ARBITRATION AND LITIGATION

Section 78 sets out the circumstances in which mediation may terminate. Mediation ends where the parties reach a settlement, where the mediator declares that further efforts are unlikely to resolve the dispute, where the parties jointly terminate the process, where a mediation provider declares the mediation concluded, or where one party notifies the other party and the mediator that it wishes to terminate the mediation.

A simple illustration may be drawn from a commercial supply dispute in Onitsha Main Market. A wholesaler supplying imported electronics to several retailers may agree to mediate a dispute concerning allegedly defective goods. If negotiations produce an agreed price reduction or replacement arrangement, the mediation terminates by settlement. If discussions reach an impasse and the mediator concludes that compromise is unlikely, the mediator may declare the mediation terminated under Section 78.

Section 79 introduces an important safeguard for the neutrality of the mediation process. Unless the parties agree otherwise, a mediator may not subsequently act as arbitrator in the same dispute, in a dispute arising out of the same contract, or in any related legal relationship. Section 81 complements this rule by granting immunity to mediators and mediation providers for acts or omissions in the performance of their functions, except where bad faith is established.

Section 80 is one of the most practically significant provisions in Part II. Where parties have agreed to attempt mediation and have undertaken not to commence arbitral or judicial proceedings for a specified period or until a specified event occurs, courts and arbitral tribunals are required to give effect to that undertaking, except where proceedings are necessary to preserve a party's rights.

In the context of commercial trade, where wholesalers and retailers in markets such as Onitsha Main Market by any chance include dispute resolution clauses in supply agreements requiring mediation before litigation. If a retailer immediately files a lawsuit without first attempting mediation, a court may stay the proceedings until the agreed mediation step has been attempted. Importantly, commencing proceedings in such circumstances does not automatically terminate the mediation agreement.

The practical significance of Section 80 is that it prevents mediation clauses from being treated as merely aspirational. Where drafted with sufficient clarity, mediation clauses may operate as enforceable conditions precedent to litigation or arbitration, thereby strengthening the role of mediation as a structured step in commercial dispute resolution.

11.8 SETTLEMENT AGREEMENTS: FORM, EFFECT AND DOMESTIC ENFORCEMENT

The central outcome of mediation is the settlement agreement, and Sections 82–86 of the Arbitration and Mediation Act 2023 establish the legal framework for how such agreements are created and enforced.

Section 82 addresses the preparation and legal effect of the settlement agreement. Where the parties reach a settlement, the mediator may assist in preparing and drafting the settlement terms if the parties agree. Once signed, the agreement becomes binding on the parties and may be enforced in court as a contract, a consent judgment, or a consent award.

This structure allows mediation to interact closely with arbitration. For example, Section 45 of the Act allows an arbitral tribunal to record a settlement as an award on agreed terms, giving the settlement the same legal status as a normal arbitral award.

A practical example can be drawn from a commodity trading dispute. A rice importer in Lagos contracts with a wholesaler to supply several containers of rice for distribution to supermarkets. A disagreement later arises when the wholesaler claims that the rice delivered does not meet the agreed quality. The parties agree to mediate. During mediation, they settle on revised delivery terms and partial reimbursement. The mediator assists them in drafting a written settlement agreement. Once signed, the agreement becomes legally binding. If the importer later fails to honour the agreed refund, the wholesaler may enforce the settlement in court as a contract or have it entered as a consent judgment.

Section 83 explains what a party must provide to rely on a mediated settlement before a court. The applicant must submit the signed settlement agreement and evidence showing that the agreement resulted from mediation. This evidence may include the mediator's signature on the agreement, a document signed by the mediator confirming the mediation, an attestation from a mediation provider, or any other proof acceptable to the court. Electronic signatures or electronic communications may satisfy the signature requirement if they reliably identify the parties and demonstrate their intention to conclude the agreement. Courts may also require translations or other supporting documents and are expected to handle such applications expeditiously.

For instance, if the rice importer and wholesaler signed the settlement electronically after an online mediation session, the electronic signatures and confirmation from the mediator may serve as proof that the settlement arose from mediation.

Section 86 highlights another important function of settlement agreements. They may be used not only to enforce rights but also to defend against further litigation. If one party attempts to reopen a dispute that has already been settled through mediation, the other party may rely on the settlement agreement to demonstrate that the dispute has already been resolved.

Nigerian case law on consent judgments provides useful guidance on how courts treat settlement agreements. In **Nigeria Water Resources Development Ltd v. Jaiyesimi**[257], the courts explained the nature of consent judgments. In **Woluchem v. Wokoma**[258], the Supreme Court emphasised that a valid consent judgment requires genuine agreement between the parties. Similarly, **Vulcan Gases Ltd v. G.F. Industries Ltd**[259] shows that a consent judgment may be challenged where there was no true agreement or where consent was obtained improperly. In **Race Auto Supply Co Ltd v. Akib**[260], the courts affirmed that settlement terms recorded by the court become binding on the parties.

Although these cases were decided before the enactment of Part II of the Act, they remain relevant because Section 82 places mediated settlements within familiar Nigerian legal categories such as contracts and consent judgments.

Section 84 sets out the grounds on which a court may refuse to grant relief based on a mediated settlement agreement. Relief may be refused where a party lacked legal capacity, where the agreement is void or incapable of being performed, where it is not binding or final, where it has been subsequently modified, or where the obligations under the settlement have already been performed. Refusal may also occur where the mediator failed to disclose circumstances that could create doubts about impartiality or independence and that failure materially influenced a party's

---

[257] (1983) 1 SCNLR 454.
[258] (1974) 3 SC 153.
[259] (2001) 9 NWLR (Pt 719) 610 (SC).
[260] (1977) 11 NSCC 343 (SC).

decision to settle. Courts may also refuse enforcement if doing so would violate public policy or if the dispute itself was not legally capable of being resolved through mediation.

A simple illustration may involve a distribution dispute in which a manufacturer agrees during mediation to compensate a distributor for delayed shipments. If it later emerges that the distributor was legally incapacitated to enter the agreement—for example, because the company had already been dissolved—enforcement of the settlement may be refused.

Finally, Section 85 addresses situations where related proceedings are pending before a court or arbitral tribunal. In such circumstances, the court may adjourn the proceedings and may require appropriate security while the question of enforcement or validity of the mediated settlement is resolved.

Taken together, Sections 82–86 create a structured framework that ensures mediated settlements are legally binding, procedurally enforceable, and integrated with the wider dispute resolution system, while also preserving safeguards against unfair or defective agreements.

11.9 INTERNATIONAL SETTLEMENT AGREEMENTS AND THE SINGAPORE CONVENTION

Section 87 internationalises the Nigerian regime. It provides that where enforcement is sought in Nigeria for an international settlement agreement made in another State/Country, the Singapore Convention applies, provided that the other State is a party to the Convention and the dispute arises from a commercial legal relationship under Nigerian law. UNCITRAL describes the Convention as a harmonised legal framework for invoking and enforcing international commercial settlement agreements resulting from mediation. Nigeria signed the Convention on 7 August 2019, ratified it on 27 November 2023, and the Convention entered into force for Nigeria on 27 May 2024.

This link to the Singapore Convention is one of the clearest reasons mediation is a focused innovation of the 2023 Act. The repealed ACA knew conciliation, but it did not connect Nigerian law to the emerging global enforcement architecture for mediated commercial settlements. By combining domestic enforceability under Sections 82–86 with treaty-backed recognition under Section 87, the AMA gives mediated settlements something closer to the cross-border functional value that the New York Convention long gave arbitral awards.

At the same time, the commercial focus of the international enforcement framework should not be overlooked. The United Nations Convention on International Settlement Agreements Resulting from Mediation (Singapore Convention on Mediation)[261] and the settlement-enforcement provisions of the UNCITRAL Model Law on International Commercial Mediation and International Settlement Agreements Resulting from Mediation 2018[262] are primarily directed at commercial disputes, and Section 87 of the Arbitration and Mediation Act 2023 follows the same orientation.

This creates an interesting structural feature within Part II of the Act. Section 67 brings a broad range of civil disputes within the mediation framework, meaning that mediation may be used for both commercial and non-commercial matters. However, Section 87 and related provisions dealing with the enforcement of mediated settlements are clearly designed with commercial transactions in mind, particularly those with an international element.

---

[261] Singapore Convention on Mediation 2019.

[262] UNCITRAL Model Law

The practical implication is that Nigerian courts may eventually need to clarify how far the enhanced enforcement regime applies where a mediation concerns a non-commercial civil dispute that nevertheless falls within the mediation framework of Section 67. The statutory design therefore appears to combine wide procedural coverage for mediation generally with a more commercially focused enforcement structure for internationally mediated settlements.

11.10 CRITICAL APPRAISAL OF PART II AS A FOCUSED INNOVATION

Part II of the Arbitration and Mediation Act 2023 can rightly be described as a focused innovation in Nigerian dispute resolution law for several reasons.

First, it moves Nigerian law beyond the older and relatively brief conciliation framework under the repealed Arbitration and Conciliation Act and replaces it with a comprehensive mediation regime. The Act now provides clearer rules on how mediation begins, how it is conducted, how it ends, and how settlements reached through mediation can be enforced.

Second, the Act broadens the scope of mediation. It allows mediation to be used not only for commercial disputes but also for ordinary civil disputes, while still maintaining a special framework for international commercial settlement enforcement through instruments such as the United Nations Convention on International Settlement Agreements Resulting from Mediation (Singapore Convention on Mediation).

For example, mediation can now be used to resolve:

a. A business dispute between two companies over a supply contract, or

b. A civil dispute between neighbours over property boundaries.

However, if a mediated settlement arises from an international commercial transaction, the Act also allows it to benefit from cross-border enforcement mechanisms linked to the Singapore Convention.

Third, the Act introduces several practical protections for parties who choose mediation. These include rules that suspend limitation periods while mediation is ongoing, confidentiality obligations protecting discussions during mediation, restrictions on using mediation communications as evidence in later proceedings, and provisions that allow courts to enforce agreements requiring parties to attempt mediation before starting litigation or arbitration.

To illustrate, two construction companies may agree in their contract that any dispute must first go to mediation before arbitration. Under the Act, that mediation clause can be treated as a binding procedural step, and a court may pause litigation until the parties have attempted mediation.

Fourth, the Act gives clear legal status to mediated settlements. A settlement agreement reached through mediation can operate as:

i. a binding contract,

ii. a consent judgment entered by a court, or

iii. a consent award recorded by an arbitral tribunal.

This clarity strengthens the credibility of mediation because parties know that a negotiated settlement can be legally enforced if necessary.

Fifth, the Act aligns Nigeria with modern international mediation standards developed by United Nations Commission on International Trade Law. The legislation also expressly recognises the international origin of these rules and allows courts to consult the preparatory materials of the UNCITRAL instruments when interpreting the Act. This encourages Nigerian courts to interpret the mediation framework in a manner consistent with international practice.

Despite these strengths, some issues will likely require judicial clarification over time.

For instance, the Act requires parties to participate in mediation in good faith, which is an important principle. However, the statute does not fully explain what happens if a party refuses to participate sincerely or deliberately frustrates the mediation process. Courts may therefore need to determine how this obligation should be applied in practice.

Another practical issue concerns the procedural path by which mediated settlements become consent judgments. While the Act recognises this possibility, the exact procedure will often depend on existing court rules and practices.

There are also some technical questions within the drafting of the statute. Section 67 excludes settlement efforts conducted by judges or arbitrators unless the parties agree otherwise. At the same time, Section 91 recognises mediation providers, which may include mediation schemes connected with courts. Courts may therefore need to clarify how these provisions interact in practice.

The grounds on which a court may refuse to enforce a mediated settlement under the Arbitration and Mediation Act 2023 broadly follow the approach taken in the UNCITRAL Model Law on International Commercial Mediation and International Settlement Agreements Resulting from Mediation 2018. However, the Nigerian Act adopts a slightly narrower approach.

Under the Model Law, enforcement may be refused where there has been a serious breach of applicable mediation standards. The Nigerian statute does not expressly include this general ground. Instead, it focuses more specifically on situations where the mediator failed to disclose circumstances that could create doubts about impartiality or independence, and that failure influenced a party's decision to settle.

A simple example illustrates the difference. Suppose two companies mediate a dispute over a construction contract. If the mediator secretly has a business relationship with one of the companies and fails to disclose it, the settlement may be challenged because the mediator's lack of disclosure affected the fairness of the process.

By contrast, imagine that the mediator simply handled the discussions poorly for example, by rushing the negotiations or failing to give both parties equal time to speak. Under the UNCITRAL Model Law, such conduct might potentially fall within the broader idea of a serious breach of mediation standards. Under the Nigerian Act, however, the challenge may be harder to frame unless it can be linked to bias, non-disclosure, public policy, or some defect affecting the validity of the agreement itself.

In practical terms, this narrower drafting may reduce the number of procedural challenges to mediated settlements. At the same time, it means that complaints about how the mediation was conducted may sometimes need to be argued under broader legal principles, such as public policy or lack of genuine consent to the settlement.

Finally, there is a practical consideration. Because the mediation provisions of the 2023 Act are relatively new, there are still few reported Nigerian appellate decisions interpreting Sections 67–87. In the meantime, judges and practitioners are likely to rely on three main sources of guidance:

a. Existing Nigerian case law on consent judgments and settlements,

b. Comparative case law from other jurisdictions on mediation and ADR enforcement, and

c. The international materials produced by UNCITRAL, including the Model Law and the Singapore Convention.

In the authors' view, this is not a weakness of the legislation. Rather, it reflects the normal evolution of a new legal framework, in which judicial interpretation gradually clarifies how the statutory provisions operate in practice.

11.11 CONCLUSION

Mediation under the Arbitration and Mediation Act, 2023 is best understood as the statute's most deliberate institutional innovation. The new Act does not simply rename conciliation. It creates a broader, denser and more enforceable mediation framework; integrates mediation with court and arbitral processes; protects parties through limitation suspension, confidentiality and evidentiary rules; and gives mediated settlements both domestic enforceability and, in qualifying cases, an international treaty pathway through the Singapore Convention.

The 2023 Act repositions mediation from a soft, optional appendage of ADR into a legally structured process with serious procedural consequences and serious settlement value. Its focused innovation lies not merely in encouraging parties to talk, but in making what they say, and what they finally sign, matter within domestic law and across borders.

INDEX